£m	$m
26	**Montedison SpA** Milano	I	933·0	2239·2
27	**Rhone-Poulenc SA** 22 Avenue Montaigne Paris 8e	F	903·8	2169·1
28	**Regie-Renault** Billancourt	F	890·3	2136·7
29	**Mannesman AG** Düsseldorf, Mannesmannufer 2	D	860·8	2064·0
30	**Gutehoffnungshütte Aktienverein** Oberhausen	D	855·8	2053·9
31	**Compagnie Francaise De Raffingage** 5 Rue Michel-Ange, Paris 16 ième	F	823·2	1975·7
32	**Compagnie Generale D'Electricite** 54 Rue la Boétie, Paris 8e	F	811·4	1947·4
33	**Compagnie De Saint-Gobain-Pont A Mousson SA** "St Gobain", 62 Boulevard Victor Hugo, Neuilly-sur-Seine, Hauts de Seine	F	793·4	1904·2
34	**Petrofina SA** 31 Rue de la Loi, Bruxelles	B	785·8	1885·9
35	**Fried Krupp Hüttenwerke AG** Alleestr 165, Bochum	D	769·3	1846·3
36	**Erap-Elf** 7 Rue Nélabon, Paris 15e	F	764·0	1833·6
37	**Ciba-Geigy AG** Basel	CH	762·6	1830·2
38	**Finsider** Via Castro Pretorio, 122, Roma	I	748·7	1796·9
39	**AGIP SpA** Pizzala E, Mattei 1, Roma	I	735·5	1765·2
40	**Rheinisch-Westfälische Boden-Credit-Bank** Koln	D	728·6	1748·6
41	**Peugeot SA** 75 Avenue de la Grande-Armée, Paris	F	698·3	1675·9
42	**Rheinstahl AG** Essen 1, Postfach 1364	D	682·7	1638·5
43	**Courtaulds Ltd** 18 Hanover Square, London W1A 2BB	GB	681·5	1635·6
44	**Esso Petroleum Company Ltd** Esso House, Victoria Street, London SW1E 5JW	GB	677·4	1625·8
45	**Robert Bosch GmbH** 7 Stuttgart 1, Breitscheidstrasse 4	D	670·7	1609·7
46	**Flick Group** Düsseldorf	D	669·5	1606·8
47	**Ford Werke AG** 5 Köln-Niew, Henry Ford-Straße	D	662·2	1589·3
48	**Denain Nord-Est Longwy** 25 Rue de Clichy, Paris 9e	F	648·8	1557·1
49	**Karstadt AG** Berliner Platz 1, Essen	D	625·2	1500·5
50	**Associated British Foods Ltd** 40 Berkeley Square, London W1X 6BR	GB	612·5	1470·0

BUSINESS ATLAS
OF WESTERN EUROPE

ATLAS DES AFFAIRES
DE L'EUROPE OCCIDENTALE

HANDELSATLAS
WESTEUROPAS

ATLAS COMERCIAL
DE EUROPA OCCIDENTAL

Gower Economic Publications

First published in Great Britain by
Gower Press Ltd, Epping, Essex, England

© Gower Press Limited 1974

ISBN 0 7161 0148 3

GOWER ECONOMIC PUBLICATIONS

Gower Economic Publications is the subsidiary imprint
of Gower Press specialising in the research and
publication of surveys and reviews covering a broad
area of management interest. All publications contain
the latest economic statistics and are regularly updated.

EUROPEAN BUSINESS ATLAS SERIES

This series is designed to identify and chart varying
economic and business conditions across Western
Europe. All atlases are produced to a high, full colour,
specification with emphasis placed on the ready
interpretation of the business data.

Printed by Dai Nippon Printing Co. (Hong Kong) Ltd.,
Hong Kong.

Contents

Table des matières

Inhalts-verzeichnis

Indice

Introduction

This atlas is designed to provide essential information for those interested in international business. The very rapid growth of international trade, the formation of a considerable number of multi-national concerns and, above all, the emergence of Europe as one major market through the expansion of the EEC require economic information to be presented across the whole of Western Europe.

For the purposes of this survey Western Europe has been defined as that area to the west of a line from the Adriatic to the Baltic. The countries which have been included through this definition are:

Austria **A**	United Kingdom **GB**
Belgium **B**	Italy **I**
Switzerland **CH**	Ireland (Irish Republic) **IRL**
West Germany (Federal	Luxembourg **L**
German Republic,	Norway **N**
including West Berlin) **D**	Netherlands **NL**
Denmark **DK**	Portugal **P**
Spain **E**	Sweden **S**
France **F**	Finland **SF**

The information which has been selected for inclusion within this Atlas has been drawn from a great number of sources. In many cases adjustments have been made and estimates formulated to bring this information onto comparative bases.

Two principal bases have been formulated. Information throughout the Atlas is structured either by country or, in the more detailed surveys, by region. The maps and graphical analyses which follow therefore allow decisions to be made both at the international and regional levels.

Set out on the following map is the survey area of Western Europe together with the outline of the regions adopted. These regions follow wherever possible the official regions within each country. In certain cases official regions have been consolidated to allow for more accurate comparative data to be included or to enhance the presentation.

In format the Atlas divides into four main parts. Each part is a self-contained unit and deals with three related aspects of essential information, industry data and consumer standards. The final part presents special statistical information on each of the sixteen countries.

Each part commences with an introduction and divides under a number of key section headings. The part titles are set out in the list of contents on page 3 and the section headings can be found at the beginning of each part.

The main elements in the preparation of this Atlas were detailed searches drawn from many sources, both official and private, and from all the countries surveyed. A detailed list of sources is to be found on page 9.

The use of such varied information has posed many problems in arriving at comparative data between countries and regions. Information has been included only where it is considered reliable. In certain instances omissions have been made on the maps and graphical analyses, where the editors were not satisfied with the reliability of information available.

Introduction

Cet atlas est destiné à fournir des renseignements essentiels à ceux qui s'intéressent aux affaires internationales. La croissance très rapide du commerce international, la formation d'un nombre considérable d'entreprises multi-nationales et avant tout l'émergence de l'Europe en tant qu'un seul et important marché par suite de l'expansion de la Communauté Economique Européenne, nécessitent des renseignements de marketing couvrant la totalité de l'Europe Occidentale.

Pour les besoins de cette étude, l'Europe Occidentale est définie comme la région s'étendant à l'ouest d'une ligne allant de l'Adriatique à la Baltique. De ce fait, les pays qui sont inclus sont les suivants:

L'Autriche **A**	Le Royaume-Uni **GB**
La Belgique **B**	L'Italie **I**
La Suisse **CH**	L'Irlande (République
L'Allemagne de l'Ouest	d'Irlande) **IRL**
(République Fédérale	Le Luxembourg **L**
Allemande, y compris	La Norvège **N**
Berlin Ouest) **D**	Les Pays-Bas **NL**
Le Danemark **DK**	Le Portugal **P**
L'Espagne **E**	La Suède **S**
La France **F**	La Finlande **SF**

Les renseignements choisis pour être compris dans cet Atlas ont été puisés à partir d'un grand nombre de sources. Dans nombre de cas, il a été nécessaire de recourir à des mises au point ainsi qu'à des estimations pour formuler les données recueillies sur des bases comparatives.

Deux formules fondamentales ont été élaborées pour servir de base, à savoir: les renseignements contenus dans cet Atlas sont présentés soit par pays, soit par suite d'études plus détaillées, par régions. Les cartes géographiques et les analyses graphiques incluses permettent donc de prendre des décisions tant à un niveau international qu'à un niveau régional.

La carte ci-après couvre la superficie de l'Europe Occidentale qui est l'objet de cette étude et fournit une esquisse des régions choisies. Ces régions suivent autant que possible les frontières officielles de ces dites régions à l'intérieur de chaque pays. Dans certains cas, les régions officielles ont été "consolidées" pour offrir des données comparatives plus précises ou pour rehausser la présentation.

Cet Atlas est divisé en quatre parties principales. Chaque partie forme un tout et traite de trois aspects apparentés de renseignements essentiels, de données industrielles et du genre de vie des consommateurs. La partie finale est composée de données statistiques spéciales pour chacun des seize pays.

Chaque partie comporte une introduction et se divise en plusieurs sections principales. Les titres des parties figurent dans la table des matières à la page 3 et les titres des sections sont placés en tête de chaque partie.

Les principaux éléments fondamentaux qui ont servi à la préparation de cet Atlas proviennent de recherches approfondies, recueillies à partir de nombreuses sources, tant officielles que privées, et de tous les pays étudiés. Une liste détaillée de ces sources d'information figure à la page 9.

L'utilisation de renseignements aussi variés a posé beaucoup de problèmes pour l'élaboration de données comparables entre pays et entre régions. Dans certains cas, des détails ont été omis sur les cartes et les analyses graphiques, en raison des doutes des éditeurs quant à la validité des renseignements disponibles.

Einführung

Dieser Atlas ist dazu bestimmt, wichtige Informationen für diejenigen zu liefern, die am internationalen Handel interessiert sind. Das außerordentlich schnelle Anwachsen des internationalen Handels, die Bildung übernationaler Gemeinschaften und darüber hinaus die Tatsache, daß Europa durch die Erweiterung der EWG zu einem der größten Absatzgebiete wird, fordern Marketing-Informationen für ganz Westeuropa.

In unserer Untersuchung ist Westeuropa das Gebiet westlich einer Linie von der Adria zur Ostsee. In die Untersuchung wurden folgende Länder einbezogen:

Österreich	A	Italien	I
Belgien	B	Irland (Republik)	IRL
Schweiz	CH	Luxemburg	L
Westdeutschland (BDR und Westberlin)	D	Norwegen	N
Dänemark	DK	Holland	NL
Spanien	E	Portugal	P
Frankreich	F	Schweden	S
England	GB	Finnland	SF

Die Informationen im Atlas stammen aus vielen Quellen. In vielen Fällen wurden die Angaben geändert und Schätzungen vorgenommen, um eine Vergleichsgrundlage zu schaffen.

Es wurden zwei Hauptgrundlagen geschaffen. Im Atlas sind die Informationen entweder nach Ländern aufgeteilt oder nach Gebieten, wenn es sich um genauere Untersuchungen handelt. Aus den folgenden Karten und grafischen Analysen kann man daher Schlüsse auf internationaler und regionaler Ebene ziehen.

Auf der folgenden Karte ist Westeuropa als untersuchtes Gebiet eingetragen, ebenfalls die Grenzen der besprochenen Gebiete. Wo möglich, stimmen diese Gebiete mit den offiziellen Gebieten des entsprechenden Landes überein. In bestimmten Fällen wurden mehrere offizielle Gebiete zusammengefaßt, um genauere Vergleichszahlen zu erhalten und diese hier einzuschließen oder ihre Präsentation zu verbessern.

Der Atlas hat vier Teile. Jeder Teil ist in sich abge-schlossen und behandelt drei miteinander verwandte Aspekte wichtiger Informationen, Industriedaten und Verbrauchernormen. Im letzten Teil sind besondere An-gaben aus den Statistiken eines jeden der sechzehn Länder enthalten.

Jeder Teil beginnt mit einer Einführung und ist in mehrere Hauptüberschriften geteilt. Die Titel der einzelnen Teile sind im Inhaltsverzeichnis auf Seite 9 enthalten und die Untertitel zu Beginn eines jeden Teils.

Dieser Atlas wurde durch Untersuchungen aus offiziellen und privaten Quellen aller untersuchter Länder zusammengestellt. Im Anhang befindet sich eine genaue Aufstellung der Quellen.

Bei der Benutzung derartig unterschiedlicher Angaben stellten sich viele Probleme, bevor wir für die Länder und Gebiete Vergleichsdaten erzielen konnten. Informationen wurden nur dann aufgenommen, wenn sie als zuverlässig bezeichnet werden konnten. In gewissen Fällen haben Karten und grafische Darstellungen Auslassungen, wo wir mit der Zuverlässigkeit der Informationen nicht zufrieden waren.

Introducción

La finalidad de este atlas es ofrecer la información esencial a aquellas personas interesadas en el comercio internacional. La gran rapidez en el incremento de los intercambios comerciales, el número considerable de empresas multi-nacionales que se forman y, sobre todo, el resurgimiento de Europa como un gran mercado a través de la expansión del Mercado Común Europeo, requiere que la información de marketing sea presentada a través de toda Europa Occidental.

Europa Occidental a fines de este estudio ha sido definida como el área al oeste de una línea desde el Adriático al Báltico. Los países incluidos dentro de esta definición son:

Austria	A	Reino Unido	GB
Bélgica	B	Italia	I
Suiza	CH	Irlanda (República de Irlanda)	IRL
Alemania del Oeste (República Federal Alemana, incluido Berlín Occidental)	D	Luxemburgo	L
		Noruega	N
Dinamarca	DK	Holanda	NL
España	E	Portugal	P
Francia	F	Suecia	S
		Finlandia	SF

La información seleccionada para ser incluida en este Atlas, se ha obtenido a través de numerosas fuentes. En mucho casos se ha tenido que efectuar ajustes y formular estimaciones a fin de poner esta información sobre bases comparativas.

Se han formulado dos bases principales. La información a través del Atlas se ha estructurado sea por país o, por región en el estudio más detallado. Los mapas y análisis gráficos que le sigue permite por lo tanto tomar decisiones a niveles internacionales y regionales.

Expuesto en el mapa que sigue hay el examen del área de Europa Occidental conjuntamente con el contorno de las regiones adoptadas. Estas regiones siguen adonde posible las regiones oficiales dentro de cada país. En algunos casos las regiones oficiales se han consolidado a fin de permitir incluir datos comparativos más exactos o para mejorar le presentación del mismo.

El formato del Atlas se divide en cuatro partes principales. Cada parte es una unidad completa y trata con tres aspectos relacionados entre ellos sobre información esencial, datos de la industria y niveles de consumo. La parte final presenta información especial estadística de cada uno de los dieciséis países.
Las búsquedas en muchas fuentes ha sido el elemento principal en la preparación de este Atlas, y por cada país estudiado las fuentes fueron tanto privadas como oficiales. Una lista detallada de las mismas se encuentra la página 9.

El uso de tanta información variada puso bastantes problemas para llegar a los datos comparativos entre países y regiones. La información que se ha incluido, es la que se ha considerado fidedigna. En algunos casos se han hecho omisiones en los mapas y en los análisis gráficos, adonde no estábamos satisfechos de la veracidad de la información disponible.

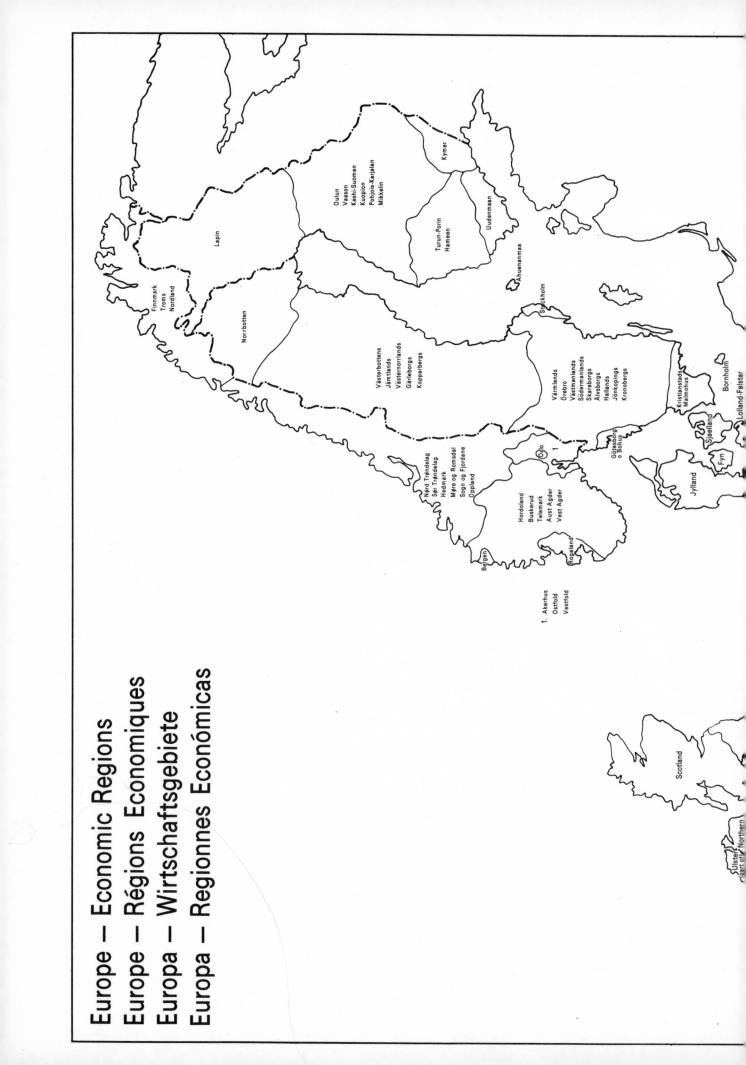

Europe – Economic Regions
Europe – Régions Economiques
Europa – Wirtschaftsgebiete
Europa – Regionnes Económicas

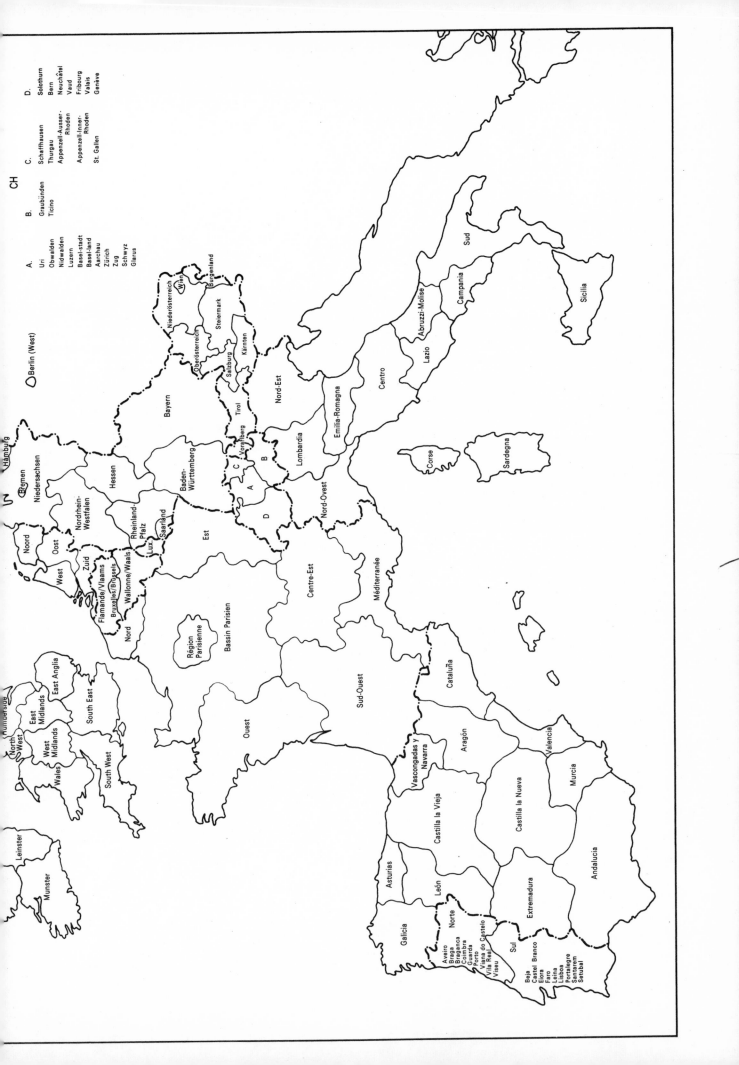

Sources of information

Sources de renseignements

Informations- quellen

Fuentes de información

The following publications constitute the primary sources of information for the analyses prepared in this Atlas, and were supplemented by material provided by the publishers' field research unit. Titles in the list below for which no publisher is given are produced by government agencies in each case.

Les publications suivantes constituent les sources primaires d'où ont été puisés les renseignements pour les analyses qui figurent dans cet ouvrage et qui furent complétées par les documents fournis par l'équipe de recherche de la rédaction. Les ouvrages ci-dessous ne portant pas le nom d'une maison d'édition sont des publications d'agences gouvernementales.

In erster Linie waren die folgenden Publikationen für die in diesem Atlas aufgestellten Analysen maßgebend. Sie wurden durch eigenes Untersuchungsmaterial des Herausgebers ergänzt. Wenn in der untenstehenden Liste kein Herausgeber angegeben ist, handelt es sich um Publikationen staatlicher Stellen.

Las siguientes publicaciones forman las fuentes primarias de información para los análisis que han sido preparados en este estudio, y fueron suplementados con material compilado por la unidad de investigación de operaciones externas de la Editorial. En la lista a continuación en la cual no se nombra editor alguno, los títulos en cada caso han sido compilados por agencias gubernamentales.

A
Statistisches Handbuch für die Republik Österreich
Austria, Facts and Figures Federal Press Service

B
Annuaire Statistique de la Belgique

CH
Statistisches Jahrbuch der Schweiz
Switzerland and her Industries Swiss Office for the Development of Trade
Switzerland in Figures Schweizerische Bankgesellschaft
Switzerland 1971 Kummerly and Frey

D
Statistisches Jahrbuch für die Bundesrepublik Deutschland

DK
Statistisk Årbog

E
Anuario Estadístico de España
Economic Report: Spain, July 1970 Lloyds Bank Ltd
Quarterly Economic Review: Spain 1971 The Economist Intelligence Unit
OECD Economic Surveys: Spain Organisation for Economic Co-operation and Development
The Spanish Economy in Figures Banco de Bilbao

F
Annuaire Statistique de la France
Economic Report: France, December 1970 Lloyds Bank Ltd

Quarterly Economic Review: France 1971 The Economist Intelligence Unit
OECD Economic Surveys: France Organisation for Economic Co-operation and Development

GB
Annual Abstract of Statistics
Abstract of Regional Statistics
Census 1971: Preliminary Report
Quarterly Economic Review: United Kingdom 1971 The Economist Intelligence Unit

I
Annuario Statistico Italiano

IRL
Statistical Abstract of Ireland

L
Annuaire Statistique

N
Statistisk Årbok

NL
Jaarcijfers voor Nederland
Economic Report: The Netherlands, March 1971 Lloyds Bank Ltd
Quarterly Economic Review: Netherlands 1971 The Economist Intelligence Unit
OECD Economic Surveys: Netherlands Organisation for Economic Co-operation and Development

P
Anuário Estatístico

Quarterly Economic Review: Sweden 1971 The Economist Intelligence Unit
OECD Economic Surveys: Sweden Organisation for Economic Co-operation and Development
Some Data about Sweden, 1971–72 Stockholms Enskilda Bank
Industrial Sweden The Swedish Institute

S
Statistisk Årsbok for Sverige
Economic Report: Sweden, February 1971 Lloyds Bank Ltd

SF
Suomen Tilastollinen Vuosikirja

General
Information Générale
Allgemein
Información General
The Scandinavian Market 1971 Nordfinanz Bank Zürich, Banque Nordique de Commerce
The Common Market and the Common Man European Communities Press and Information
European Community, The Facts European Communities Press and Information
OECD Economic Outlook, July 1971 Organisation for Economic Co-operation and Development
Labour Force Statistics 1958–1969 Organisation for Economic Co-operation and Development
International Finance Statistics International Monetary Fund
Institute of Directors' Guide to Europe Thornton Cox
Cook's Continental Timetable Thos Cook and Son Ltd
Jane's Major Companies of Europe Sampson Low, Marston and Co Ltd
The Times 1000 Times Newspapers Ltd
The Top 300 Annual Review The Banker

1

BASIC MARKET INFORMATION

RENSEIGNEMENTS FONDAMENTAUX DE MARKETING

GRUNDLEGENDE MARKETING - INFORMATIONEN

INFORMACION BASICA DE MARKETING

Introduction to Part 1

This first part of the Atlas provides background data of basic interest to those involved in international marketing. A number of key business factors are covered in summary form from population distribution to finance and trade information.

An understanding of the distribution of market data shown in Part 1 is essential to fundamental marketing decisions. The broad and diverse elements covered do not allow this data to be categorised either in Part 2 (The Major Industries of Europe) or Part 3 (The European Consumer).

Introduction de la Ière partie

Cette première partie de l'Atlas fournit des données générales d'un intérêt fondamental à ceux qui sont engagés dans le marketing international. Nombre de facteurs commerciaux de base sont couverts sous une forme condensée, allant de la distribution de la population aux renseignements financiers et commerciaux.

La compréhension de la distribution des données du marché qui paraissent dans la Première Partie est essentielle pour permettre la mise à exécution de décisions fonda-mentales relatives au marketing. L'étendue et la diversité des connaissances réunies ne permettent de catégoriser ces données ni dans la Deuxième Partie (Les Principales Industries de l'Europe) ni dans la troisième Partie (Le Consommateur Européen).

Einführung zu Teil 1

Im ersten Teil des Atlas sind grundlegende Daten enthalten, die für alle interessant sind, die mit internationalem Marketing zu tun haben. Einige der wichtigsten geschäftlichen Faktoren wie Verteilung der Bevölkerung und Informationen über Finanzen und Handel, sind zusammengefaßt.

Für die Grundentscheidungen im Marketing ist ein Verständnis der Marktangaben in Teil I wichtig. Da alle Elemente eingehend und umfassend einbezogen wurden, konnten diese Angaben in Teil II (die größten Industriezweige Europas) oder Teil III (der europäische Verbraucher) nicht untergebracht werden.

Introducción a la 1ª Parte

Esta primera parte del Atlas proporciona datos de fondo de interés básico para aquellos que están implicados en el marketing internacional. Un número de negocios claves han sido cubiertos en forma de recompila-ción, yendo desde la distribución de la población a finanzas e información comercial.

Es indispensable a fin de tomar decisiones de marketing, una comprensión de los datos referentes a la distribución de mercado expuestos en la Iª Parte. Los amplios y diversos elementos cubiertos no permiten que dichos datos se categoricen en la 2ª Parte (Las Principales Industrias de Europa) o en la 3ª Parte (El Consumidor Europeo).

Contents

Table des matières

Inhaltsverzeichnis

Indice

A

Politics, language and
religion

La politique, la langue
et la religion

Politik, Sprache und
Religion

Política, idioma y religión

Austria

Austria, a democratic republic, is a Federal State comprising nine independent provinces, each administered by a Provincial Government. The Federal President and Federal Government as the executive authority are elected by general election every six years. The legislative bodies are the Nationalrat (National Council) representing 25 constituencies and the Bundesrat (Federal Council) representing the provinces.

Language: German 98%

Religion: Roman Catholic 90%

Autriche

L'Autriche, république démocratique, est un état fédéral qui comprend neuf provinces indépendantes, chacune administrée par un gouvernement provincial. Le président de la fédération et le gouvernement fédéral qui assurent le pouvoir exécutif sont élus lors d'élections générales tous les six ans. Les corps législatifs sont le Nationalrat (le Conseil National) qui représente 25 circonscriptions électorales et le Bundesrat (le Conseil Fédéral) qui représente les provinces.

Langue: l'allemand 98%

Religion: Le catholicisme romain 90%

Österreich

Österreich, eine demokratische Republik, ist ein Bundesstaat mit neun eigenständigen Bundesländern, die alle ihre eigene Landesregierung haben. Bundespräsident und Bundesregierung – die Staatsregierung – werden alle sechs Jahre durch allgemeine Wahlen gewählt. Gesetzgebende Körperschaften sind Nationalrat mit 25 Wahlkreise und Bundesrat für die Ländervertretungen.

Sprache: Deutsch 98%

Religion: röm. katholisch 90%

Austria

Austria es una república democrática y Estado Federal, con nueve provincias independientes y cada una de ellas administradas por un Gobierno Provincial. El Presidente Federal y Gobierno Federal como autoridades ejecutivas son elegidos cada seis años a través de elecciones generales. Los cuerpos legislativos son el Nationalrat (Consejo Nacional) representando a 25 electorados y el Budesrat (Consejo Federal) en representación de las provincias.

Idioma: Alemán 98%

Religión: Católica romana 90%

Belgium

Belgium is a constitutional monarchy with a two-chamber parliamentary system. Executive power resides with the monarch whose acts must be countersigned by a minister. The diversity of the Belgian political and social scenes has meant that successive governments are not only coalitions from the three major political parties, but must also include proportions of both Flemish and French speaking members.

Languages: Flemish 60%, mainly in north, French 40%

Religion: Roman Catholic

Belgique

La Belgique est une monarchie constitutionnelle avec un système parlementaire à deux Chambres. Le pouvoir exécutif est entre les mains du monarque dont les décisions doivent être ratifiées par un ministre. La diversification politique et sociale de la Belgique est telle que les gouvernements successifs ne sont pas seulement des coalitions des trois principaux partis politiques, mais comprennent aussi une proportion de membres parlant le flamand et de membres parlant le français.

Langues: le flamand 60%, surtout dans le Nord, le français 40%

Religion: le catholicisme romain

Belgien

Belgien ist eine konstitutionelle Monarchie mit zwei Parlamentshäusern. Die Executive übt der König nach Gegenzeichnung eines Ministers aus. Die Unterschiedlichkeit des belgischen politischen und sozialen Gefüges brachte es mit sich, daß eine Reihe von Regierungen nicht nur Koalitionen der drei großen politischen Parteien waren, sondern daß in ihnen auch Anteile flämisch und französisch sprechender Mitglieder vorhanden sein mußten.

Sprachen: Flämisch 60% hauptsächlich im Norden, Französisch 40%

Religion: röm katholisch

Bélgica

Bélgica es una monarquía constitucional con sistema parlamentario de dos cámaras. Los poderes ejecutivos residen con el Monarca cuyos actos tienen a su vez que ser contrafirmados por un ministro. La diversidad política Belga y panoramas sociales ha resultado en que consecutivos gobiernos no sólo han sido formados por la coalición de los tres principales partidos pero también incluyen una proporción de miembros de habla flamenca y francesa.

Idiomas: Flamenco 60%, en su mayoría en el norte, francés 40%

Religión: Católica romana

Switzerland

Switzerland, a democracy, is a confederation of over 3000 communities forming twenty-two cantons, each with a great deal of administrative autonomy. Legislative power resides with the Federal Assembly which elects the government (the Federal

Suisse

La Suisse, une démocratie, est une confédération de plus de 3000 communautés formant vingt-deux cantons, chacun avec une grande autonomie administrative. L'Assemblée Fédérale a le pouvoir législatif et c'est elle qui élit le Gouvernement (le

Schweiz

Die Schweiz, eine Demokratie, ist ein Bund von über 3000 Gemeinden, die 22 Kantone bilden, von denen jeder weitgehend autonom ist. Gesetzgeber ist die Bundesversammlung, die die Regierung wählt (den Bundesrat). Jedes

Suiza

Suiza es una democracia, siendo una federación de 3000 comunidades y formando veintidós cantones, cada uno de ellos con gran autonomía administrativa. El poder legislativo reside en la Asamblea Federal, la cual elige al gobierno

Council). Each of the seven members of the Federal Council acts as President for one year in rotation.

Languages : German 72%, French 20%, Italian 6%

Religions : Protestant 53%, Roman Catholic 46%

Conseil Fédéral). Chacun des sept membres du Conseil Fédéral remplit les fonctions de président pour un an à tour de rôle.

Langues : l'allemand 72%, le français 20%, l'italien 6%

Religions : le protestantisme 53%, le catholicisme romain 46%

der sieben Mitglieder des Bundesrates ist abwechselnd ein Jahr lang Bundespräsident.

Sprachen : deutsch 72%, französisch 20%, italienisch 6%

Religionen : reformiert 53%, röm. katholisch 46%

(Consejo Federal). Cada uno de los siete miembros del Consejo Federal actúa como Presidente durante un año y en rotación.

Idiomas : Alemán 72%, francés 20%, italiano 6%

Religiones : Protestante 53%, Católica romana 46%

West Germany

West Germany is a federal republic comprising 10 Länder (regions). It has a two-chamber Parliament with 10 state parliaments. The federal President is elected by national convention for a term of five years and the federal and Land parliaments for four years.

Language : German

Religions : Evangelical 50%, Roman Catholic 45%

Allemagne de L'Ouest

L'Allemagne de l'Ouest est une république fédérale qui comprend 10 Länder (régions). Elle a un parlement à deux Chambres avec 10 parlements régionaux. Le président fédéral est élu par convention nationale pour une période de cinq ans et le parlement fédéral et les parlements régionaux pour quatre ans.

Langue : l'allemand

Religion : l'Eglise évangélique 50%, le catholicisme romain 45%

Westdeutschland

Die Bundesrepublik Westdeutschland besteht aus 10 Ländern. Sie hat zwei Parlamentshäuser mit 10 Länderregierungen. Der Bundespräsident wird von der Bundesversammlung auf 5 Jahre gewählt, Bundesregierung und Länderregierungen auf vier Jahre.

Sprache : deutsch

Religionen : evangelisch 50%, röm. katholisch 45%

Alemania Occidental

Alemania occidental es una república federal con 10 Länder (regiones). Tiene un Parlamento con dos cámaras y 10 parlamentos de estado. El Presidente Federal se elige para un término de cinco años por medio de una convención nacional. Los parlamentos federales y del Land por un período de cuatro años.

Idioma : Alemán

Religiones : Evangélica 50%, Católica romana 45%

Denmark

Denmark, a monarchy, has a multi-party system. Members are elected to Parliament (the Foketing) by proportional representation, but never has a single party majority been produced ; the country being ruled by coalitions and minority governments.

Language : Danish

Religion : Danish Lutheran Church 95%

Danemark

Le Danemark est une monarchie avec un système à multi-partis politiques. Les représentants sont élus au parlement (le Foketing) par représentation proportionnelle mais aucun parti n'a jamais obtenu une majorité. Le pays est gouverné par des coalitions et des minorités.

Langue : le danois

Religion : l'Eglise danoise luthérienne 95%

Dänemark

Die Monarchie Dänemark hat mehrere politische Parteien. Ins Parlament (Foketing) werden Mitglieder der Parteien anteilsmäßig gewählt. Eine Partei hat bisher nie die Mehrheit erhalten. Das Land wird durch Koalitionen und Minoritätsregierungen geführt.

Sprache : Dänisch

Religion : dänische lutherische Kirche 95%

Dinamarca

Dinamarca es una monarquía con un sistema de partidos múltiples (Foketing) por representación proporcional, pero nunca se ha producido la mayoría de un partido ; el país se gobierna a través de coaliciones y gobiernos de minoría.

Idioma : Danés

Religión : Iglesia luterana danesa 95%

Spain

Spain is defined in the Act of Succession as a 'traditional, catholic, social and representative monarchy'. Legislation is the responsibility of the Cortes (Parliament) and the Judiciary is independent. Under the Head of State is the

Espagne

L'Espagne est définie selon l'Acte de Succession comme étant "une monarchie traditionnelle, catholique, sociale et représentative". Le Cortes (le Parlement) est responsable pour la législation, et la judicature est indépendante. Au-

Spanien

Spanien wird im Thronfolgegesetz als 'traditionelle katholische, soziale und repräsentative Monarchie' bezeichnet. Das Parlament (Cortes) ist Gesetzgeber. Die Justizgewalt ist unabhängig. Unter dem Staatsoberhaupt gibt es

España

España se define en el Acta de Sucesión como "una monarquía, tradicional, católica, social y representativa". Las Cortes (Parlamento) son responsables de legislar y el sistema judicial es independiente. El Consejo del Reino está bajo el Jefe

Council of the Realm which delegates a Prime Minister for a term of five years.
Languages : Spanish, Basque (north), Catalan (north-east)
Religion : Roman Catholic

dessous du Chef de l'Etat se trouve le Conseil du Royaume qui nomme un premier ministre pour une période de cinq ans.
Langues : l'espagnol, le basque (au nord), le catalan (au nord-est)
Religion : le catholicisme romain

einen Reichsrat mit einem Premierminister, dessen Amtszeit fünf Jahre beträgt.
Sprachen : spanisch, baskisch (Norden), katalanisch (Nord-Osten)
Religion : römisch katholisch

del Estado, el cual delega en un Primer Ministro por un período de cinco años.
Idiomas : Castellano, vascuence (norte), catalán (nordeste)
Religión : Católica romana

France

France is a republic whose president is elected by general election. The Prime Minister, appointed by the President, recommends the members of his Cabinet. Parliament consists of two houses, the National Assembly and the Senate.
Language : French
Religion : Roman Catholic 90%

France

La France est une république dont le président est élu lors d'élections générales. Le premier ministre, nommé par le président, recommande les membres de son cabinet. Le parlement consiste de deux Chambres, l'Assemblée Nationale et le Sénat.
Langue : le français
Religion : le catholicisme romain 90%

Frankreich

Frankreich ist eine Republik. Sein Präsident wird durch allgemeine Wahl gewählt. Der Premierminister, der vom Präsidenten eingesetzt wird, empfiehlt die Kabinettsmitglieder. Das Parlament besteht aus zwei Häusern, der Nationalversammlung und dem Senat.
Sprache : französisch
Religion : röm. katholisch 90%

Francia

Francia es una república con un Presidente el cual es elegido por elecciones generales. El Primer Ministro es nombrado por el Presidente y le recomienda los miembros del Gabinete. El Parlamento consiste de dos cámaras, la Asamblea Nacional y el Senado.
Idioma : Francés
Religión : Católica romana 90%

UK

The UK is a parliamentary democracy with a two-chamber parliament. Executive power is invested in Her Majesty's Government, headed by a Prime Minister who is leader of the largest party in the lower house (House of Commons). General elections take place at least every five years.
Language : English
Religion : Church of England

Royaume-Uni

Le Royaume-Uni est une démocratie parlementaire avec un parlement à deux Chambres. Le pouvoir exécutif est confié au Gouvernement de Sa Majesté, à le tête duquel se trouve le premier ministre qui est le chef du plus grand parti de la Chambre Basse House of Commons Les élections générales ont lieu au moins tous les cinq ans.
Langue : l'anglais
Religion : l'Eglise anglicane

Vereinigtes Königreich

Das Vereinigte Königreich ist eine parlamentarische Demokratie, dessen Parlament zwei Häuser hat. Die Regierung Ihrer Majestät hat die Executive. Ihr steht ein Premierminister vor, der der Vorsitzende der größten Partei im Unterhaus (House of Commons) ist. Mindestens alle fünf Jahre finden allgemeine Wahlen statt.
Sprache : englisch
Religion : Englische Hochkirche

Reino Unido

El Reino Unido es una democracia parlamentaria con dos cámaras de Parlamento. El poder ejecutivo reside en el Gobierno de Su Majestad, y encabeza el mismo un Primer Ministro, el cual es también el jefe del partido más numeroso en la Cámara Baja (House of Commons). Las elecciones generales tienen lugar al menos cada cinco años.
Idioma : Inglés
Religión : Iglesia anglicana

Italy

Italy, a republic, is a parliamentary democracy. The two houses of Parliament (Chamber of Deputies and Senate) possess very similar powers. The President holds a powerful position and is elected every seven years by both houses of Parliament and representatives from the regional assemblies.
Language : Italian
Religion : Roman Catholic

Italie

L'Italie, une république, est une démocratie parlementaire. Les deux Chambres du Parlement (Chambre des Députés et le Sénat) possédent des pouvoirs identiques. Le président occupe une position d'autorité et est élu tous les sept ans par les deux Chambres du Parlement et par les représentants des assemblées régionales.
Langue : l'italien
Religion : le catholicisme romain

Italien

Die italienische Republik ist eine parlamentarische Demokratie. Die beiden Parlamentshäuser (Abgeordnetenhaus und Senat) haben sehr ähnliche Befugnisse. Der Präsident hat viel Macht und wird alle sieben Jahre von beiden Parlamentshäusern und von Vertretern der Regionalregierungen gewählt.
Sprache : italienisch
Religion : röm. katholisch

Italia

Italia es una república democrática parlamentaria. Las dos Cámaras del Parlamento (Cámara de Diputados y Senado) tienen poderes muy parecidos. El Presidente tiene una posición poderosa y es elegido cada siete años por las dos Cámaras de Parlamento y por los representantes de las regiones.
Idioma : Italiano
Religión : Católica romana

Ireland

Ireland is a parliamentary democracy with a two-chamber Parliament with a President as Head of State. The two houses of Parliament are the Dail, lower house, and Senate, upper house. Elections for the Dail take place at least every five years.

Languages : Irish and English

Religion : Roman Catholic 95%

Irlande

L'Irlande est une démocratie parlementaire avec un parlement à deux Chambres et avec un président comme Chef d'Etat. Les deux Chambres du Parlement sont le Dail, ou Chambre Basse et le Sénat ou Chambre Haute. Les élections pour le Dail ont lieu au moins tous les cinq ans.

Langue : l'irlandais et l'anglais

Religion : le catholicisme romain 95%

Irland

Irland ist eine parlamentarische Demo-kratie mit zwei Parla-mentshäusern und einem Präsidenten als Staatsoberhaupt. Die beiden Parlamentshäuser sind Dail – das Unterhaus – und der Senat – das Oberhaus. Mindestens alle fünf Jahre finden Wahlen für das Unterhaus statt.

Sprachen : irisch und englisch

Religion : röm. katholisch 95%

Irlanda

Irlanda es una democracia parlamentaria con un Parlamento de dos cámaras y con un Presidente como Jefe de Estado. Las dos Cámaras del Parlamento son el Dail, Cámara Baja, y el Senado, Cámara Alta. Las elecciones para el Dail se efectuan cada cinco años.

Idiomas : Irlandés e inglés

Religión : Católica romana 95%

Luxembourg

Luxembourg's government is headed by the Grand Duke and a cabinet. The Grand Duke nominates a Council of State of 21 members. Governments are elected for terms of five years.

Languages : German, French

Religion : Roman Catholic 95%

Luxembourg

A la tête du Gouverne-ment du Luxembourg est le Grand Duc et un Cabinet de Ministres. Le Grand Duc nomme un Conseil d'Etat de 21 membres. Les gouverne-ments sont élus pour une période de cinq ans.

Langues : l'allemand, le français

Religion : le catholicisme romain 95%

Luxemburg

Der Luxemburger Regierung steht der Großherzog und ein Kabinett vor. Der Großherzog ernennt einen Staatsrat mit 21 Mitgliedern. Die Regierung wird für fünf Jahre gewählt.

Sprachen : deutsch, französisch

Religion : röm. katholisch 95%

Luxemburgo

El Gran Duque encabeza el gobierno de Luxemburgo con su gabinete. El Gran Duque nomina a los 21 miembros del Consejo de Estado. Los gobiernos se eligen por un término de cinco años.

Idiomas : Alemán, francés

Religión : Católica romana 95%

Norway

Norway is a monarchy. The Storting (Parliament) consists of two Houses, Lagting (Upper House), and Odelsting (Lower House).

Language : Forms of Norwegian : Bokmal 80%, Landsmal 20%

Religions : Evangelical, Lutheran

Norvège

La Norvège est une monarchie. Le Storting (Parlement) est composé de deux Chambres : Lagting (Chambre Haute) et Odelsting (Chambre Basse).

Langues : (dialectes du norvégien) Bokmal 80%, Landsmal 20%

Religions : l'Eglise évangélique, l'Eglise luthérienne

Norwegen

Norwegen ist eine Monarchie. Das Parlament (Storting) besteht aus zwei Häusern, dem Oberhaus (Lagting) und dem Unterhaus (Odelsting).

Sprache : norwegische Dialekte : Bokmal 80%, Landsmal 20%

Religionen : reformiert, lutherisch

Noruega

Noruega es una monarquía. El Storting (Parlamento) consiste de dos cámaras, Lasting (Cámara Alta) y Odelsting (Cámara Baja).

Idiomas : formas de Noruego : Bokmal 80%, Landsmal 20%

Religión : Evangélica, luterana

Netherlands

Netherlands is a monarchy. Parliament consists of the Eerste Kamer (First Chamber) and the Tweede Kamer (Second Chamber). Members of the former are elected by the Provincial Diets every six years, whilst members for the latter are elected

Pays-Bas

Les Pays-Bas sont un état monarchique. Le parlement comprend l'Eerste Kamer (la Première Chambre) et le Tweede Kamer (la Deuxième Chambre). Les membres de la Première Chambre sont élus par les Diètes Provinciales tous les

Holland

Holland ist eine Monarchie. Das Parlament besteht aus Erster und Zweiter Kammer. Die Mitglieder der ersten Kammer werden alle sechs Jahre von den Provinzregierungen gewählt, während Mitglieder der zweiten Kammer alle vier Jahre

Países Bajos

Holanda es una monarquía. El Parlamento consiste del Eerste Kamer (Cámara Primaría) y Tweede Kamer (Cámara Secundaría). Los miembros de la Primaría se eligen cada seis años por las Dietas provinciales, mientras que

by general election for a period of four years.
Language : Dutch
Religions : Roman Catholic 40%, Protestant 40%

six ans, tandis que les membres de la Deuxième Chambre sont élus aux élections générales pour une période de quatre ans.
Langue : le hollandais
Religions : le catholicisme romain 40%, le protestantisme 40%

durch allgemeine Wahl gewählt werden.
Sprache : holländisch
Religionem : röm. Katholisch 40%, Protestantisch 40%

los miembros de la Secundaría son elegidos por elecciones generales por un término de cuatro años.
Idioma : Holandés
Religión : Católica romana 40%, protestante 40%

Portugal

Portugal is a republic whose President is elected for a term of seven years by an electoral college. He appoints a Prime Minister and other government members on the Prime Minister's advice. There is a single-chamber legislative body (Assembleia Nacional) of 130 elected members.
Language : Portuguese
Religion : Roman Catholic

Portugal

Le Portugal est une république dont le président est élu pour une période de sept ans par un collège électoral. Il nomme son premier ministre, ainsi que les autres membres du Gouvernement selon le conseil de son premier ministre. Il y a une seule assemblée législative (Assembleia Nacional) composée de 130 membres élus.
Langue : le portugais
Religion : le catholicisme romain

Portugal

Portugal ist eine Republik, deren Präsident für die Dauer von sieben Jahren durch ein Wahlkollegium gewählt wird. Er ernennt einen Premierminister und sonstige Mitglieder der Regierung, die der Premierminister vorschlägt. Es gibt eine gesetzgebende Körperschaft (Assembleia Nacional) von 130 gewählten Mitgliedern.
Sprache : portugiesisch
Religion : röm. katholisch

Portugal

Portugal es una república cuyo Presidente es elegido por un término de siete años por un colegio electoral. El Presidente nombra al Primer Ministro y a sugerencia del Primer Ministro a los otros miembros del Gobierno. El cuerpo legislativo es de cámara única (Assembleia Nacional) con 130 diputados elegidos.
Idioma : Portugués
Religión : Católica romana

Sweden

Sweden is a monarchy. The one-chamber Diet (Riksdag) contains three hundred and fifty members who are elected for terms of three years. A Council of Ministers (Statråd) is responsible to the Riksdag.
Language : Swedish
Religion : Lutheran Protestant

Suède

La Suède est une monarchie. La Diète qui est une seule chambre de députés (Riksdag) comprend trois cent cinquante membres qui sont élus pour une période de trois ans. Un Conseil de Ministres (Statråt) est responsable envers le Riksdag.
Langue : le suédois
Religion : le protestantisme luthérien

Schweden

Schweden ist eine Monarchie. Der Reichstag (Riksdag) mit einem Haus hat 350 Mitglieder, die auf drei Jahre gewählt werden. Der Minsterrat (Statråd) ist dem Reichstag unterstellt.
Sprache : Schwedisch
Religion : lutherisch

Suecia

Suecia es una monarquía con Dieta a una cámara (Riksdag) teniendo trescientos cincuenta miembros, los cuales son elegidos por un período de tres años. Un Consejo de Ministros (Statrad) es responsable al Rikdag.
Idioma : Sueco
Religión : Protestante luterana

Finland

Finland is a democratic republic with a one-chamber Parliament. The President has wide powers by the written constitution and has the initiative in foreign policy. General elections are held every four years.
Language : Finnish 93%
Religion : National Lutheran Church 95%

Finlande

La Finlande est une république démocratique avec un parlement à une seule Chambre. La constitution donne des pouvoirs étendus au président qui est entièrement responsable pour la politique étrangère. Les élections générales ont lieu tous les quatre ans.
Langue : le finlandais 93%
Religion : l'Eglise nationale luthérienne

Finnland

Finnland ist eine Demokratie mit einem Parlamentshaus. Das Grundgesetz verleiht dem Präsidenten weitgehende Befugnisse und Initiative in der Auslandspolitik. Alle vier Jahre finden allgemeine Wahlen statt.
Sprache : finnisch 93%
Religion : Nationale lutherische Kirche 95%

Finlandia

Finlandia es una república popular con un parlamento de cámara única. El Presidente tiene extensos poderes escriturados en la constitución teniendo la iniciativa en política exterior. Las elecciones generales se efectúan cada cuatro años.
Idioma : Finlandés
Religión : Iglesia Nacional Luterana

On 25th March 1957, six nations signed the Rome Treaty in order to bring into operation in 1958 the European Economic Community. These countries, Belgium, France, Italy, Luxembourg, the Netherlands and West Germany agreed on a basic objective for their Common Market. This objective was 'the constant improvement of the living and working conditions of their peoples', with special emphasis placed on developing the economic standards in the less fortunate regions.

In 1972, the governments of four other countries, Denmark, the Irish Republic, Norway and the United Kingdom, held concluding negotiations with the Common Market in order to join the Market in 1973. However, in a referendum, the Norwegian people voted against entering the Common Market. There are, therefore, nine members of the enlarged European Economic Community.

The EEC has a population of nearly 250m, including 63.5m people who reside in the three newer member countries. Thus the Common Market now contains over three quarters of the entire population of Western Europe.

Le 25 mars 1957, six nations apposèrent leur signature au Traité de Rome qui préludait à la mise en oeuvre en 1958 de la Communauté Economique Européenne. Ces pays, la Belgique, la France, l'Italie, le Luxembourg, les Pays-Bas et l'Allemagne de l'Ouest se mirent d'accord sur un objectif fondamental pour leur Marché Commun. Cet objectif était 'l'amélioration constante du niveau de vie et des conditions de travail des populations de la CEE' et une importance toute particulière devait être donnée au développement économique des régions les moins favorisées.

En 1972, les gouvernements de quatre autres pays, le Danemark, la République Irlandaise, la Norvège et le Royaume-Uni, ont abouti à la conclusion des négociations poursuivies avec les pays du Marché Commun dans le but de devenir membres de la CEE en 1973. Toutefois, le peuple norvégien, consulté par référendum, a voté contre l'entrée dans le Marché Commun. La Communauté Economique Européenne élargie compte, par conséquent, neuf membres.

La CEE a une population de près de 250 millions, dont 63,5 millions résident dans les trois nouveaux venus parmi les pays membres. Le Marché Commun contient donc maintenant les trois quarts du total de la population de l'Europe Occidentale.

Am 25. März 1957 unterzeichneten sechs Länder den Vertrag von Rom um im Jahre 1958 die Europäische Wirtschaftsgemeinschaft zu verwirklichen. Diese Länder, Belgien, Frankreich, Italien, Luxemburg, Holland und Westdeutschland einigten sich auf ein Grundziel für den Gemeinsamen Markt. Dieses Ziel bestand in der 'stetigen Verbesserung der Lebens- und Arbeitsbedingungen ihrer Bevölkerungen', wobei besondere Betonung auf die Entwicklung des Wirtschaftsniveaus der weniger begünstigten Gebiete gelegt wurde.

Im Jahre 1972 fanden abschließende Verhandlungen der Regierungen von vier weiteren Ländern, Dänemark, der irischen Republik, Norwegen und dem Vereinigten Königreich mit dem Gemeinsamen Markte statt zwecks Beitritt dieser Länder im Jahre 1973. Bei einer Abstimmung entschied sich jedoch das norwegische Volk gegen den Eintritt in den Gemeinsamen Markt. Die erweiterte Europäische Wirtschaftsgemeinschaft wird daher neun Mitglieder umfassen.

Die EWG weist eine Bevölkerung von fast 250 Mio auf, einschließlich von 63,5 Mio, die in den drei neueren Mitgliedländern leben. Der Gemeinsame Markt umfaßt daher nunmehr über Dreiviertel der Gesamtbevölkerung Westeuropas.

El 25 de marzo de 1957, seis naciones firmaron el Tratado de Roma con objeto de poner en práctica en 1958 la Comunidad Económica Europea. Estos países. Alemania Occidental, Bélgica, Francia, Italia, Luxemburgo y Países Bajos se pusieron de acuerdo sobre un objetivo básico para formar un Mercado Común. Dicho objetivo era: 'la mejora constante de las condiciones de vida y de trabajo de sus pueblos', haciendo especial hincapié en el desarrollo de los niveles económicos en las regiones menos afortunadas.

En 1972, los gobiernos de otros cuatro países, a saber, Dinamarca, Noruega, el Reino Unido y la República de Irlanda, finalizaron negociaciones con los países del Mercado Común europeo a fin de unirse al mismo en 1973. Sin embargo, en un referéndum celebrado en Noruega, la mayoría del pueblo noruego votó en contra del ingreso al Mercado Común. Por lo tanto, existen actualmente nueve países miembros en la Comunidad Económica Europea así ampliada.

La C.E.E. cuenta con una población de cerca de 250 millones de habitantas, incluyendo a 63,5 millones que residen en los tres nuevos países miembros. Así, pues, los países que forman el Mercado Común cuentan con más de las tres cuartas partes de toda la población de la Europa Occidental.

Legend

European Economic Community	Communauté Economique Européenne	Europäische Wirtschaftsgemeinschaft	Comunidad Económica Europea
European Free Trade Area	Zone Européenne de Libre Echange	Europäische Freies handelsgebiete	Zona Europea de Libre Comercio
* associate member	* membre associé	* außerordentliches Mitglied	* miembro asociado

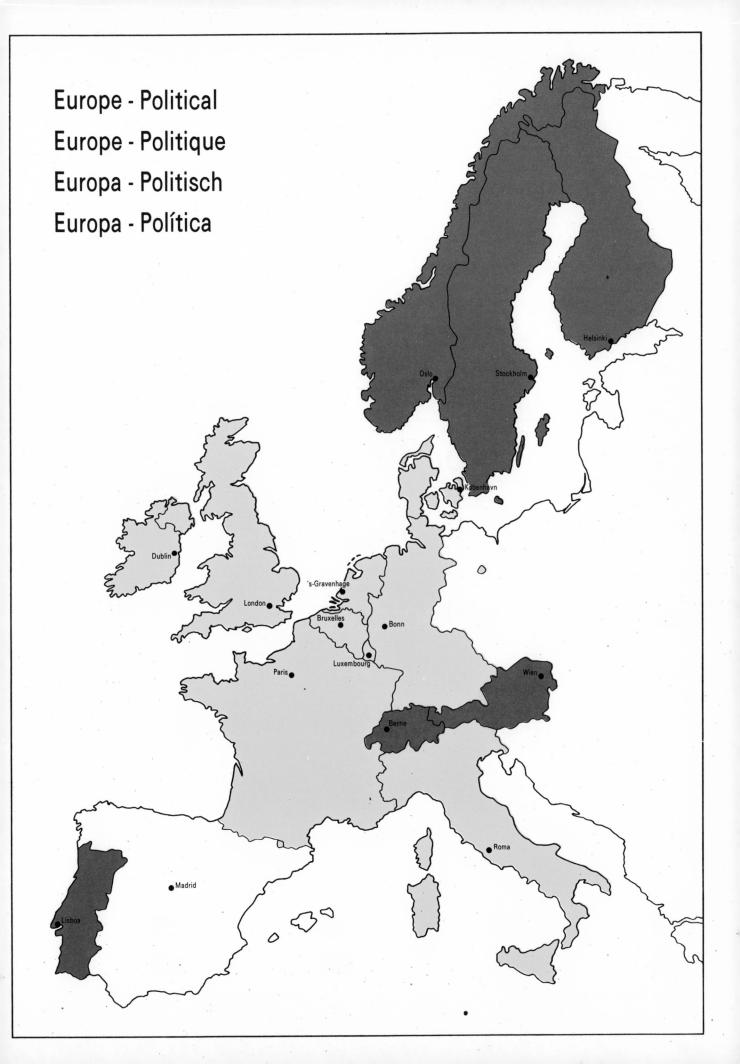

Europe - Political
Europe - Politique
Europa - Politisch
Europa - Política

B

Population

La population

Einwohnerzahlen

Población

This section covers the fundamental marketing aspects of population size, distribution and growth across Western Europe.

Maps and data in this section include:

- National population densities and growth characteristics.
- Regional population densities.
- 100 key urban centres.

The zone of strongest concentration extends from the centre of the UK to northern Italy and includes the Benelux countries, the west part of West Germany, and northern Switzerland. Outside this zone densely populated areas are only to be found surrounding the key cities, especially West Berlin and the immediate surrounds of Paris, Roma, Napoli, Wien, Stockholm, Oslo, Bergen and København.

The basic pattern of population distribution is displayed in the map showing national densities. This shows that the countries with the highest densities are the Netherlands, Belgium, West Germany, United Kingdom and Italy.

Cette section traite des aspects fondamentaux du marketing, de la dimension de la population, de la distribution et de l'accroissement à travers l'Europe Occidentale.

Les cartes et les données de cette section comprennent:

- Les densités des populations nationales et les caractéristiques d'accroissement.
- Les densités des populations régionales.
- 100 principaux centres urbains.

La zone à concentration maximum de population s'étend de la région centrale du Royaume-Uni au Nord de l'Italie et comprend les pays du Benelux, la région ouest de l'Allemagne de l'Ouest et le Nord de la Suisse. En dehors de cette zone, les zones à fortes densités de population se retrouvent autour des villes principales, surtout Berlin Ouest et les régions limitrophes de Paris, Roma, Napoli, Wien, Stockholm, Oslo, Bergen et København.

La modalité fondamentale de la distribution de la population est indiquée sur la carte des densités des populations nationales. Cette carte montre que les pays à densités très élevées sont les Pays-Bas, la Belgique, l'Allemagne de l'Ouest, le Royaume-Uni et l'Italie.

Dieser Abschnitt behandelt die grundlegenden Marketing-Aspekte von Einwohnerzahlen, Bevölkerungsverteilung und-zunahme in Westeuropa.

Karten und Angaben dieses Abschnittes enthalten folgende Einzelheiten:

- Bevölkerungsdichte der einzelnen Länder und Zuwachs.
- Bevölkerungsdichte der einzelnen Regionen.
- Die 100 größten Städte.

Die Zone der stärksten Konzentration reicht von Mittelengland bis Norditalien einschließlich den Beneluxländern, dem westlichen Teil Westdeutschlands und der Nordschweiz. Außerhalb dieser Zone findet man dicht besiedelte Gebiete nur um die großen Städte herum, besonders um Westberlin und in unmittelbarer Umgebung von Paris, Roma, Napoli, Wien, Stockholm, Oslo, Bergen und København.

Das eigentliche Bild der Bevölkerungsdichte wird auf der Karte mit den Bevölkerungsdichten der einzelnen Länder gezeigt. Hier sieht man, daß Holland, Belgien, Westdeutschland, England und Italien die größten Bevölkerungsdichten aufweisen.

Esta sección cubre los aspectos fundamentales de marketing y referentes a la división de la población, distribución y crecimiento a través de Europa Occidental.

Los mapas y datos en esta esta sección incluyen:

- Densidades de las poblaciones regionales.
- Densidades de las poblaciones nacionales y las características del crecimiento.
- 100 centro urbanos claves.

La zona de más fuerte concentración se extiende desde el centro del Reino Unido a Italia del norte, e incluye los países del Benelux, la parte occidental de Alemania del Oeste y el norte de Suiza. Areas densamente pobladas fuera de esta zona, se encuentran tan sólo alrededor de las ciudades claves y especialmente en Berlin occidental y en los alrededores inmediatos de París, Roma, Napoli, Wien, Stockholm, Oslo, Bergen y København.

El mapa nos muestra el patrón básico sobre la distribución de poblaciones y densidades nacionales. Esto nos dice que los países de mayor densidad son, Holanda, Bélgica, Alemania Occidental, Reino Unido e Italia.

National Populations   **Populations nationales**   **Nationale Bevölkerung**   **Poblaciones Nacionales**

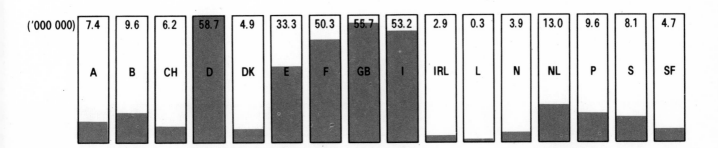

('000 000)	7.4	9.6	6.2	58.7	4.9	33.3	50.3	55.7	53.2	2.9	0.3	3.9	13.0	9.6	8.1	4.7
	A	B	CH	D	DK	E	F	GB	I	IRL	L	N	NL	P	S	SF

The Netherlands, Spain, Portugal and Luxembourg have experienced the highest rates of population growth in Western Europe during recent years. These countries, however, do not possess other similar population characteristics. Luxembourg and the Netherlands are both more densely populated than Spain and Portugal. Furthermore, they are also more industrialised nations.

Finland and Austria have the lowest rates of growth of population. They are both countries with relatively low population densities. However their working populations have different characteristics. Finland has a higher proportion of its labour force in agriculture and mining.

Les Pays-Bas, l'Espagne, le Portugal et le Luxembourg sont les pays d'Europe Occidentale dont les populations ont connu ces dernières années les taux d'accroissement les plus élevés. Par ailleurs, toutefois, les populations de ces pays ne possèdent pas de similarités. Le Luxembourg et les Pays-Bas ont tous deux une densité plus forte que l'Espagne et le Portugal. Et ce sont aussi des pays plus industrialisés.

La Finlande et l'Autriche ont les taux les plus bas d'accroissement de population et ce sont deux pays à densité relativement faible. Mais leurs populations actives présentent des caractéristiques différentes. En Finlande, une plus large proportion de la main-d'oeuvre est employée à l'agriculture et dans les mines.

Der größte Bevölkerungszuwachs in Westeuropa erfolgte in den letzten Jahren in Holland, Spanien, Portugal und Luxemburg. Diese Länder besitzen jedoch sonst keine ähnlichen Bevölkerungsmerkmale. Luxemburg und Holland sind beide dichter bevölkert als Spanien und Portugal. Sie sind darüber hinaus höher industrialisierte Länder.

Finnland und Österreich weisen den niedrigsten Bevölkerungszuwachs auf. Es sind beides Länder mit verhältnismäßig niedrigen Bevölkerungsdichten. Die arbeitenden Bevölkerungen haben jedoch verschiedene Besonderheiten. Finnland hat einen größeren Anteil seiner Arbeiterschaft in der Landwirtschaft und im Bergbau.

Los Países Bajos, España, Portugal y Luxemburgo han experimentado el aumento más elevado de la población en Europa Occidental durante los últimos años. No obstante, estos países no poseen otras características similares en la población. Luxemburgo y los Países Bajos tienen mayor densidad de población que España y Portugal. Además, aquéllas son también naciones más industrializadas.

Finlandia y Austria cuentan con el crecimiento más bajo de la población. Son ambos países con densidades de población relativamente bajas. Sin embargo, las características de su población obrera son distintas. Finlandia tiene una proporción más elevada de su mano de obra en la agricultura y en la minería.

Population Growth

Increase over 5 years

Accroissement de Population

Accroissement sur 5 ans

Bevolkerungswachstum

Zuwachs uber 5 Jahre

Aumento de la Poblacion

Aumento en 5 anos

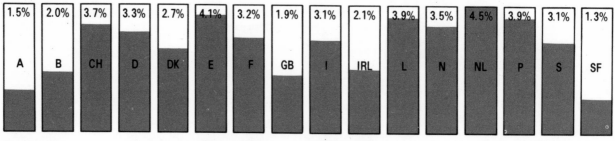

| 1.5% A | 2.0% B | 3.7% CH | 3.3% D | 2.7% DK | 4.1% E | 3.2% F | 1.9% GB | 3.1% I | 2.1% IRL | 3.9% L | 3.5% N | 4.5% NL | 3.9% P | 3.1% S | 1.3% SF |

Average increase for Western Europe 3.0%

Augmentation moyenne pour l'Europe occidentale 3.0%

Durchschnittlicher Zuwachs für Westeuropa 3.0%

Aumento medio para Europa Occidental 3.0%

Population Density

number of inhabitants per km²

Densité de la Population

nombre d'habitants au km²

Bevölkerungsdichte

Einwohnerzahl pro km²

Densidad de Población

número de habitantes por Km²

| Under 100 | 100 + | 150 + | 200 + | 300 + |

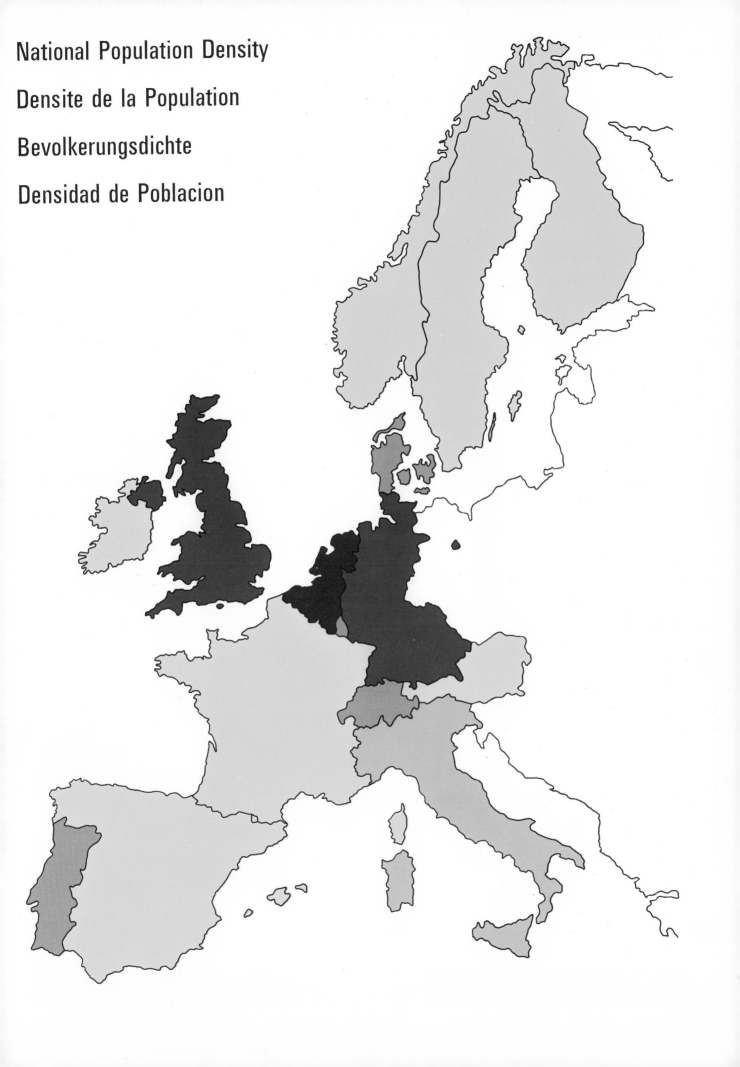

National Population Density

Densite de la Population

Bevolkerungsdichte

Densidad de Poblacion

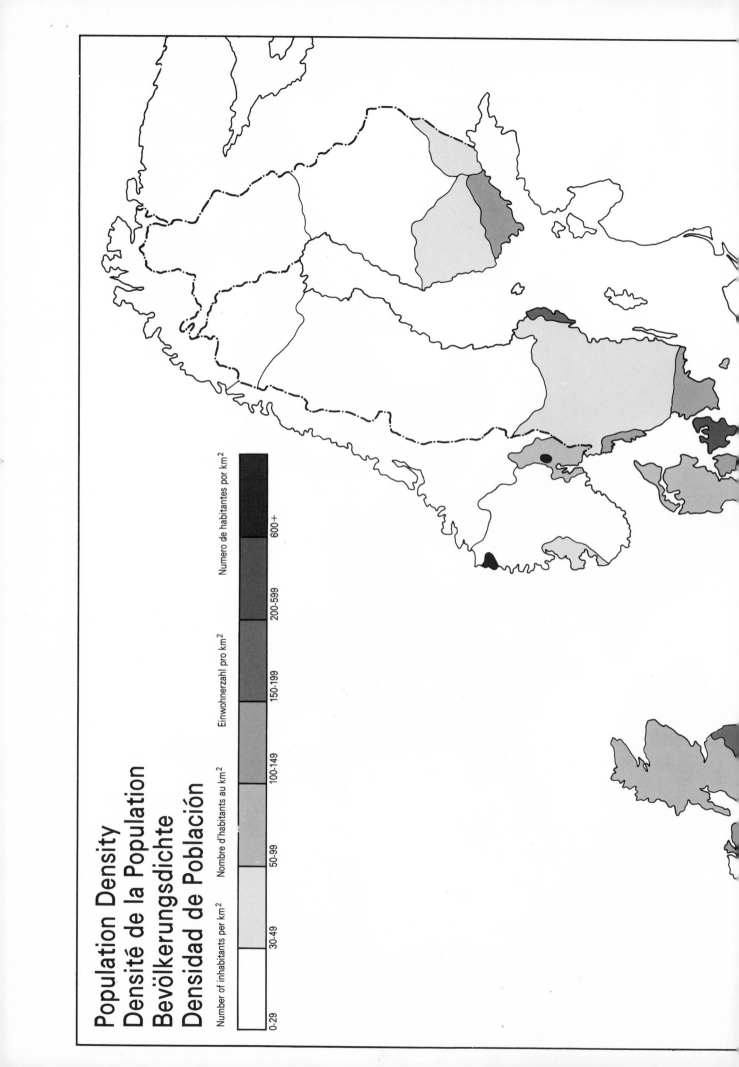

Population Density
Densité de la Population
Bevölkerungsdichte
Densidad de Población

Number of inhabitants per km²   Nombre d'habitants au km²   Einwohnerzahl pro km²   Numero de habitantes por km²

| 0-29 | 30-49 | 50-99 | 100-149 | 150-199 | 200-599 | 600+ |

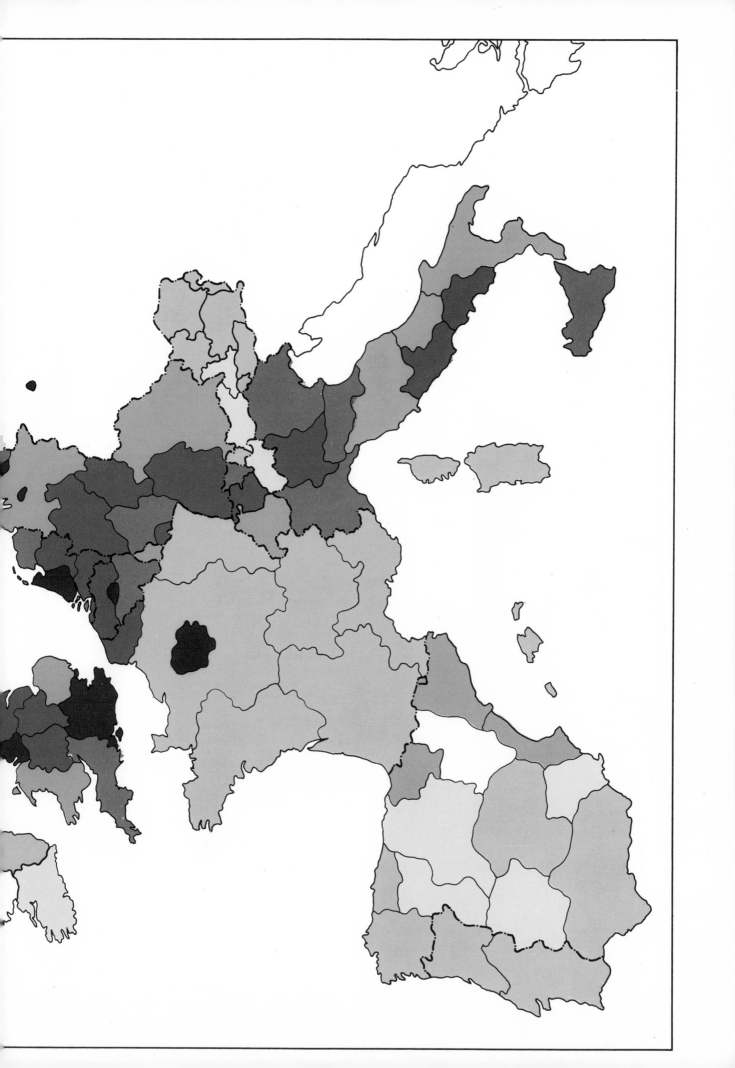

Top 100 major urban centres

Les 100 principaux centres urbains

Die 100 grössten Städte

Los principales 100 centros urbanos

These centres are ranked by size of population.

Ces centres sont classés suivant le nombre d'habitants.

nach Einwohnerzahl geordnet.

Estos centros están clasificados por el tamaño de su población.

City / Ville / Stadt / Ciudad	Population / Population / Einwohner / Población ('000)
1 Paris	8,850
2 London	7,379
3 Berlin-West	5,150
4 Hamburg	3,975
5 Milano	3,365
6 Madrid	2,900
7 Roma	2,810
8 Barcelona	2,375
9 München	2,335
10 Bruxelles	2,070
11 Wien	2,015
12 Napoli	1,875
13 Amsterdam	1,805
14 Köln	1,655
15 Essen	1,625
16 Frankfurt-am-Main	1,520
17 Torino	1,480
18 Stuttgart	1,470
19 Lisboa	1,450
20 København	1,381
21 Stockholm	1,280
22 Mannheim	1,210
23 Birmingham	1,013
24 Rotterdam	1,095
25 Düsseldorf	1,075
26 Antwerpen	1,040

City / Ville / Stadt / Ciudad	Population / Population / Einwohner / Población ('000)
27 Glasgow	960
28 Lyon	920
29 Genova	890
30 Marseille	870
31 Lille	865
32 s'-Gravenhage	840
33 Porto	810
34a Hannover	765
34b Valencia	765
36 Dublin	760
37 Zürich	745
38 Helsinki	710
39 Nürnberg	690
40 Oslo	685
41 Bremen	675
42 Palermo	651
43 Liverpool	607
44 Firenze	595
45 Liège	575
46 Göteborg	565
47 Sevilla	549
48 Wiesbaden	545
49 Manchester	541
50 Basel	530
51a Bologna	520
51b Sheffield	520

City / Ville / Stadt / Ciudad	Population / Population / Einwohner / Población ('000)
53 Leeds	495
54 Bordeaux	480
55 Edinburgh	468
56 Utrecht	435
57 Bristol	425
58 Venezia	415
59 Wuppertal	413
60 Catania	407
61 Belfast	398
62 Teesside	395
63 Zaragoza	393
64 Karlsrühe	370
65 Gent	350
66 Bari	345
67a Coventry	335
67b Genève	335
67c Nantes	335
70 Toulouse	324
71 Málaga	322
72a Krefeld	320
72b Strasbourg	320
74 Augsberg	310
75 Nottingham	300
76 Kassel	295
77 Bradford	294
78 Nice	293

City / Ville / Stadt / Ciudad	Population / Population / Einwohner / Población ('000)
79 St Etienne	290
80 Kingston-upon-Hull	285
81 Leicester	283
82 Trieste	281
83 Eindhoven	280
84a Braunschweig	278
84b Cardiff	278
86 Kiel	270
87a Messina	269
87b Wolverhampton	269
89 Bern	266
90 Stoke-on-Trent	265
91 Cagliari	255
92 Malmö	254
93a Graz	252
93b Verona	252
95 Lübeck	243
96 Plymouth	239
97a Bergen	222
97b Newcastle upon Tyne	222
99 Padova	221
100 Derby	219

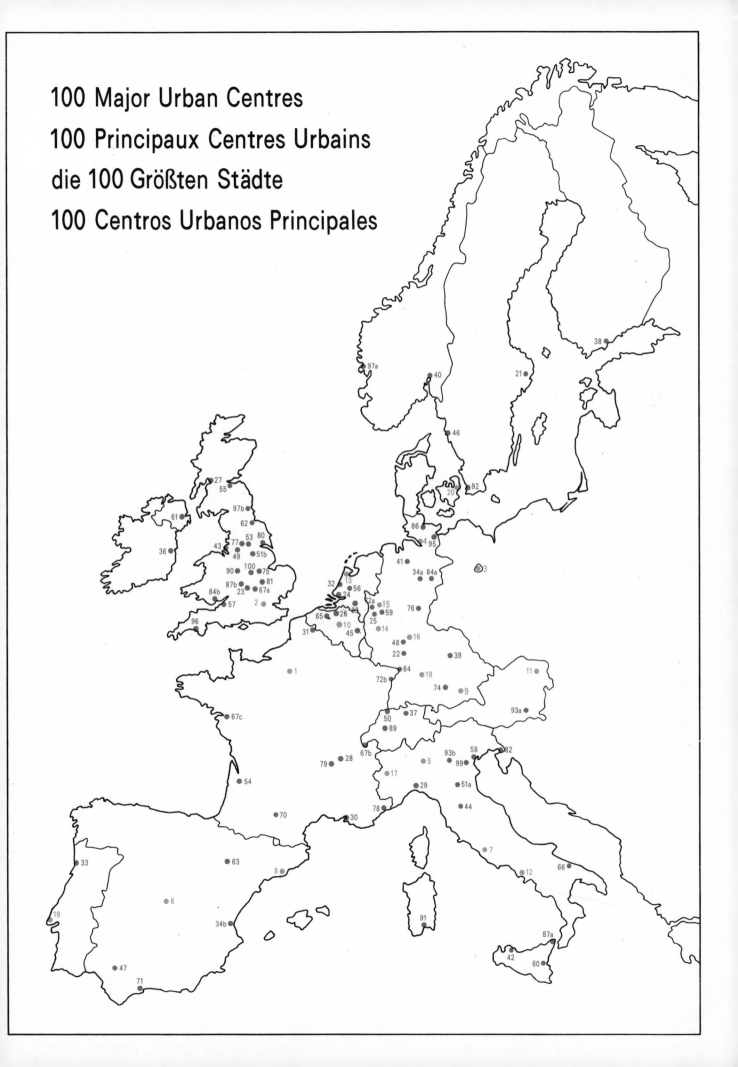

100 Major Urban Centres

100 Principaux Centres Urbains

die 100 Größten Städte

100 Centros Urbanos Principales

C

Labour

La main-d'œuvre

Der Arbeitsmarkt

Mano de obra

Set out in this section are national and regional data covering the related aspects of employment profiles, activity rates and stoppages through industrial disputes.

Maps and data in this section include:
- National employment profiles.
- Distribution of employment in manufacturing by region.
- Unemployment rates by country and region.
- Days lost and numbers of industrial disputes.

Cette section concerne les données nationales et régionales traitant des généralités relatives au profil de la main d'œuvre, aux taux d'activités et d'arrêts de travail à la suite de conflits industriels.

Les cartes et les données de cette section comprennent:
- les profils de la main d'œuvre nationale.
- la répartition de la main-d'œuvre par région.
- les taux de chômage par pays et par région.
- les journées de travail perdues et le nombre de conflits industriels.

Dieser Abschnitt enthält Angaben über nationale und regionale Struktur der Arbeitsstellenverteilung, Beschäftigung und Arbeitsunterbrechung durch Streiks.

In diesem Abschnitt sind Karten und Angaben über folgende Themen zu finden:
- Nationale Arbeitsstellenverteilung.
- Verteilung der Arbeitsstellen in der Produktion in den einzelnen Regionen.
- Höhe der Arbeitslosigkeit nach Ländern und Gebieten aufgeteilt.
- Arbeitsausfälle in Tagen und Anzahl der Streiks.

Esta sección suministra los datos nacionales y regionales relacionados con los perfiles de los empleos, la proporción de actividades y de paros causados por disputas industriales.

Los mapas y datos de esta sección incluyen:
- Perfiles sobre los empleos nacionales.
- Distribución por región de los empleos en fabricaciones.
- Proporciones del desempleo por país y región.
- Número de días perdidos y de disputas industriales.

Employment profiles: national survey

Profils de la main-d'œuvre: enquête nationale

Arbeitsstellen-verteilung: aus nationaler Sicht

Perfiles sobre los empleos: estudio nacional

From the national employment profiles the fact emerges that agriculture still plays a very important part in the economies of Italy, Portugal and Spain. Over 50% of the working population are now involved in commerce and other services in 10 of the 16 countries surveyed.

The manufacturing employment profile shows that industrial Europe is concentrated mainly in:

1 south east France and north west Italy.

2 Belgium, West Germany and Netherlands.

3 Midlands and northern regions of the UK.

De l'étude des profils de la main-d'œuvre nationale il ressort que l'agriculture joue encore un rôle très important dans l'économie de l'Italie, du Portugal et de l'Espagne. Plus de 50% de la population active est maintenant engagée dans le commerce ou autres institutions dans 10 des 16 pays étudiés.

Une profil de la main-d'œuvre manufacturière montre que l'Europe industrielle est concentrée surtout:

1 Dans la région sud-est de la France et celle du nord-ouest de l'Italie.

2 En Belgique, en Allemagne de l'Ouest et aux Pays-Bas.

3 Dans les Midlands et le nord du Royaume-Uni.

Aus der Arbeitsstellenverteilung der einzelnen Länder geht hervor, daß die Landwirtschaft in der Wirtschaft Italiens, Portugals und Spaniens noch immer eine sehr große Rolle spielt. Über 50% der arbeitenden Bevölkerung wird im Handel und in anderen Dienstleistungsbetrieben in 10 der 16 untersuchten Länder beschäftigt.

Die Arbeitsstellenverteilung in der Produktion zeigt, daß die europäischen Industriegebiete sich auf folgende Länder konzentrieren:

1 Südost-Frankreich und Nordwest-Italien.

2 Belgien, Westdeutschland und Holland.

3 Mittelengland und Nordengland.

De los perfiles sobre los empleos nacionales, sale a relucir el hecho de que la agricultura tiene una parte muy importante en las economías de Italia, Portugal y España. En 10 de los 16 paises estudiados más del 50% de la población trabajadora se dedica al comercio u otros servicios.

El perfil de los empleos en fabricaciones nos muestra que las concentraciones principales se encuentran en:

1 Sudeste de Francia y Noroeste de Italia.

2 Bélgica, Alemania Occidental y Países Bajos.

3 Midlands y regiones norte del Reino Unido.

Total Number of Persons Employed in Manufacturing Industries

calculated to nearest 10,000

Nombre total de personnes employées dans les industries de fabrication

calcul à 10.000 personnes pres

Gesamtzahl der in der Produktion Beschäftigten

auf 10.000 auf- oder abgerundet

Número Total de Personas Empleadas en la Industria Fabril

cálculo redondeado a la cifra 10.000 más próxima

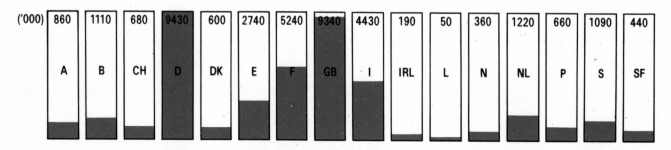

| ('000) | 860 | 1110 | 680 | 9430 | 600 | 2740 | 5240 | 9340 | 4430 | 190 | 50 | 360 | 1220 | 660 | 1090 | 440 |
| | A | B | CH | D | DK | E | F | GB | I | IRL | L | N | NL | P | S | SF |

National employment profiles

Agriculture, fishing, forestry

Mining, quarrying

Manufacturing

Construction

Services

Profil de l'emploi par pays

Agriculture, pêche, sylviculture

Mines, carrières

Fabrication

Construction

Services

Das nationale Beschäftigungsbild

Landwirtschaft, Fischerei, Forstwirtschaft

Bergbau, Steinbruch

Produktion

Bau

Dienstleistungen

Perfiles nacionales de Empleo

Agricultura, pesca, silvicultura

Minería, cantería

Fabricación

Construcción

Servicios

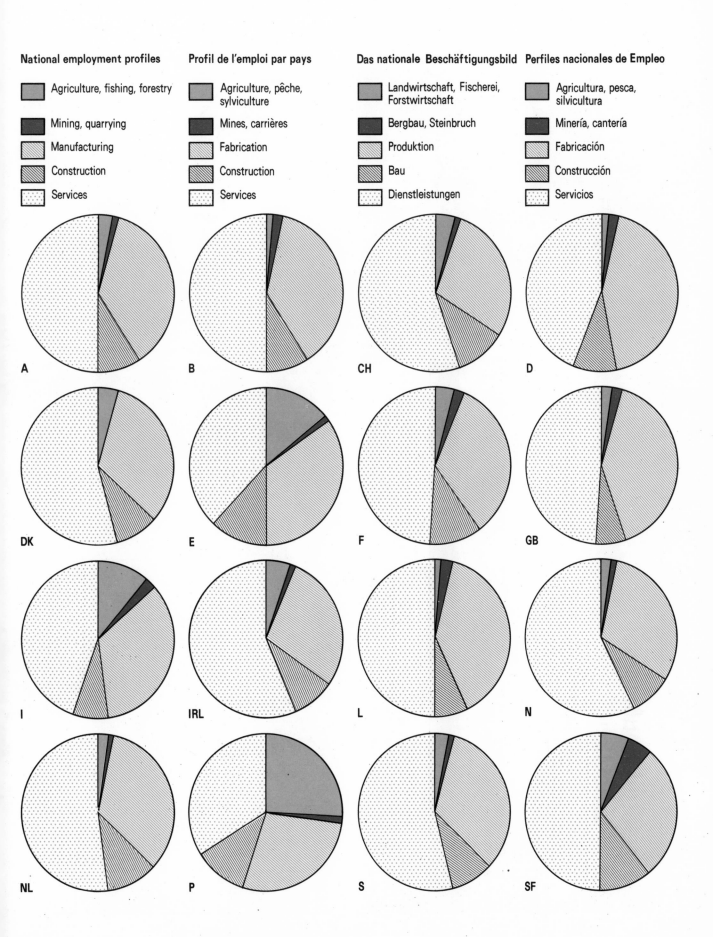

A

B

CH

D

DK

E

F

GB

I

IRL

L

N

NL

P

S

SF

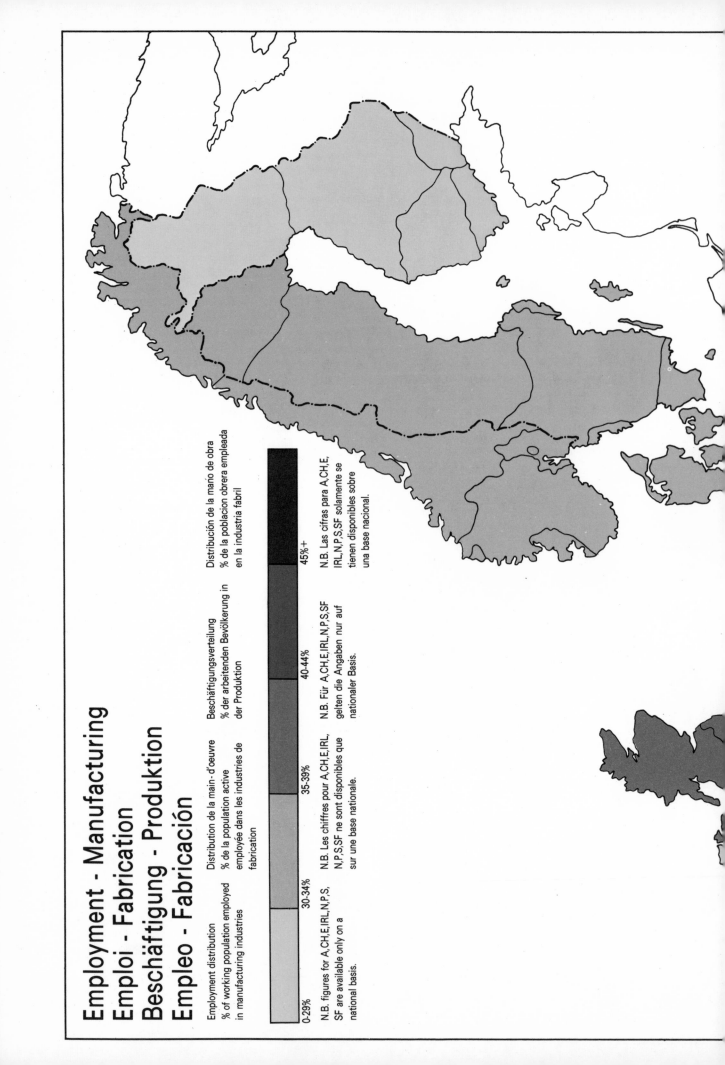

Employment - Manufacturing
Emploi - Fabrication
Beschäftigung - Produktion
Empleo - Fabricación

Employment distribution
% of working population employed in manufacturing industries

Distribution de la main-d'oeuvre
% de la population active employée dans les industries de fabrication

Beschäftigungsverteilung
% der arbeitenden Bevölkerung in der Produktion

Distribución de la maño de obra
% de la poblacion obrera empleada en la industria fabril

0-29%   30-34%   35-39%   40-44%   45%+

N.B. figures for A,CH,E,IRL,N,P,S, SF are available only on a national basis.

N.B. Les chiffres pour A,CH,E,IRL, N,P,S,SF ne sont disponibles que sur une base nationale.

N.B. Für A,CH,E,IRL,N,P,S,SF gelten die Angaben nur auf nationaler Basis.

N.B. Las cifras para A,CH,E, IRL,N,P,S,SF solamente se tienen disponibles sobre una base nacional.

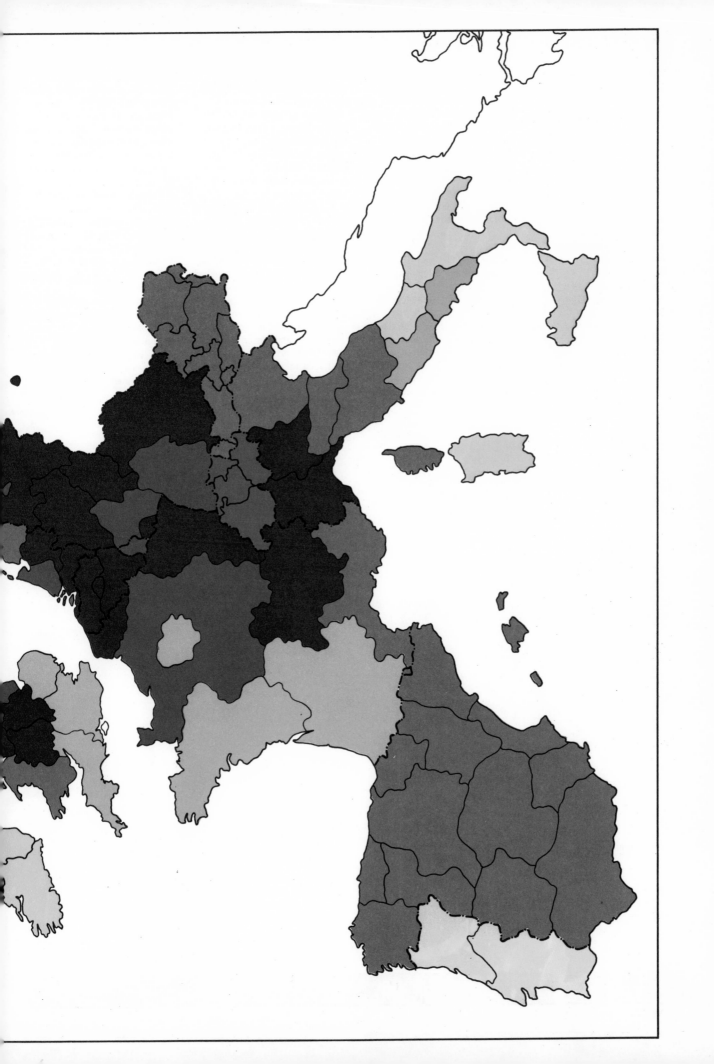

Unemployment

Unemployment rates in the Western European countries for which reliable statistics are available have remained low in recent years. It can be seen from the national map that Ireland has recorded the highest unemployment rates in recent times averaging 5% over five years.

Reliable figures are not available for the Iberian peninsula but it is thought that unemployment rates in Spain and Portugal are relatively high. Estimates of unemployment in Spain range around 8%.

A regional analysis shows that the Northern Ireland region of UK and the Sud region of Italy have experienced the highest unemployment rates in Western Europe.

Le chômage

Les taux de chômage dans les pays de l'Europe Occidentale, pour lesquels existent des statistiques bien fondées, sont demeurés bas au cours de ces dernières années. Il est à constater sur la carte nationale que l'Irlande a enregistré les taux de chômage les plus élevés, une moyenne de 5% sur une période de cinq ans.

Des données sûres ne sont pas disponibles pour la Péninsule Ibérique, mais il est vraisemblable que les taux de chômage en Espagne et au Portugal soient relativement élevés. Le chômage en Espagne est estimé à environ 8 %.

Une analyse par région montre que la région de Northern Ireland dans le Royaume-Uni et la région Sud de l'Italie ont connu les taux de chômage les plus élevés de l'Europe Occidentale.

Arbeitslosigkeit

In den westeuropäischen Ländern, für die Statistiken zur Verfügung stehen, war die Arbeitslosigkeit in den letzten Jahren gering. Aus den Karten für die einzelnen Länder geht hervor, daß Irland kürzlich die stärkste Arbeitslosigkeit zu verzeichnen hatte, da diese fünf Jahre lang über 5% lag.

Für die iberische Halbinsel gibt es keine verläßlichen Angaben. Es wird jedoch angenommen, daß die Arbeitslosigkeit in Spanien und Portugal relativ hoch ist. In Spanien wird die Arbeitslosigkeit auf ca. 8 Prozent geschätzt.

Eine Analyse nach Gebieten zeigt, daß das Gebiet von Northern Ireland im Vereinigten Königreich und das Sud-Gebiet von Italien das höchste Maß an Arbeitslosigkeit in Westeuropa aufwiesen.

Desempleo

En los países de Europa Occidental y en los cuales existen estadísticas fidedignas, la proporción del desempleo se ha mantenido bajo. Puede verse que Irlanda en el mapa nacional ha tenido un récord en el desempleo, hebiendo tenido un promedio del 5% en los últimos años.

Referente a la Peninsula Ibérica no existen cifras fidedignas aunque se calcula que las proporciones de desempleados en España y Portugal es bastante alta. Se estima que la cifra de desempleo gira sobre el 8%.

Mediante un análisis por regiones se pone de relieve que el territorio británico Northern Ireland y la región Sud de Italia, han experimentado los niveles más elevados de desempleo en la Europa Occidental.

Unemployment

average unemployment rate
  over 5 years
N.B. figures for P, CH are not
  available

Chômage

moyenne du taux de chômage
  sur cinq ans
N.B. les chiffres pour P, CH ne
  sont pas disponibles

Arbeitslosigkeit

durchschnittliche Arbeitslosigkeit
  der letzten 5 Jahre
N.B. für P, CH sind keine
  Angaben vorhanden

Desempleo

proporción media de desempleo
  durante 5 años
N.B. no se cuenta con las cifras
  para P. CH

0-0·9%	1-1·9%	2-2·9%	3-3·9%	4%+

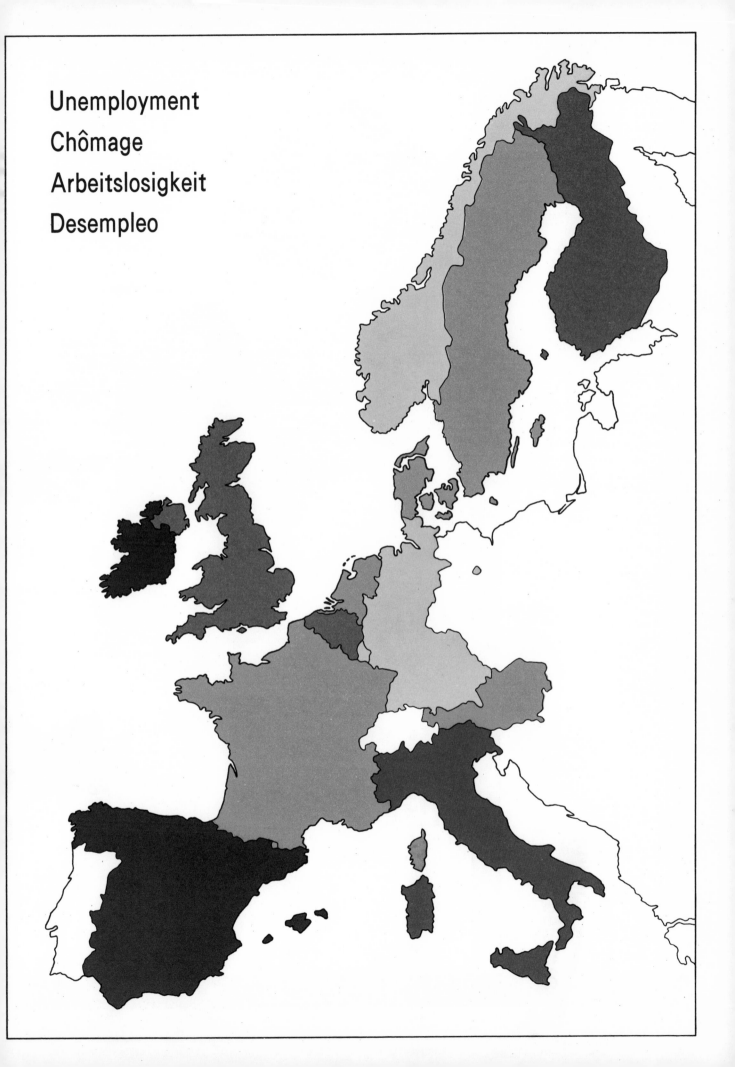

Unemployment

Chômage

Arbeitslosigkeit

Desempleo

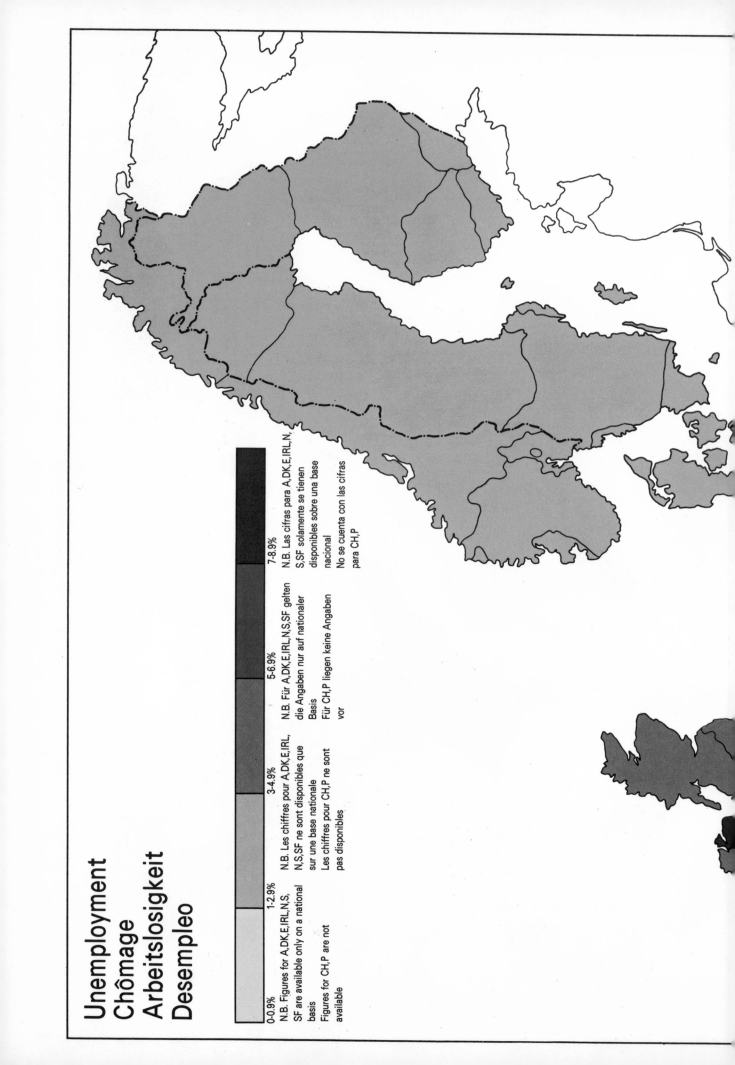

Unemployment
Chômage
Arbeitslosigkeit
Desempleo

0-0.9% 1-2.9% 3-4.9% 5-6.9% 7-8.9%

N.B. Figures for A,DK,E,IRL,N,S,SF are available only on a national basis

Figures for CH,P are not available

N.B. Les chiffres pour A,DK,E,IRL, N,S,SF ne sont disponibles que sur une base nationale

Les chiffres pour CH,P ne sont pas disponibles

N.B. Für A,DK,E,IRL,N,S,SF gelten die Angaben nur auf nationaler Basis

Für CH,P liegen keine Angaben vor

N.B. Las cifras para A,DK,E,IRL,N, S,SF solamente se tienen disponibles sobre una base nacional

No se cuenta con las cifras para CH,P

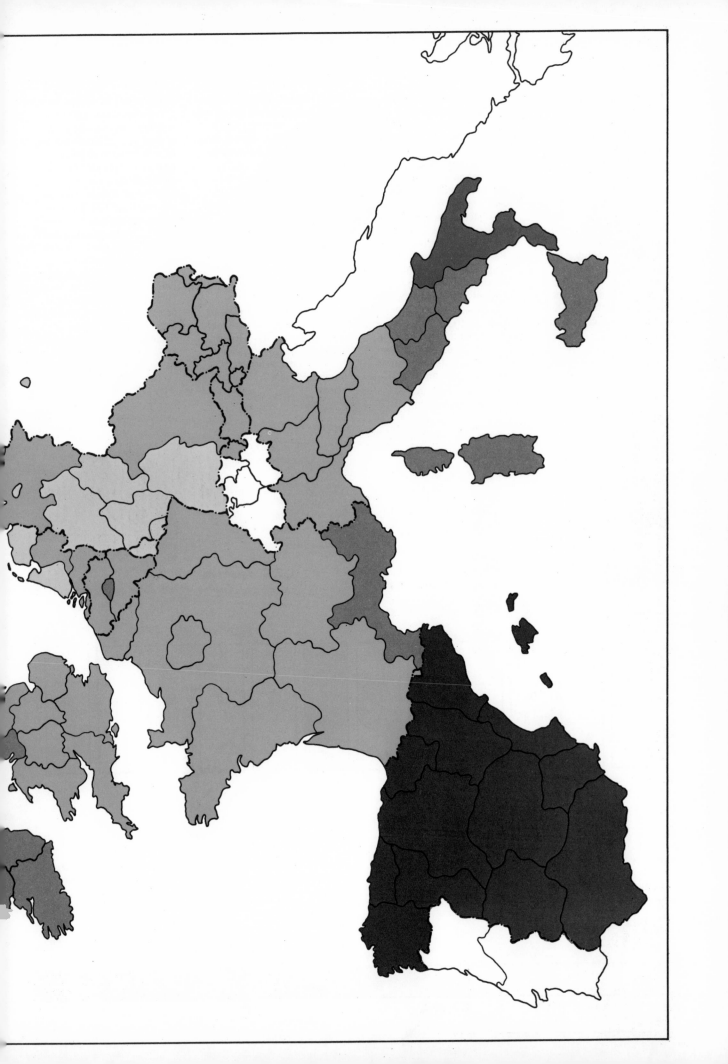

Industrial disputes

A substantial number of countries surveyed have enjoyed good industrial relations in recent years. Indeed an analysis of days lost per worker, identifies two countries – Switzerland and Sweden – which lose less than 0.0001 days per worker each year in labour disputes.

Ireland and Italy, in contrast, have experienced the most troubled labour conditions in terms of days lost per worker. Measured purely in terms of numbers of strikes, the graph below is headed by Italy, UK and France with over 1500 disputes in one year.

Conflits industriels

Un nombre important de pays étudiés ont joui de bonnes relations industrielles dans le courant des années passées. En effet, l'analyse des journées de travail perdues par travailleur et rapportées sur la carte, reconnaît deux pays – la Suisse et la Suède – qui perdent moins de 0,0001 journée de travail par ouvrier par an à la suite de conflits industriels.

Par contre, l'Irlande et l'Italie ont éprouvé le plus grand nombre de troubles en terme de journées de travail perdues per travailleur En se basant seulement sur le nombre de grèves, le graphique ci-après montre que l'Italie, le Royaume-Uni et la France sont en tête de la liste avec plus de 1500 conflits par an.

Streiks

In den letzten Jahren bestanden in den untersuchten Ländern gute Beziehungen zwischen Arbeit-gebern und Arbeitnehmern. In der Analyse der pro Arbeitnehmer ausgefallenen Tage zeigt es sich, daß zwei Länder – die Schweiz und Schweden – weniger als 0,0001 Tage pro Arbeitnehmer pro Jahr an Ausfällen durch Streiks zu verzeichnen hatten.

Im Gegensatz dazu waren die Bedingungen in Irland und Italien am meisten gestört, was die Ausfalltage pro Arbeit-nehmer betrifft. Bei der Anzahl der Streiks zeigt sich, daß laut untenstehender Grafik Italien, das vereinigte Königreich und Frankreich mit mehr als 1500 Streiks in einem Jahr führend waren.

Disputas industriales

De los países estudiados un buén número han tenido buenas relaciones industriales en estos últimos años. Suecia y Suiza se identifican en el mapa que analiza los días perdidos por trabajador, como los países cuyas pérdidas en disputas laborales son menos de 0,0001 días de trabajador por año.

Por contraste Irlanda e Italia son los países que han experi-mentado más transtornos laborales en términos de días perdidos por trabajador. Medido puramente en términos de huelgas, el gráfico a continuación está encabezado por Italia, Reino Unido y Francia, con más de 1500 disputas en un año.

Total Number of Industrial Disputes Resulting in Stoppages of Work

N.B. figures for A, L, P, D are not available

Nombre total de conflits dans l'industrie ayant causé des arrêts de travail

N.B. les chiffres pour A, L, P, D ne sont pas disponibles

Gesamtzahl der Streiks, die Arbeitsunterbrechungen verursachten

N.B. Für A, L, P, D liegen keine Angaben vor

Número Total de Disputas Industriales que se Convirtie-ron en Interrupciones de Trabajo

N.B. no se cuenta con las cifras para A, L, P, D

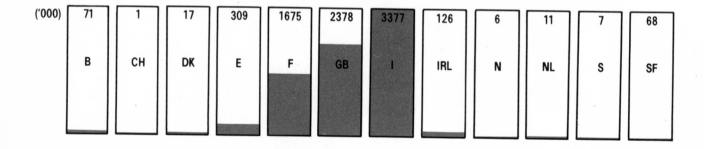

('000)

71	1	17	309	1675	2378	3377	126	6	11	7	68
B	CH	DK	E	F	GB	I	IRL	N	NL	S	SF

Industrial Disputes

number of working days lost per stoppage
N.B. figures for A, L, P, D are not available

Conflits dans l'industrie

nombre de jours perdus par arrêt de travail
N.B. les chiffres pour A, L, P, D ne sont pas disponibles

Industriestreiks

pro Arbeitsunterbrechung ausgefallene Tage
N.B. Für A, L, P, D liegen keine Angaben vor

Disputas Industriales

número de días laborables perdidos debido a interrup-ciones
N.B. no se cuenta con las cifras para A, L, P, D

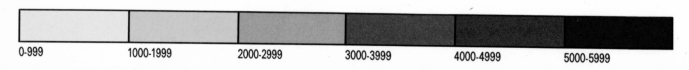

| 0-999 | 1000-1999 | 2000-2999 | 3000-3999 | 4000-4999 | 5000-5999 |

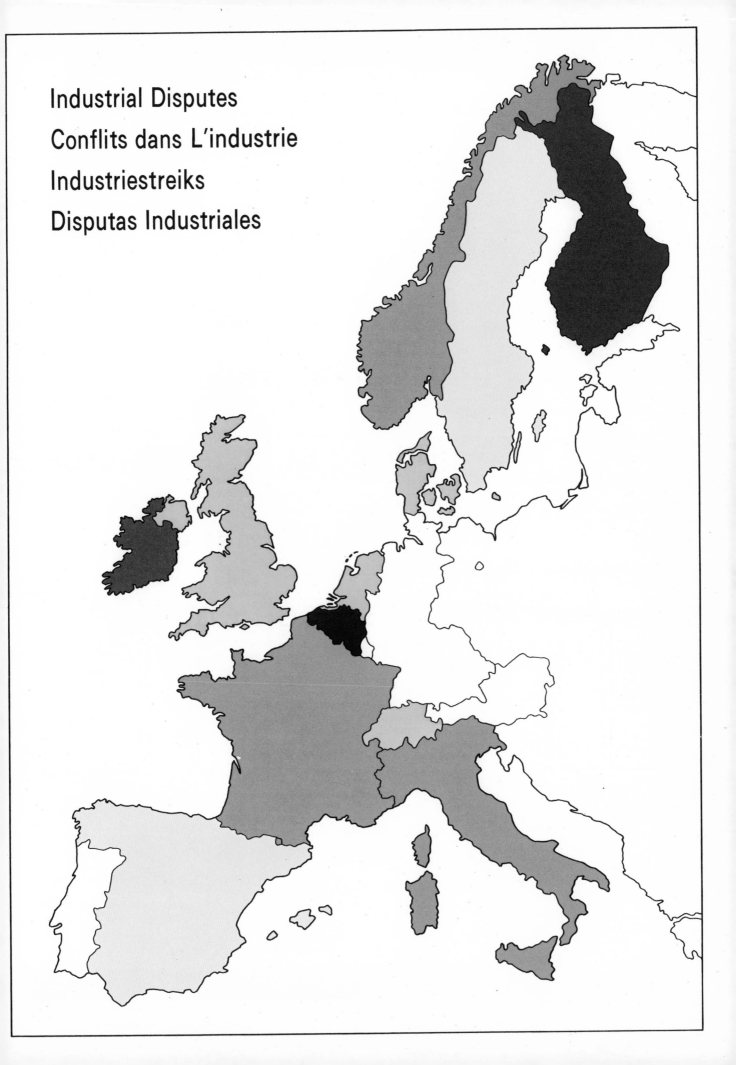

Industrial Disputes

Conflits dans L'industrie

Industriestreiks

Disputas Industriales

D

Finance and trade

La finance et le commerce

Finanzen und Handel

Finanzas y comercio

This final section of Part 1 sets out basic indicators to the financial background and trading status of each country.

Maps and data include:
- Notes and coinage in current usage.
- Names and locations of key European banks.
- Principal trading links.

Cette dernière section de la 1ère partie établit les indications fondamentales de l'arrière-plan financier et de la position commerciale de chaque pays.

Les cartes et les données comprennent:
- Les billets et les pièces de monnaie en usage.
- Les noms et les emplacements des principales banques européennes.
- Les principales liaisons commerciales.

Dieser letzte Abschnitt von Teil 1 beschreibt die Grundlagen des finanziellen Geschehens und der Handelsstellung eines jeden Landes.

Karten und Angaben enthalten:
- Banknoten und Münzen.
- Namen und Anschriften der großen europäischen Banken.
- Die großen Handelsverbindungen.

En esta sección final de la 1ª Parte se han expuesto los indicadores básicos del fondo financiero y rango comercial de cada país.

Los mapas y datos incluyen:
- Billetes y monedas de uso actual.
- Nombre y ubicación de los principales bancos Europeos.
- Los principales enlaces comerciales.

Notes and coins in general use

Papier-monnaie et pièces en circulation

Im Umlauf befindliche Noten und Münzen

Billetes y monedas en uso general

Monetary unit / Unité monétaire / Währungseinheit / Unidades monetarias	Sub-units / Sous-unités / Kleingeld / Sub-unidades	Country / Pays / Land / Nacion	Notes / Papier-monnaie / Banknoten / Billetes	Coins / Pièces de monnaie / Münzen / Monedas
Schilling	100 groschen	A	Schilling : 1,000, 500, 100, 50, 20	Schilling : 50, 25, 10, 5, 1 Groschen : 50, 10, 5, 2, 1
Franc	100 centimes	B	Francs : 5,000, 1,000, 500, 100, 50, 20	Francs : 100, 50, 10, 5, 1 Centimes : 50, 25
Franc	100 centimes	CH	Francs : 1,000, 500, 100, 50, 20, 10, 5	Francs : 5, 2, 1 Centimes : 50, 20, 10, 5, 2, 1
Deutsche Mark	100 Pfennig	D	Deutsche Mark : 1,000, 500, 100, 50, 20, 10, 5	Deutsche Mark : 10, 5, 2, 1 Pfennig : 50, 10, 5, 2, 1
Krone	100 ore	DK	Kroner : 500, 100, 50, 10	Kroner : 5, 1 Ore : 25, 10, 5, 2, 1
Peseta	100 céntimos	E	Pesetas : 1,000, 500, 100, 50	Pesetas : 100, 50, 25, 5, $2\frac{1}{2}$, 1 Céntimos : 50, 10
Franc 1 Franc=100 anciens francs	100 centimes	F	Francs : 500, 100, 50, 10, 5	Francs : 10, 5, 1, $\frac{1}{2}$ Anciens francs : 2, 1 Centimes : 20, 10, 5, 1
Pound	100 pence	GB	Pounds : 20, 10, 5, 1	Pence : 50, 10, 5, 2, $2\frac{1}{2}$ (6d), 1, $\frac{1}{2}$
Lira	100 centesimi	I	Lire : 100,000, 50,000, 10,000, 5,000, 1,000, 500	Lire : 1,000, 500, 100, 50, 20, 10, 5, 2, 1
Pound	100 pence	IRL	Pounds : 100, 50, 20, 10, 5, 1	Pence : 50, 10, 5, 2, 1, $\frac{1}{2}$
Franc	100 centimes	L	Francs : 100, 50, 20, 10	Francs : 250, 100, 5, 1 Centimes : 25
Krone	100 ore	N	Kroner : 1,000, 500, 100, 50, 10, 5	Kroner : 5, 1 Ore : 50, 25, 10, 5, 2, 1
Florin (Guilder)	100 cents	NL	Florins : 1,000, 100, 25, 10, 5, $2\frac{1}{2}$, 1	Florins : 10, $2\frac{1}{2}$, 1 Cents : 25, 10, 5, 1
Escudo	100 centavos	P	Escudo : 1,000, 500, 100, 50, 20	Escudo : 20, 10, 5, $2\frac{1}{2}$, 1, $\frac{1}{2}$ Centavos : 20, 10
Krona	100 ore	S	Kronar : 10,000, 1,000, 100, 50, 10, 5	Kronar : 5, 2, 1 Ore : 50, 25, 10, 5, 2, 1
Markka	100 pennia	SF	Markkas : 100, 50, 10, 5, 1	Markkas : 10, 5, 1 Pennia : 50, 20, 10, 5, 1

Major banks of Europe

Les principales banques d'Europe

Die grössten Banken Europas

Los principales bancos de Europa

The following table highlights major European banks. The banks have been ranked by value of total assets for the latest available year.

Le tableau suivant fait ressortir les principales banques européennes. Les banques ont été classées suivant leurs actifs. Les chiffres cités sont ceux de l'année la plus récemment disponible.

In der folgenden Tabelle sind die größten Banken Europas enthalten. Die Banken wurden nach ihrem Gesamtvermögen des letzten Berichtsjahres bewertet.

El siguiente cuadro saca a relucir los principales bancos europeos. Los bancos se han clasificado según el valor del total de sus activos del último año disponible.

Bank Banque Bank Banco	Location of head office Siège social Hauptsitz Ubicacion de la central	Total assets Capitaux Gesamtvermögen Total del activo	
		£m	$m
1 Barclays Bank Group	London	6,598	15,796
2 National Westminster	London	5,392	12,908
3 Banca Nazionale del Lavoro	Roma	5,044	12,075
4 Banque Nationale de Paris	Paris	4,441	10,632
5 Westdeutsche Landesbank Girozentrale	Düsseldorf	4,382	10,490
6 Deutsche Bank	Frankfurt	4,380	10,485
7 Crédit Lyonnais	Paris	4,098	9,810
8 Midland Bank	London	3,690	8,834
9 Banca Commerciale Italiana	Milano	3,609	8,639
10 Société Générale	Paris	3,382	8,096
11 Cassa di Risparmio Delle Provincie Lombarde	Milano	3,214	7,694
12 Lloyds Bank	London	3,189	7,634
13 Credito Italiano	Milano	3,040	7,278
14 Dresdner Bank	Frankfurt	2,837	6,793
15 Banco di Roma	Roma	2,789	6,676
16 Swiss Bank Corp.	Basle	2,718	6,508
17 Swiss Credit Bank	Zürich	2,713	6,494
18 Union Bank of Switzerland	Zürich	2,494	5,970
19 Commerzbank	Frankfurt	2,369	5,671
20 Standard & Chartered Group	London	2,351	5,645

International Trade   Echanges internationaux   Internationaler Handel   Comercio Internacional

Imports (US $000,000)   Importations   Importe   Importaciones

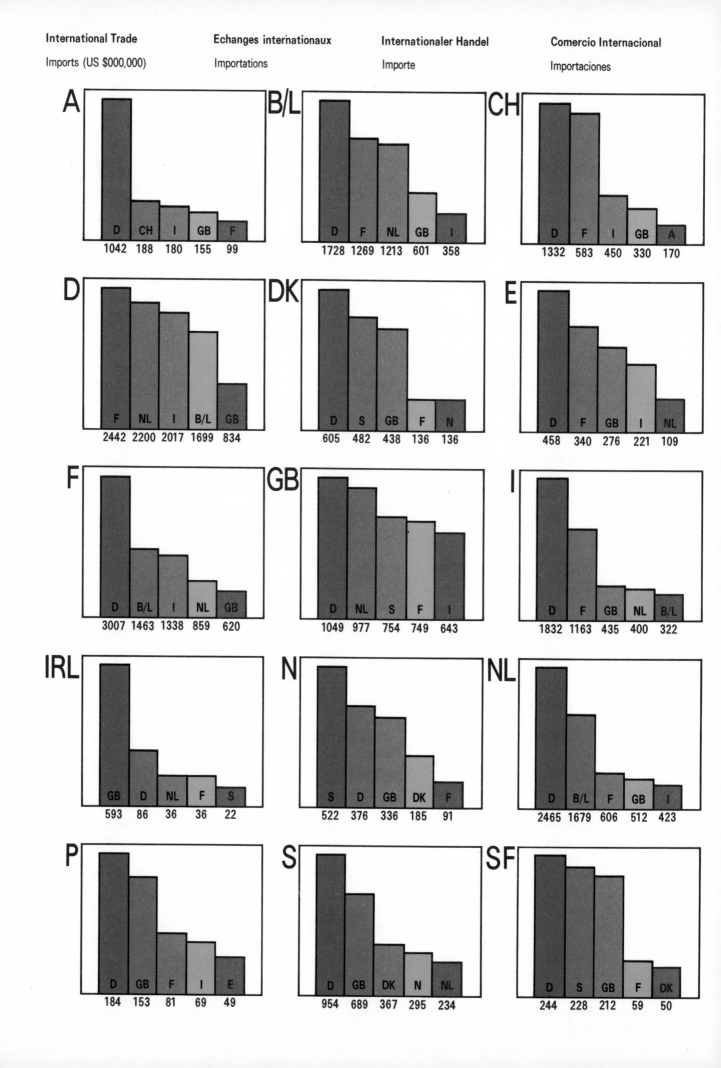

A
D	CH	I	GB	F
1042	188	180	155	99

B/L
D	F	NL	GB	I
1728	1269	1213	601	358

CH
D	F	I	GB	A
1332	583	450	330	170

D
F	NL	I	B/L	GB
2442	2200	2017	1699	834

DK
D	S	GB	F	N
605	482	438	136	136

E
D	F	GB	I	NL
458	340	276	221	109

F
D	B/L	I	NL	GB
3007	1463	1338	859	620

GB
D	NL	S	F	I
1049	977	754	749	643

I
D	F	GB	NL	B/L
1832	1163	435	400	322

IRL
GB	D	NL	F	S
593	86	36	36	22

N
S	D	GB	DK	F
522	376	336	185	91

NL
D	B/L	F	GB	I
2465	1679	606	512	423

P
D	GB	F	I	E
184	153	81	69	49

S
D	GB	DK	N	NL
954	689	367	295	234

SF
D	S	GB	F	DK
244	228	212	59	50

International Trade
Exports (US $'000 000)

Echanges internationaux
Exportations (US $'000 000)

Internationaler Handel
Exporte (US $'000 000)

Comercio Internacional
Exportaciones (US $'000 000)

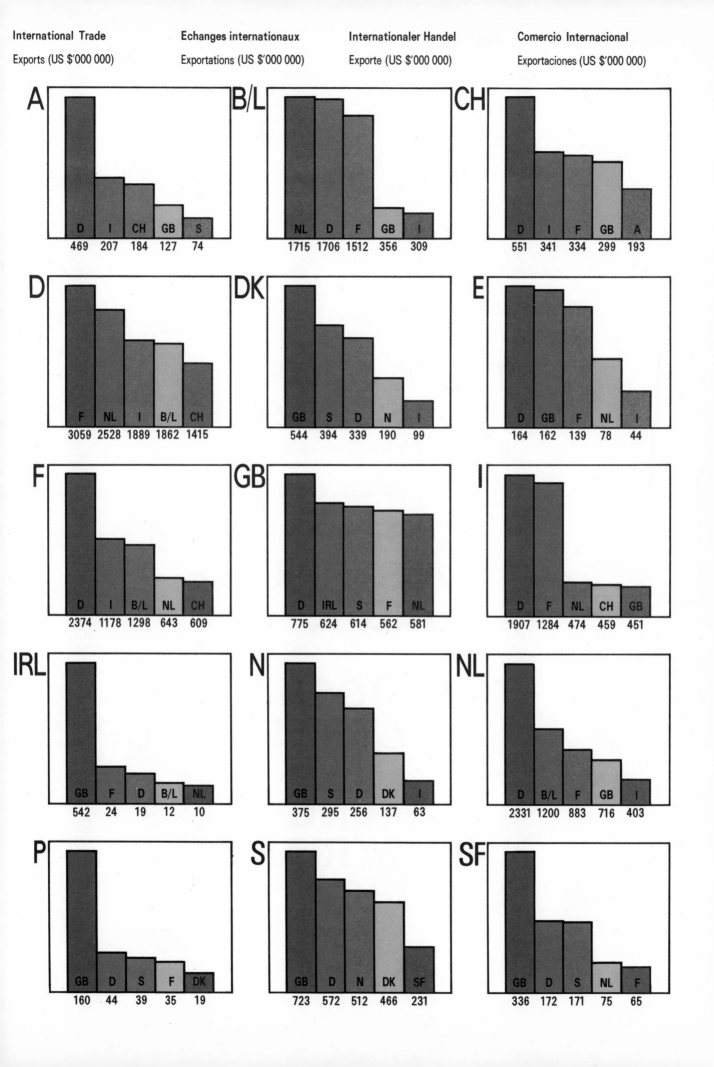

A
D	I	CH	GB	S
469	207	184	127	74

B/L
NL	D	F	GB	I
1715	1706	1512	356	309

CH
D	I	F	GB	A
551	341	334	299	193

D
F	NL	I	B/L	CH
3059	2528	1889	1862	1415

DK
GB	S	D	N	I
544	394	339	190	99

E
D	GB	F	NL	I
164	162	139	78	44

F
D	I	B/L	NL	CH
2374	1178	1298	643	609

GB
D	IRL	S	F	NL
775	624	614	562	581

I
D	F	NL	CH	GB
1907	1284	474	459	451

IRL
GB	F	D	B/L	NL
542	24	19	12	10

N
GB	S	D	DK	I
375	295	256	137	63

NL
D	B/L	F	GB	I
2331	1200	883	716	403

P
GB	D	S	F	DK
160	44	39	35	19

S
GB	D	N	DK	SF
723	572	512	466	231

SF
GB	D	S	NL	F
336	172	171	75	65

2

THE MAJOR INDUSTRIES OF EUROPE

LES PRINCIPALES INDUSTRIES DE L'EUROPE

DIE GRÖSSTEN INDUSTRIEN EUROPAS

LAS PRINCIPALES INDUSTRIAS DE EUROPA

Introduction to Part 2

Part 2 of the Atlas provides facts and analyses relative to industrial markets. The industry surveys also provide comparative data on areas of production and competing companies for readers dealing with consumer markets.

Seven key industrial sector groupings have been selected for inclusion in this survey. These groupings cover very wide areas of industry, and between them account for nearly 95% of all manufacturing output.

Each section is a self-contained summary of one industry grouping. It includes such data as employment distribution, output analyses, a listing of major companies and areas of designated key activity.

Introduction de la II ème partie

La deuxième partie de cet Atlas fournit des faits et des analyses des marchés industriels. Les enquêtes industrielles procurent aussi des données de comparaison des régions productrices et des entreprises concurrentes pour les lecteurs qui s'intéressent aux marchés des biens de consommation.

Sept groupements principaux de secteurs industriels ont été inclus dans cette étude. Les secteurs industriels les plus divers sont compris à l'intérieur de ces groupements qui, entre eux, sont responsables pour près de 95 pour cent de tout le rendement industriel.

Chaque section est un résumé indépendant d'une industrie. Elle comprend des informations telles que la distribution de la main-d'oeuvre, des analyses de la productivité, une liste des entreprises les plus importantes et les régions reconnues comme étant très actives industriellement.

Einführung zu Teil 2

Teil 2 des Atlas enthält Tatsachen und Analysen über die Industriemärkte. In der Industrie-untersuchung sind ferner Angaben über den Produktions-bereich und die Konkurrenzfirmen enthalten, die für Leser interessant sind, die sich mit dem Verbrauchermarkt befassen.

In der Untersuchung sind sieben Industriegruppen beleuchtet worden. Diese Gruppen gelten für viele Industrien und decken fast 95% der gesamten Produktion.

Jeder Abschnitt behandelt eine Industriegruppe allein. Arbeitsstellenverteilung, Leistungsanalysen und eine Liste der größten Firmen sowie Bereiche der Haupttätigkeit wurden aufgeführt.

Introducción a la 2ª Parte

En la segunda parte de este Atlas se suministran análisis y hechos sobre los mercados industriales. En el estudio industrial tembién se suministran datos comparativos de las áreas de producción y para los lectores que tratan en los mercados de consumo, se comparan sociedades.

Han sido seleccionados siete grupos de sectores industriales claves para ser incluidos en el estudio. Dichos grupos cubren extensas áreas industriales, y entre ellas suman un 95% de todas las producciones en fabricación.

Cada sección es un resumen completo de un grupo industrial. También se incluyen datos tales como la distribución de los empleos, análisis de producción, listas de las principales compañías y áreas designadas de actividad principal.

E

Agriculture

L'agriculture

Landwirtschaft

Agricultura

The GEP industry classification of agriculture includes agriculture, forestry and fishing.

The regional distribution of employment in these sectors is charted in the following map. It also includes fishing ports and areas of principal agricultural activity by main types of product.

Agriculture is accounting for a steadily declining share of employment in most Western European countries. It is in the less industrialised areas that it continues to fulfil a substantial function. Regions where agriculture remains of particular importance are central and northern Finland (timber) and southern Italy (fruit and arable farming).

La classification industrielle de l'agriculture établie par GEP comprend l'agriculture proprement dite, la syviculture et la pêche.

La répartition régionale de la main-d'oeuvre dans ces secteurs est indiquée sur la carte suivante qui comprend aussi les ports de pêche et les principales régions agricoles suivant les principaux produits cultivés.

Dans l'agriculture, la diminution de la main-d'oeuvre persiste dans la plupart des pays de l'Europe Occidentale. C'est dans les régions moins industrialisées qu'elle continue à remplir un rôle essentiel. Les régions où l'agriculture continue à revêtir une importance spéciale sont le centre et le nord de la Finlande (le bois de construction) et l'Italie du sud (l'exploitation fruitcole et la culture).

In der GEP-Klassierung für die Industrie sind Landwirtschaft, Forstwirtschaft und Fischerei in der Gruppe Landwirtschaft enthalten.

Die regionale Verteilung der Beschäftigung in diesen Gebieten wird auf der folgenden Karte gezeigt. Auf ihr sind auch die Fischereihäfen und die großen Landwirtschaftsgebiete mit ihren Hauptprodukten enthalten.

In den meisten westeuropäischen Ländern geht die Beschäftigung in der Landwirtschaft ständig zurück. Nur in den weniger industrialisierten Gebieten erfüllt sie eine wichtige Funktion. In Mittel- und Nordfinnland (Holz) sowie Süditalien (Obst und Ackerbau) hat die Landwirtschaft noch große Bedeutung.

En la clasificación del GEP de industrias de la agricultura, se incluye la agricultura, selvicultura y pesca.

En el mapa a continuación se exponen las distribución de los empleos regionales en estos sectores. También se incluyen puertos y las principales áreas de actividad agrícola por los principales tipos de productos.

En la mayoría de los países de Europa Occidental la agricultura está en declive continuo. En las áreas menos industrializadas ejerce todavía una función substancial. Las regiones a donde la agricultura es todavía de particular importancia son las siguientes: Finlandia del norte y centro (madera) e Italia meridional (frutas y tierras de arado).

Total Number of Persons Employed in Agriculture, Forestry and Fishing

Nombre total de personnes employées dans l'agriculture, la sylviculture et la pêche

Gesamtbeschäftigte in der Landwirtschaft, Forstwirtschaft und in der Fischerei

Número Total de Personas Empleadas en Agricultura, Silvicultura y Pesca

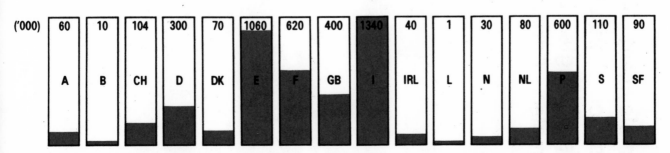

('000)	60	10	104	300	70	1060	620	400	1340	40	1	30	80	600	110	90
	A	B	CH	D	DK	E	F	GB	I	IRL	L	N	NL	P	S	SF

Employment - Agriculture
Emploi - Agriculture
Beschäftigte - Landwirtschaft
Empleo - Agricultura

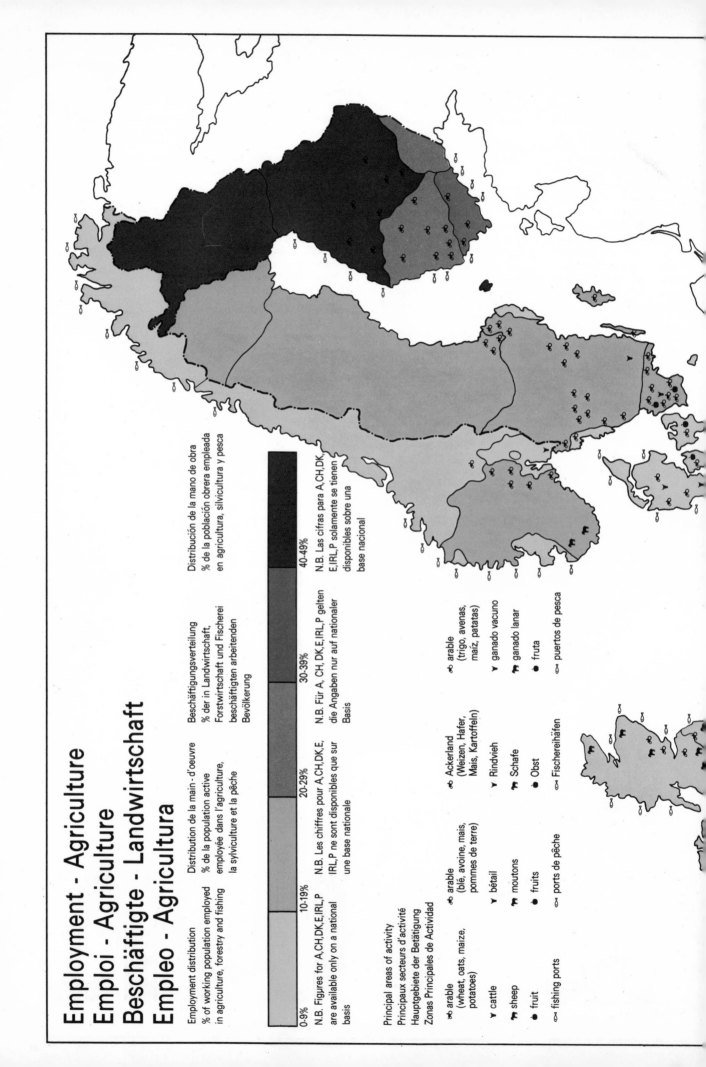

Employment distribution

% of working population employed in agriculture, forestry and fishing

N.B. Figures for A,CH,DK,E,IRL,P are available only on a national basis

Distribution de la main - d'oeuvre

% de la population active employée dans l'agriculture, la sylviculture et la pêche

N.B. Les chiffres pour A,CH,DK,E, IRL,P ne sont disponibles que sur une base nationale

Beschäftigungsverteilung

% der in Landwirtschaft, Forstwirtschaft und Fischerei beschäftigten arbeitenden Bevölkerung

N.B. Für A, CH, DK,E,IRL,P gelten die Angaben nur auf nationaler Basis

Distribución de la mano de obra

% de la población obrera empleada en agricultura, silvicultura y pesca

N.B. Las cifras para A,CH,DK, E,IRL,P solamente se tienen disponibles sobre una base nacional

0-9%   10-19%   20-29%   30-39%   40-49%

Principal areas of activity
Principaux secteurs d'activité
Hauptgebiete der Betätigung
Zonas Principales de Actividad

arable (wheat, oats, maize, potatoes)

cattle

sheep

fruit

fishing ports

arable (blé, avoine, maïs, pommes de terre)

bétail

moutons

fruits

ports de pêche

Ackerland (Weizen, Hafer, Mais, Kartoffeln)

Rindvieh

Schafe

Obst

Fischereihäfen

arable (trigo, avenas, maíz, patatas)

ganado vacuno

ganado lanar

fruta

puertos de pesca

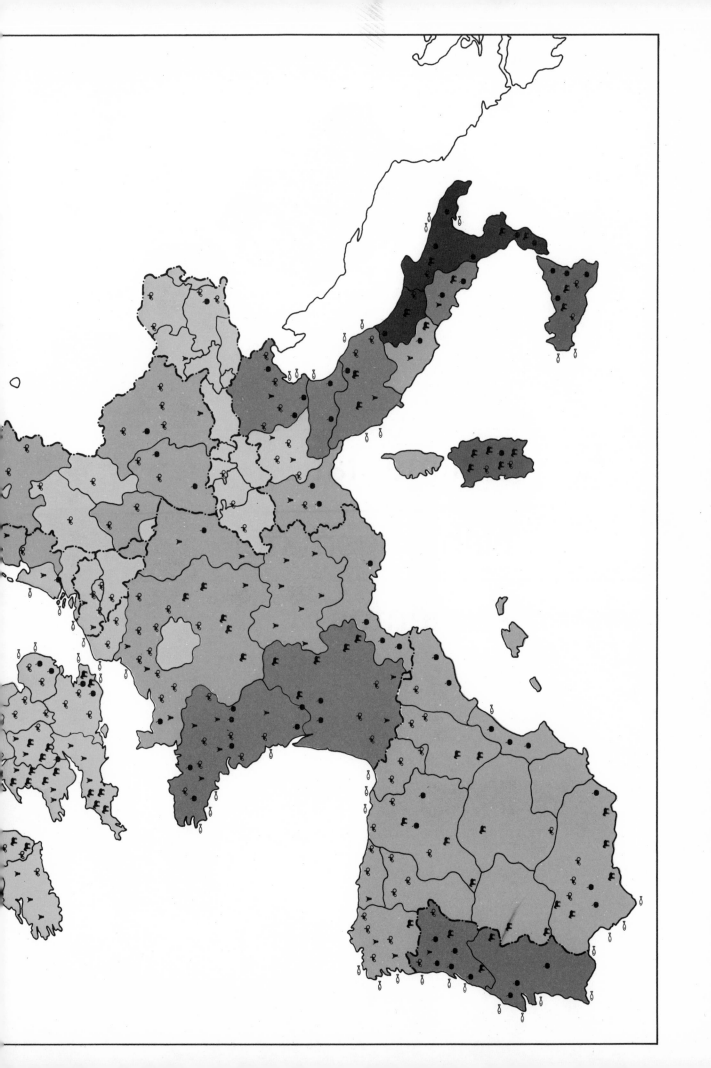

F

Food

L'alimentation

Nahrungsmittel

Alimentos

The GEP industry classification of food industries includes the manufacture of all types of food products together with drink and tobacco.

Maps and data in this section include:
- Value added per capita.
- Employment distribution.
- Major food, drink and tobacco companies.

La classification industrielle des industries alimentaires établie par GEP comprend la fabrication de tous genres de produits alimentaires ainsi que des boissons et du tabac.

Les cartes et les données de cette section comprennent:
- La valeur ajoutée par tête.
- La répartition de la main-d'oeuvre.
- Les principales sociétés engagées dans les industries alimentaires, des boissons et du tabac.

In der GEP-Klassierung für die Nahrungsmittelindustrie sind alle Hersteller von Nahrungsmit-telprodukten sowie Getränke-und Tabakhersteller enthalten.

In diesem Abschnitt enthalten Karten und Angaben:
- Leistungswert pro Kopf.
- Verteilung der Beschäftigung.
- Die größten Hersteller von Nahrungsmitteln, Getränken und Tabakwaren.

En la clasiticación de GEP de industrias del ramo de la alimentación se incluye la fabricación de todos los tipos de productos alimenticios conjunta-mente con bebidas y tabaco.

En los mapas y datos de esta sección se incluye:
- Valor añadido per cápita.
- Distribución de los empleos.
- Principales compañías de productos alimenticios, de bebidas y de tabaco.

Value of output per capita
(US $ per annum)

N.B. Figure for CH is not available

Average for Western Europe $52

Valeur ajoutée par tête
(US $ par an)

N.B. Le chiffre pour CH n'est pas disponible

Moyenne pour l'Europe occidentale $52

Leistungswert pro Kopf
(US $ pro Jahr)

N.B. Für CH liegen keine Angaben vor

Durchschnitt für Westeuropa $52

Valo de la producción por cabeza
(US $ por ano)

N.B. no se cuenta con la cifra para CH

Promedio para Europa Occidental $52

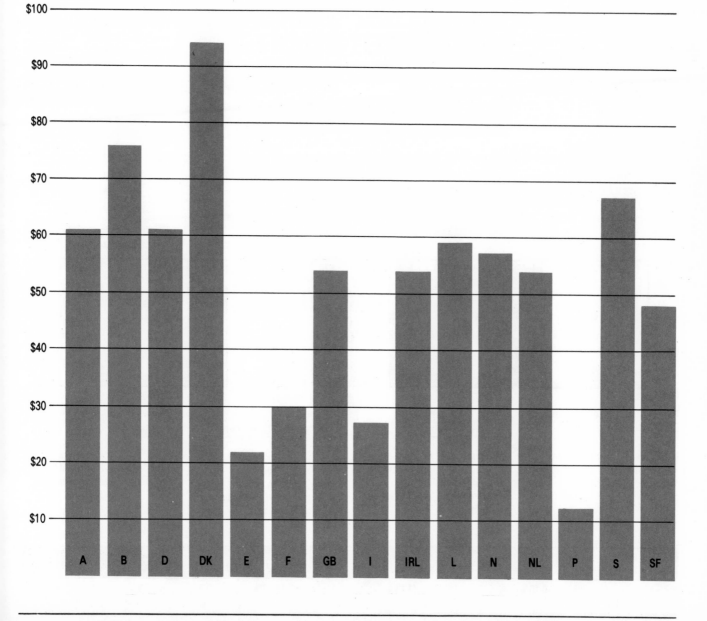

The location of the food industry in Western Europe is determined by the availability of produce (either through locally produced foodstuffs or by trade) and proximity of market. The pattern of location, whilst following the incidence of agriculture, is also influenced by the spread of population.

The four countries that are identified as having the highest proportions of the manufacturing population engaged in the food industries are Ireland, Norway, Denmark and the Netherlands. The first three have particularly large agricultural communities.

The importance of the first three countries in this respect reflects the substantial contribution to national output provided by agriculture. In the case of the Netherlands, established international trade has led to the growth of major food processing plants serving not only the Netherlands but also neighbouring countries.

In contrast the agricultural base of Italy has not required the establishment of a food processing industry of comparable size. It can be seen from the map that the level of all employees in manufacturing which is engaged in food processing is less than 10%.

L'emplacement de l'industrie alimentaire en Europe Occidentale est fonction de la disponibilité des produits (soit denrées alimentaires produites localement, soit importées) et de la proximité des marchés. La répartition de ces emplacements bien qu'elle soit liée à l'incidence agricole, est aussi influencée par le déploiement de la population.

Les quatre pays qui s'identifient par la forte proportion de leur population manufacturière engagée dans les industries alimentaires sont l'Irlande, la Norvège, le Danemark et les Pays-Bas. Les trois premiers de ces pays possèdent une très grosse population agricole.

L'importance de ces trois pays dans ce secteur industriel reflète la contribution de l'agriculture à la productivité nationale. Dans le cas des Pays-Bas, l'établissement du commerce international a entraîné l'accroissement du nombre de fabriques de produits alimentaires qui desservent non seulement le pays lui-même mais aussi les pays avoisinants.

Par contre, la structure agricole de l'Italie n'a pas nécessité l'établissement d'une industrie de produits alimentaires d'une importance comparable. Comme la carte l'indique, la main-d'oeuvre manufacturière engagée dans l'industrie des produits alimentaires est inférieure à 10%.

Die Lage der Nahrungsmittelindustrie in Westeuropa wird durch das Vorhandensein der Produkte bestimmt (entweder durch örtlich hergestellte Nahrungsmittel oder durch den Handel) und die Nähe des Absatzgebietes. Obgleich sich die Industrie in der Nähe der Landwirtschaft befindet, wird sie auch von der Verteilung der Bevölkerung beeinflußt.

Die vier Länder mit der höchsten Beschäftigung in der Nahrungsmittelbranche sind Irland, Norwegen, Dänemark und Holland. Die ersten drei haben besonders große landwirtschaftliche Gemeinschaften.

Die Bedeutung der ersten drei Länder zeigt, welchen großen Beitrag die Landwirtschaft zur Leistung des Landes leistet. In Holland haben die alten internationalen Handelsbeziehungen zum Wachstum der großen Nahrungsmittelverarbeitungsanlagen geführt, die nicht dur Holland, sondern auch Nachbarländer beliefern.

Im Gegensatz dazu brauchte das landwirtschaftliche Gebiet von Italien noch keine so große Nahrungsmittelverarbeitungsindustrie, die einem Vergleich standhielte. Aus der Karte ist ersichtlich, daß unter 10% aller Beschäftigten in der Nahrungsmittelverarbeitung tätig sind.

En Europa Occidental la ubicación de la industria de la alimentación se determina por la asequibilidad de los productos, (tanto como productos locales alimenticios o por los de comercio) y la proximidad del mercado. El cuadro de ubicación si bien sigue la incidencia de la agricultura, también es afectado por el desparramo de la población.

Irlanda, Noruega, Dinamarca y Holanda son los países con las proporciones más altas de población empleada en las industrias alimenticias. Los tres primeros países tienen comunidades agrícolas particularmente importantes.

La importancia de la agricultura en estos tres países se refleja en su contribución a la producción nacional. En el caso del comercio internacional holandés, ha ocasionado el tener que ampliar la envergadura de las instalaciones para procesar alimentos, no sólo para el mercado interior sino también para el de los mercados de los países vecinos. Por contraste Italia no ha necesitado establecer instalaciones para procesar alimentos, en la misma medida. Por el mapa puede verse que, menos del 10% de los empleados en fabricaciones trabajan en el proceso de alimentos.

Total Number of Persons Employed in the Food, Drink and Tobacco Industries

calculated to nearest 10,000

Nombre total de personnes employées dans les industries de l'alimentation, des boissons et du tabac

calcul à 10,000 personnes pres

Gesamtbeschäftigte in der Nahrungsmittel, Getränke- und Tabakwarenindustrie

auf 10.000 auf- oder agerundet

Número Total de Personas Empleadas en las Industrias de Alimentos, Bebidas y Tabaco

cálculo redondeado a la cifra 10.000 más próxima

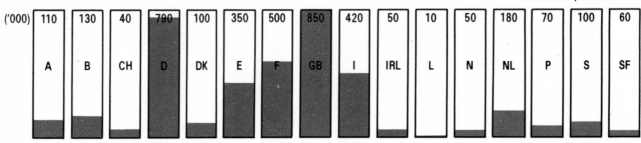

('000)	110	130	40	790	100	350	500	850	420	50	10	50	180	70	100	60
	A	B	CH	D	DK	E	F	GB	I	IRL	L	N	NL	P	S	SF

Employment – Food, Drink and Tobacco

% of manufacturing population employed in the food, drink and tobacco industries

Emploi – Alimentation, Boissons et Tabac

pourcentage de la population employée à la fabrication dans les industries de l'alimentation, des boissons et du tabac

Beschäftigte – Nahrungsmittel, Getränke, Tabakwaren

% der in der Produktion Beschäftigten in der Nahrungsmittel-, Getränke-und Tabakwarenindustrie

Empleo – Alimentos, Bebidas y Tabaco

% de la población obrera fabril empleada en las industrias de alimentos, bebidas y tabaco

6-8%	9-10%	11-13%	14-17%	18%+

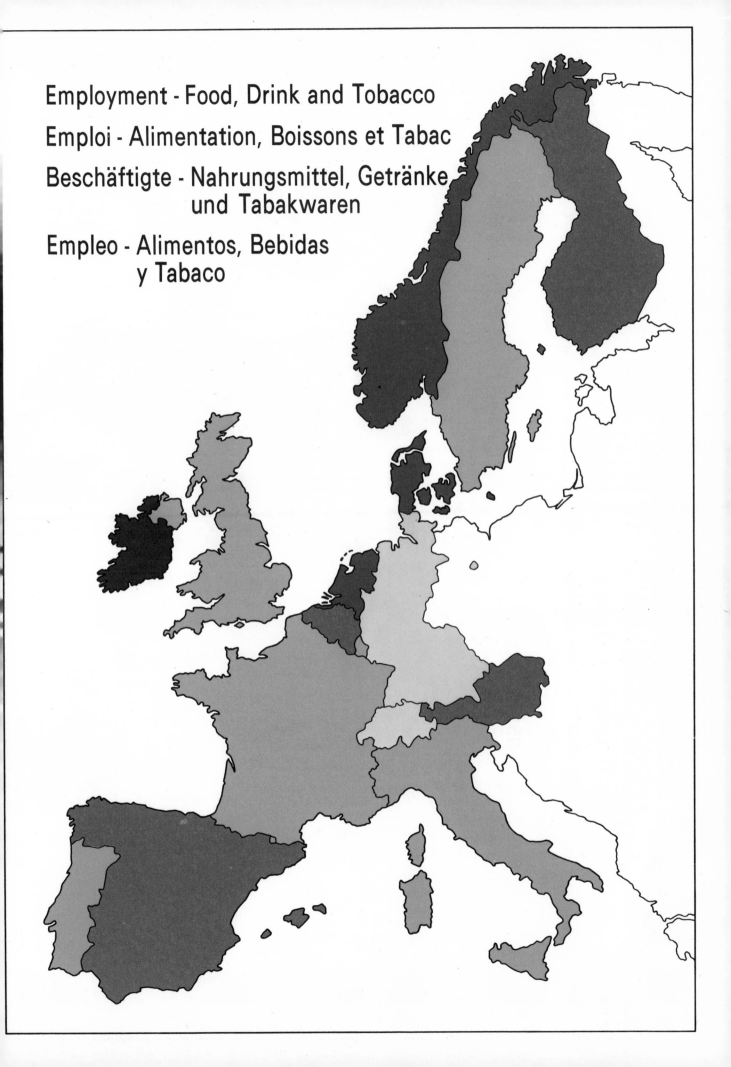

Employment - Food, Drink and Tobacco

Emploi - Alimentation, Boissons et Tabac

Beschäftigte - Nahrungsmittel, Getränke und Tabakwaren

Empleo - Alimentos, Bebidas y Tabaco

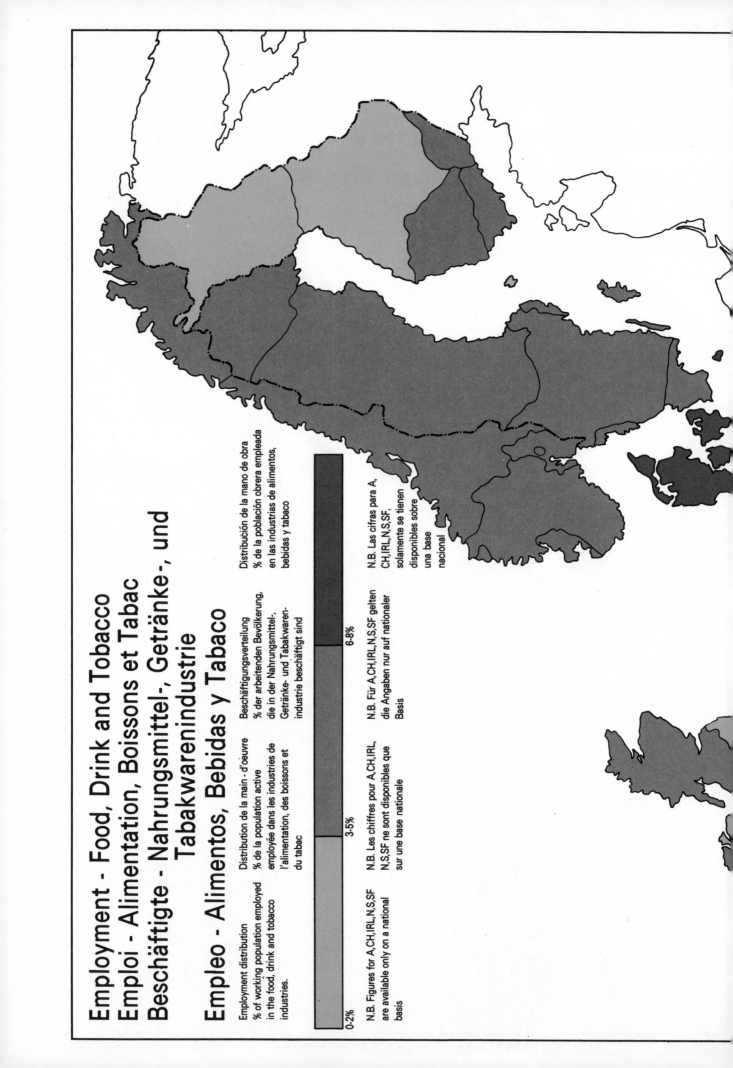

Employment - Food, Drink and Tobacco
Emploi - Alimentation, Boissons et Tabac
Beschäftigte - Nahrungsmittel-, Getränke-, und Tabakwarenindustrie
Empleo - Alimentos, Bebidas y Tabaco

Employment distribution
% of working population employed in the food, drink and tobacco industries.

Distribution de la main - d'oeuvre
% de la population active employée dans les industries de l'alimentation, des boissons et du tabac

Beschäftigungsverteilung
% der arbeitenden Bevölkerung, die in der Nahrungsmittel-, Getränke- und Tabakwarenindustrie beschäftigt sind

Distribución de la mano de obra
% de la población obrera empleada en las industrias de alimentos, bebidas y tabaco

0-2%

3-5%

6-8%

N.B. Figures for A,CH,IRL,N,S,SF are available only on a national basis

N.B. Les chiffres pour A,CH,IRL, N,S,SF ne sont disponibles que sur une base nationale

N.B. Für A,CH,IRL,N,S,SF gelten die Angaben nur auf nationaler Basis

N.B. Las cifras para A, CH,IRL,N,S,SF, solamente se tienen disponibles sobre una base nacional

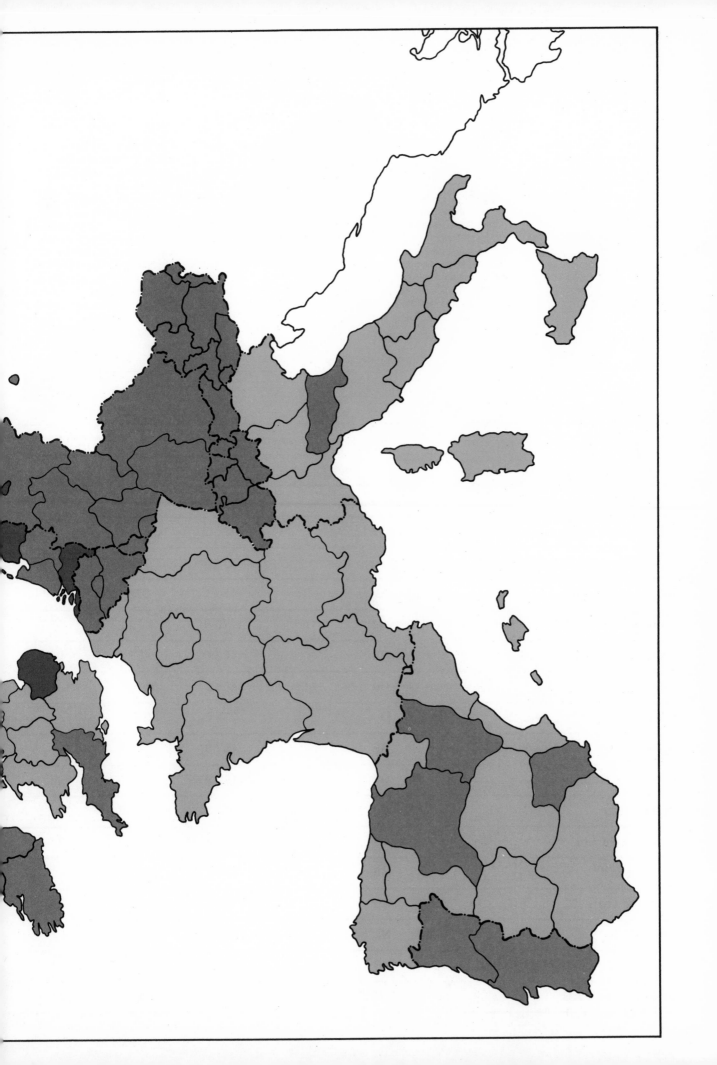

Food and non-alcoholic drink companies

Sociétés de l'alimentation et des boissons non-alcooliques

Hersteller von Nahrungsmitteln und alkoholfreien Getränken

Empresas alimenticias y de bebidas no alcohólicas

The following table lists those major European companies operating in the manufacture of food and non-alcoholic drink. Latest available turnover figures are given; and where possible the proportion of total turnover derived from these activities has been estimated Where the firm is amongst the major 100 companies of Europe its rank number has been given.

Le tableau suivant donne la liste des principales sociétés européennes engagées dans la manufacture des produits alimentaires et des boissons non-alcooliques. Il indique le dernier montant connu de leur chiffre d'affaires; et, quand cela était possible, la proportion du chiffre d'affaires qui correspond aux activités en question a été évaluée. Dans le cas où la firme se place parmi les 100 premières sociétés d'Europe, son rang a été indiqué.

In der folgenden Tabelle sind die größten europäischen Hersteller für Nahrungsmittel und alkoholfreie Getränke aufgeführt. Umsatzzahlen sind angegeben. Wo möglich, wurde der Anteil dieser Produkte am Gesamtumsatz geschätzt. Wenn sich das Unternehmen unter den 100 größten Firmen Europas befindet, ist angegeben, auf welchem Platz es sich befindet.

En la tabla que sigue constan las principales empresas europeas que se dedican a la fabricación de alimentos y bebidas no alcohólicas. Se señala las cifras del giro de negocios más recientes que ha habido disponible; y donde-quiera haya sido posible, se ha estimado el porcentaje del giro de negocios total derivado de tales actividades. Tratándose de una firma que se cuenta entre las 100 principales empresas de Europa, se indica el puesto que entre ellas ocupa.

			£m	$m	%
Associated British Foods Ltd	GB	50	612·5	1470·0	42
Beecham Group Ltd	GB		219·1	525·8	64
Brooke Bond Liebig Ltd	GB		262·9	631·0	100
Cadbury-Schweppes Ltd	GB		296·1	710·6	100
Fitch Lovell Ltd	GB		186·7	448·1	
Grand Metropolitan Hotels Ltd	GB		314·5	754·8	36
Albert Heijn NV	NL		158·1	379·4	
Imperial Tobacco Group Ltd	GB	15	1275·9	3062·2	15
J Lyons & Company Ltd	GB		189·0	453·6	63
Nestle-Alimentana SA	CH	11	1465·1	3516·2	100
Oetker Group	D		239·0	573·6	
Ranks Hovis McDougall Ltd	GB	88	407·0	976·8	96
Reckitt & Colman Ltd	GB		192·9	463·0	45
Spillers Ltd	GB		192·0	460·8	
Tate & Lyle Ltd	GB		339·6	815·0	92
Unigate Ltd	GB	89	399·2	958·1	
Unilever Ltd	GB	14	1356·8	3256·3	38
Unilever NV	NL	7	1712·2	4109·3	62
The Union International Company Ltd	GB		334·0	801·6	100
Ursina-Franck AG	CH		190·6	457·4	100

Alcoholic drink and tobacco companies

Sociétés de l'industrie des boissons alcooliques et des tabacs

Hersteller von alkoholischen Getränken und Tabakwaren

Empresas tabacaleras y de bebidas alcohólicas

The following table lists those major European companies operating in the manufacture of alcoholic drink and tobacco. Latest available turnover figures are given; and where possible the proportion of total turnover derived from these activities has been estimated. Where the firm is amongst the 100 major companies of Europe, its rank number has been given.

Le tableau suivant donne la liste des principales sociétés européennes engagées dans la manufacture des boissons alcooliques et des tabacs. Il indique le dernier montant connu de leur chiffre d'affaires; et, quand cela était possible, la proportion du chiffre d'affaires qui correspond aux activités en question a été évaluée. Dans le cas où la firme se place parmi les 100 premières sociétés d'Europe, son rang a été indiqué.

In der folgenden Tabelle sind die größten europäischen Hersteller von alkoholischen Getränken und Tabakwaren aufgeführt. Umsatzzahlen sind angegeben. Wo möglich, wurde der Anteil dieser Produkte am Gesamtumsatz geschätzt. Wenn sich das Unternehmen unter den 100 größten Firmen Europas befindet, ist angegeben, auf welchem Platz es sich befindet.

En la tabla que sigue constan las principales empresas europeas dedicadas a la fabricación de tabacos y bebidas alcohólicas. Se señala las cifras de negocios más recientes que ha habido disponible; y dondequiera haya sido posible, se ha estimado el porcentaje del giro de negocios total derivado de tales actividades. Tratándose de una firma que se cuenta entre las 100 principales empresas de Europa, se indica el puesto que entre ellas ocupa.

			£m	$m	%
Allied Breweries Ltd	GB	67	484·5	1162·8	
Bass Charrington Ltd	GB	77	440·5	1057·2	
Boussois-Souchon-Neuvesel SA	F		302·0	724·8	
Martin Brinkmann AG	D		271·9	652·6	
British-American Tobacco Company Ltd	GB	5	1846·7	4432·1	88
Courage Ltd (Imperial Tobacco Group Ltd)	GB		171·0	410·4	
De Forenede Bryggerier AS	DK		96·7	232·1	89
The Distillers Company Ltd	GB	75	442·6	1062·2	89
Gallaher Ltd	GB	71	452·9	1087·0	92
Grand Metropolitan Hotels Ltd	GB		314·5	754·8	5
Imperial Tobacco Group Ltd	GB	15	1275·9	3062·2	74
Arthur Guinness Son & Co Ltd	GB		213·4	512·2	85
Heineken NV	NL		86·3	207·1	
Pripp-Bryggerierna AB	S		152·1	365·0	
Reemtsma Group	D	51	610·9	1466·2	
Rothman's International Ltd	GB		166·7	400·1	100
Scottish & Newcastle Breweries Ltd	GB		170·6	409·4	
Tobacofina	B		148·7	356·9	
Watney Mann Ltd (Grand Metropolitan Hotels Ltd)	GB		158·4	380·2	
Whitbread & Company Ltd	GB		250·2	600·5	

G

Chemicals

Les produits chimiques

Chemikalien

Industrias químicas

The GEP industry classification of chemicals and allied industries include the manufacture and processing of chemicals, rubber, hydrocarbon products and non-metallic minerals.

Maps and data in this section include:
- Value added per capita.
- Employment distribution.
- Output of petroleum products.
- Areas of concentrated activity.
- Major chemical, petroleum and oil companies.

La classification industrielle de l'industrie chimique et des industries alliées établie par GEP comprend la fabrication et le traitement des produits chimiques, du caoutchouc, des hydrates de carbone et des minéral non-métalliques.

Les cartes et les données de cette section comprennent:
- La valeur ajoutée par tête.
- La répartition de la main-d'oeuvre.
- La production de produits pétroliers.
- Les régions à activité concentrée.
- Les principales sociétés engagées dans la fabrication de produits chimiques et pétroliers.

In der GEP-Klassifizierung für die Chemikalienindustrie und verwandte Branchen ist die Herstellung und Verarbeitung von Chemikalien, Gummi, Kohlenwasserstoffprodukten und nicht-metallischen Mineralien enthalten.

Aus Karten und Angaben dieses Abschnittes gehen hervor:
- Leistungswert pro Kopf.
- Verteilung der Beschäftigung.
- Produktion von Erdölprodukten.
- Gebiete konzentrierter Aktivität.
- Die größten Chemie- und Erdölfirmen.

En la clasificación del GEP de industrias químicas y aliadas se incluye la fabricación y procesos de productos químicos, gomas, derivados de hidrocarburos y minerales no metálicos.

Los mapas y datos de esta sección incluyen:
- Valor añadido per cápita.
- Distribución de los empleos.
- Producción de los derivados del petróleo.
- Areas de actividad concentrada.
- Las principales sociedades químicas, petrolíferas y del aceite.

Value of output per capita
(US $ per annum)

N.B. Figure for CH is not available

Average for Western Europe $54

Valeur ajoutée par tête
(US $ par an)

N.B. Le chiffre pour CH n'est pas disponible

Moyenne pour l'Europe occidentale $54

Leistungswert pro Kopf
(US $ pro Jahr)

N.B. Für CH liegen keine Angaben vor

Durchschnitt für Westeuropa $54

Valor de la producción por cabeza
(US $ por ano)

N.B. no se cuenta con la cifra para CH

Promedio para Europa Occidental $54

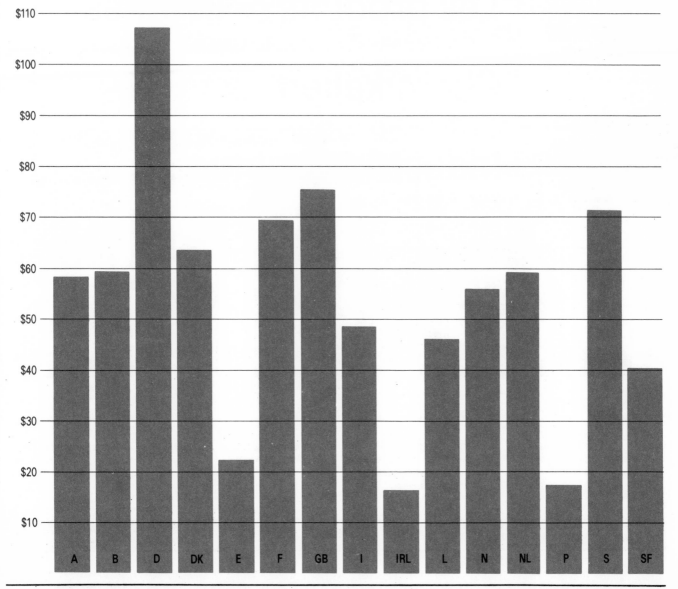

The chemical industries are among the fastest growing sectors within Western European industry. Much of the process work is essentially of a capital intensive nature.

The UK and West Germany are the two countries with over one million employees in these industries. However, Italy emerges as the country most dependent in economic terms on its chemical industry.

The international nature of this industry has been responsible for activities to be concentrated around ports and principal transport links. Two regions emerge with very strong activity in chemicals. The industry in the northern regions of the UK is based primarily on the estuaries of the rivers Tees and Tyne. In contrast the Rheinland-Pfalz region is situated away from the coast but along the principal international link of the river Rhein.

Les industries chimiques sont, parmi les secteurs industriels de l'Europe Occidentale, l'un de ceux dont le taux de croissance est le plus rapide. Une grande partie des procédés de traitement chimique nécessitent l'investissement de gros capitaux.

Le Royaume-Uni et l'Allemagne de l'Ouest sont les deux pays avec plus d'un million d'employés dans ces industries. Cependant, l'Italie est le pays qui économiquement dépend le plus sur son industrie chimique.

La nature internationale de cette industrie fait que ses centres d'activités sont concentrées autour des ports et des principales voies de transport. Deux régions se distinguent par une activité intense dans le domaine des produits chimiques : celle du nord du Royaume-Uni autour des estuaires de la Tees et de la Tyne, et celle de la région de Rheinland-Pfalz qui, par contre, est éloignée de la côte, mais sur la principale voie de communication internationale du Rhin.

In der westeuropäischen Industrie ist die chemische Industrie eines der Gebiete mit dem schnellsten Zuwachs. Viele Verarbeitungsverfahren sind besonders kapitalintensiv.

Das Vereinigte Königreich und Westdeutschland beschäftigen in diesen Branchen mehr als eine Million Arbeitnehmer. Italien wird jedoch langsam zu dem Land, das in wirtschaftlicher Hinsicht besonders stark von seiner chemischen Industrie abhängt.

Der internationale Charakter dieser Industrie war der Grund dafür, daß sie sich um Häfen und die großen Verkehrsadern angesiedelt hat. In zwei Gebieten finden wir besonders viele Unternehmen der chemischen Industrie. Die Industrie im Norden des Vereinigten Königreiches gruppiert sich besonders um die Mündungen der Flüsse Tees und Tyne. Im Gegensatz dazu liegt das Gebiet von Rheinland-Pfalz nicht an der Küste, jedoch an der großen internationalen Verkehrsader, dem Rhein.

Entre las industrias de Europa Occidental la química es una de las industrias en el sector de crecimiento más rápido. Gran parte del proceso de trabajo es esencialmente por naturaleza de capital intensivo.

Los países con más de un millón de empleados en estas industrias son el Reino Unido y Alemania Occidental. No obstante, Italia emerge como uno de los países que en términos económicos depende más de su industria química.

La naturaleza internacional de estas industrias ha hecho que sus actividades sean concentradas alrededor de puertos y los puntos principales de enlace de transporte. Dos regiones de actividades fuertes emergen en la química. La industria en las regiones septentrionales del Reino Unido está basada principalmente en los estuarios de los ríos Tees y Tyne. Por contraste la región Rheinland-Pfalz está situada lejos de la costa aunque al borde del enlace principal del Rin.

Total Number of Persons Employed in the Chemical Industries

calculated to nearest 10,000

Nombre total de personnes employées dans les industries chimiques

calcul à 10,000 personnes pres

Gesamtbeschäftigte in der chemischen Industrie

auf 10.000 auf- oder abgerundet

Número Total de Personas Empleadas en las Industrias Químicas

cálculo redondeado a la cifra 10.000 más próxima

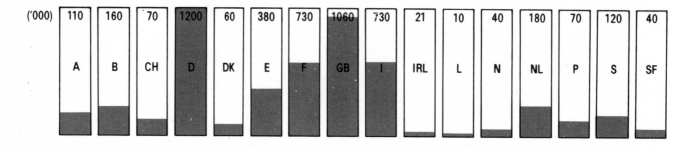

('000)	110	160	70	1200	60	380	730	1060	730	21	10	40	180	70	120	40
	A	B	CH	D	DK	E	F	GB	I	IRL	L	N	NL	P	S	SF

Employment – Chemicals

% of manufacturing population employed in chemicals and allied industries

Emploi – Produits chimiques

pourcentage de la population employée à la fabrication dans les industries chimiques et les industries connexes

Beschäftigte – Chemikalien

% der in der Produktion Beschäftigten in der Chemikalienindustrie und verwandten Industrien

Empleo – Productos Químicos

% de la población obrera fabril empleada en las industrias de productos químicos y análogos

9-10%	11-12%	13-14%	15%+

Employment-Chemicals

Emploi-Produits Chimiques

Beschäftigte-Chemikalien

Empleo-Productos Químicos

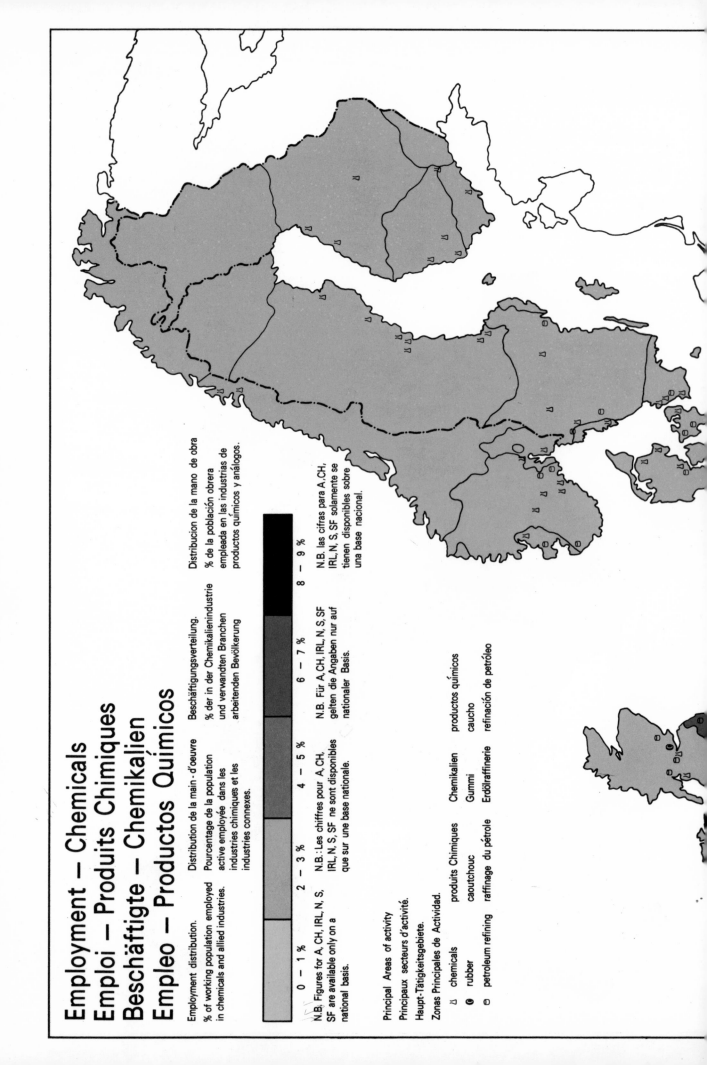

Employment – Chemicals
Emploi – Produits Chimiques
Beschäftigte – Chemikalien
Empleo – Productos Químicos

Employment distribution.

% of working population employed in chemicals and allied industries.

Distribution de la main - d'oeuvre

Pourcentage de la population active employée dans les industries chimiques et les industries connexes.

Beschäftigungsverteilung.

% der in der Chemikalienindustrie und verwandten Branchen arbeitenden Bevölkerung

Distribucion de la mano de obra

% de la población obrera empleada en las industrias de productos químicos y análogos.

0 – 1 %   2 – 3 %   4 – 5 %   6 – 7 %   8 – 9 %

N.B. Figures for A, CH, IRL, N, S, SF are available only on a national basis.

N.B.: Les chiffres pour A, CH, IRL, N, S, SF ne sont disponibles que sur une base nationale.

N.B. Für A,CH, IRL, N, S, SF gelten die Angaben nur auf nationaler Basis.

N.B. las cifras para A,CH, IRL, N, S, SF solamente se tienen disponibles sobre una base nacional.

Principal Areas of activity
Principaux secteurs d'activité.
Haupt-Tätigkeitsgebiete.
Zonas Principales de Actividad.

chemicals   produits Chimiques   Chemikalien   productos químicos
rubber   caoutchouc   Gummi   caucho
petroleum refining   raffinage du pétrole   Erdölraffinerie   refinación de petróleo

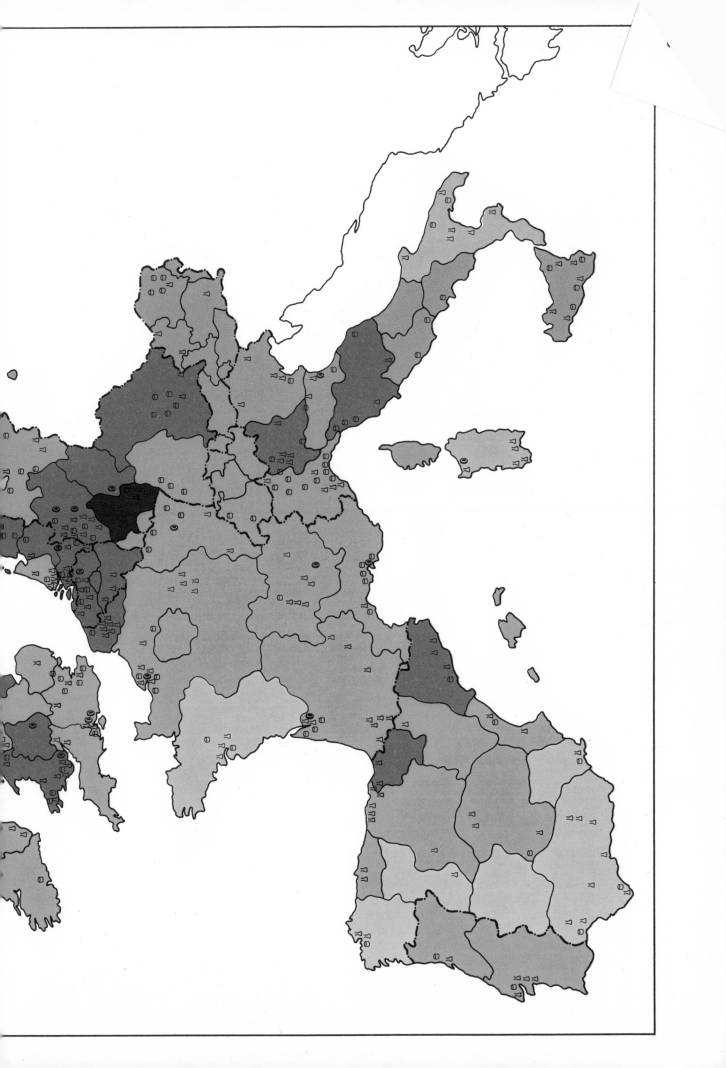

Chemical companies

Sociétés de produits chimiques

Hersteller von chemischen Produkten

Empresas químicas

The following table lists those major European companies operating in the manufacture of chemicals, and allied products. Latest available turnover figures have been given; and where possible the proportion of total turnover derived from these activities has been estimated. Where the firm is amongst the 100 major companies of Europe its rank number has been given.

Le tableau suivant donne la liste des principales sociétés européennes engagées dans la manufacture des produits chimiques et des produits associés. Il indique le dernier montant connu de leur chiffre d'affaires; et, quand cela était possible, la proportion du chiffre d'affaires qui correspond aux activités en question a été évaluée. Dans le cas où la firme se place parmi les 100 premières sociétés d'Europe, son rang a été indiqué.

In der folgenden Tabelle sind die größten europäischen Hersteller von chemischen und verwandten Produkten aufgeführt. Umsatzzahlen sind angegeben. Wo möglich, wurde der Anteil dieser Produkte am Gesamtumsatz geschätzt. Wenn sich das Unternehmen unter den 100 größten Firmen Europas befindet, ist angegeben, auf welchem Platz es sich befindet.

En la tabla que sigue constan las principales empresas europeas dedicadas a la fabricación de productos químicos y similares. Se señala las cifras de negocios más recientes que ha habido disponible; y dondequiera haya sido posible, se ha estimado el porcentaje del giro de negocios total derivado de tales actividades. Tratándose de una firma que se cuenta entre las 100 principales empresas de Europa, se indica el puesto que entre ellas ocupa.

			£m	$m	%
Akzo NV	NL	25	969·2	2326·1	
Badische Anilin & Soda-Fabrik AG	D	12	1449·3	3478·3	
Ciba-Geigy AG	CH	37	762·6	1830·2	100
Compagnie de Saint-Gobain-Pont à Mousson	F	33	793·4	1904·2	
Courtaulds Ltd	GB	43	681·5	1635·6	10
Farbenfabriken Bayer AG	D	13	1427·8	3426·7	100
Farbwerke Hoechst AG	D	10	1523·2	3655·7	
Finsider	I	38	748·7	1796·9	
Henkel GmbH	D	80	431·2	1034·9	
Imperial Chemical Industries Ltd	GB	9	1524·4	3658·6	56
F Hoffman-la Roche & Co	CH	57	580·0	1392·0	
Mannesmann AG	D	29	860·0	2064·0	
Montedison SpA	I	26	933·0	2239·2	
Pechiney-Ugine-Kuhlmann	F	22	1020·4	2449·0	
Rhône-Poulenc SA	F	27	903·8	2169·1	
Royal Dutch/Shell Group	GB/NL	1	5030·6	12073·4	12
Solvay & Cie SA	B	90	395·1	948·2	
Unilever Ltd	GB	14	1356·8	3256·3	26
Unilever NV	NL	7	1712·2	4109·3	7
Veba AG	D	21	1125·9	2702·2	

Oil and petroleum companies

Sociétés pétrolières

Öl- und Erdölfirmen

Empresas de Petróleo

The following table lists those major European companies operating in the manufacture and/or distribution of oil, petroleum or petroleum products. Latest available turnover figures are given; and where possible the proportion of total turnover derived from these activities has been estimated. Where the firm is amongst the 100 major companies of Europe its rank number has been given.

Le tableau suivant donne la liste des principales sociétés européennes engagées dans la manufacture et/ou la distribution du pétrole, de l'essence ou des produits pétroliers. Il indique le dernier montant connu de leur chiffre d'affaires; et, quand cela était possible, la proportion du chiffre d'affaires qui correspond aux activités en question a été évaluée. Dans le cas où la firme se place parmi les 100 premières sociétés d'Europe, son rang a été indiqué.

In der folgenden Tabelle sind die größten europäischen Hersteller und Händler in der Öl-, Erdöl- und Erdölprodukt-branche aufgeführt. Umsatzzahlen sind angegeben. Wo möglich, wurde der Anteil dieser Produkte am Gesamtumsatz geschätzt. Wenn sich das Unternehmen unter den 100 größten Firmen Europas befindet, ist angegeben, auf welchem Platz es sich befindet.

En la tabla que sigue constan las principales empresas europeas dedicadas a la fabricación y/o distribución de petróleo y productos petroleros. Se señala las cifras de negocios más recientes que ha habido disponible; y dondequiera haya sido posible, se ha estimado el porcentaje del giro de negocios total derivado de tales actividades. Tratándose de una firma que se cuenta entre las 100 principales empresas de Europa, se indica el puesto que entre ellas ocupa.

			£m	$m	%
AGIP SpA	I	39	735·5	1765·2	
British Petroleum UK Ltd	GB	2	3153·0	7567·2	
Compagnie Française des Pétroles	F	23	991·7	2380·1	
Compagnie Française de Raffinage	F	31	823·2	1975·7	
Deutsche Shell AG	D	87	412·0	988·8	100
Erap-Elf	F	36	764·0	1833·6	
Esso Petroleum Company Ltd	GB	44	677·4	1625·8	
Petrofina SA	B	34	785·8	1885·9	100
Royal Dutch/Shell Group	GB/NL	1	5030·6	12073·4	86
Shell Mex-BP Group Ltd	GB	17	1230·0	2952·0	100

Output of Petroleum Products

('000) metric tons
calculated to nearest 1000 metric tons

Production de produits pétroliers

en milliers de tonnes
calcul à 1.000 tonnes près

Produktion von Erdölprodukten

(in tausend Tonnen)
auf die nächsten 1.000 t auf- oder abgerundet

Producción de Productos Petrolíferos

toneladas métricas (en miles)
cálculo redondeado a la cifra de 1.000 toneladas más próxima

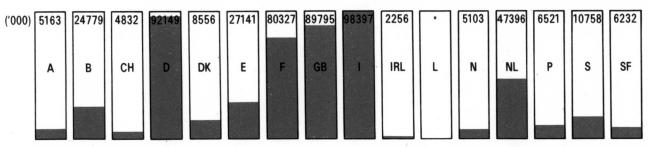

('000)	5163	24779	4832	92149	8556	27141	80327	89795	98397	2256	*	5103	47396	6521	10758	6232
	A	B	CH	D	DK	E	F	GB	I	IRL	L	N	NL	P	S	SF

* less than 1000 tons

* moins de 1000 tonnes

* unter 1000 tonnen

* menos de 1000 toneladas

H

Metals

Les métaux

Metall

Metales

The GEP industry classification of metal manufacture includes activity in both ferrous and non-ferrous metal processing. The methods adopted for the compilation of international data on employment do not allow an analysis specific to metal manufacture. Consequently the data has been based on output information.

Maps and data in this section include:
- Value added per capita.
- Output and consumption of steel.
- Output of principal non-ferrous metals.
- Areas of concentrated activity.

La classification industrielle de la fabrication des métaux établie par GEP comprend le traitement des métaux ferreux et non-ferreux. Les méthodes adoptées pour la compilation des données internationales sur la main-d'oeuvre ne permettent pas une analyse spécifique de la fabrication des métaux. Par conséquent, les données ont été établies à partir des chiffres de productivité.

Les cartes et les données de cette section comprennent:
- La valeur ajoutée par tête.
- La production et la consommation de l'acier.
- La productivité des principaux métaux non-ferreux.
- Les régions à activité concentrée.

In der GEP-Klassifizierung sind Verarbeitungsbetriebe für Eisen- und NE-Metalle enthalten. Aus der Zusammenstellung inter-nationaler Angaben über die Beschäftigung konnten wir keine Analyse speziell für die Metall-industrie vornehmen. Die Angaben basieren daher auf Angaben über die Produktions-leistung.

Karten und Angaben enthalten:
- Leistungswert pro Kopf.
- Produktion und Verbrauch von Stahl.
- Produktion der wichtigsten NE-Metalle.
- Gebiete konzentrierter Aktivität.

En la clasificación del GEP de industrias de fabricaciones en metal se incluyen las actividades de procesar metales tanto férricos como no férricos. Los métodos usados para la recompilación de datos internacionales sobre los puestos de trabajo, en el caso de la fabricación en metal no permite un análisis específico. Por consiguiente, dichos datos han sido basados sobre la información de la producción.

Los mapas y datos de esta sección incluyen:
- Valor añadido per cápita.
- Producción y consumos de acero.
- Producción de los principales metales no férricos.
- Áreas de actividad concen-trada.

Value of output per capita
(US $ per annum)

N.B. Figure for CH is not available

Average for Western Europe $170

Valeur ajoutée par tête
(US $ par an)

N.B. Le chiffre pour CH n'est pas disponible

Moyenne pour l'Europe occidentale $170

Leistungswert pro Kopf
(US $ pro Jahr)

N.B. Für CH liegen keine Angaben vor

Durchschnitt für Westeuropa $170

Valor de la producción por cabeza
(US $ por ano)

N.B. no se cuenta con la cifra para CH

Promedio para Europa Occidental $170

Level	A	B	D	DK	E	F	GB	I	IRL	L	N	NL	P	S	SF

The production of steel is undertaken in all sixteen Western European countries. Of the heavily industrialised countries, annual consumption and production levels are generally in balance. The remaining countries, with the exception of Austria, are net importers of steel.

Over 25% of consumption requirements of steel have to be imported by seven countries. These are Denmark, Finland, Ireland, Norway, Portugal, Spain and Switzerland. In contrast Austria, Belgium and Luxembourg are the only countries where production is considerably higher than consumption.

Tous les seize pays de l'Europe Occidentale sont engagés dans la production de l'acier. La consommation annuelle et le niveau de productivité des pays fortement industrialisés s'équilibrent. Les autres pays, à l'exception de l'Autriche, ne sont pas des importateurs d'acier.

Plus de 25% de leurs besoins en acier doivent être importés par sept pays. Ce sont le Danemark, la Finlande, l'Irlande, la Norvège, le Portugal, l'Espagne et la Suisse. Par contre, l'Autriche, la Belgique et le Luxembourg sont les seuls pays où la production est considérablement plus élevé que la consommation.

Alle sechzehn westeuropäischen Länder stellen Stahl her. Bei den sehr industrialisierten Ländern halten sich Verbrauch und Herstellung eines Jahres im allgemeinen die Waage. Die restlichen Länder, mit Ausnahme von Österreich, sind Netto-importeure von Stahl.

Sieben Länder müssen über 25% ihres Bedarfs einführen. Darunter befinden sich Dänemark, Finnland, Irland, Norwegen, Portugal, Spanien und die Schweiz. Im Gegensatz dazu sind Österreich, Belgien und Luxemburg die einzigen Länder, deren Produktion sehr viel höher als ihr Verbrauch ist.

En Europa Occidental los dieciséis países son productores de acero. En los países fuertemente industrializados, los niveles de producción y de consumos anuales están a la par. Con excepción de Austria, el resto de los países no importan acero.

Más del 25% del acero requerido para su consumo tiene que ser importado por los siguientes países:- Dinamarca, Finlandia, Irlanda, Noruega, Portugal, España y Suiza. Por contraste los países donde la producción es considerablemente más alta que el consumo son los siguientes: Austria, Bélgica y Luxemburgo.

Steel – Output and Consumption

total annual output ('000) metric tons

Acier – Production et Consommation

production totale annuelle en milliers de tonnes

Stahl – Erzeugung und Verbrauch

Jahres-Gesamterzeugung (in tausend)

Acero – Producción y Consumo

producción anual total en (miles de) toneladas.

('000)						
0-999	1000-4999	5000-9999	10000-14999	15000-19999	20000+

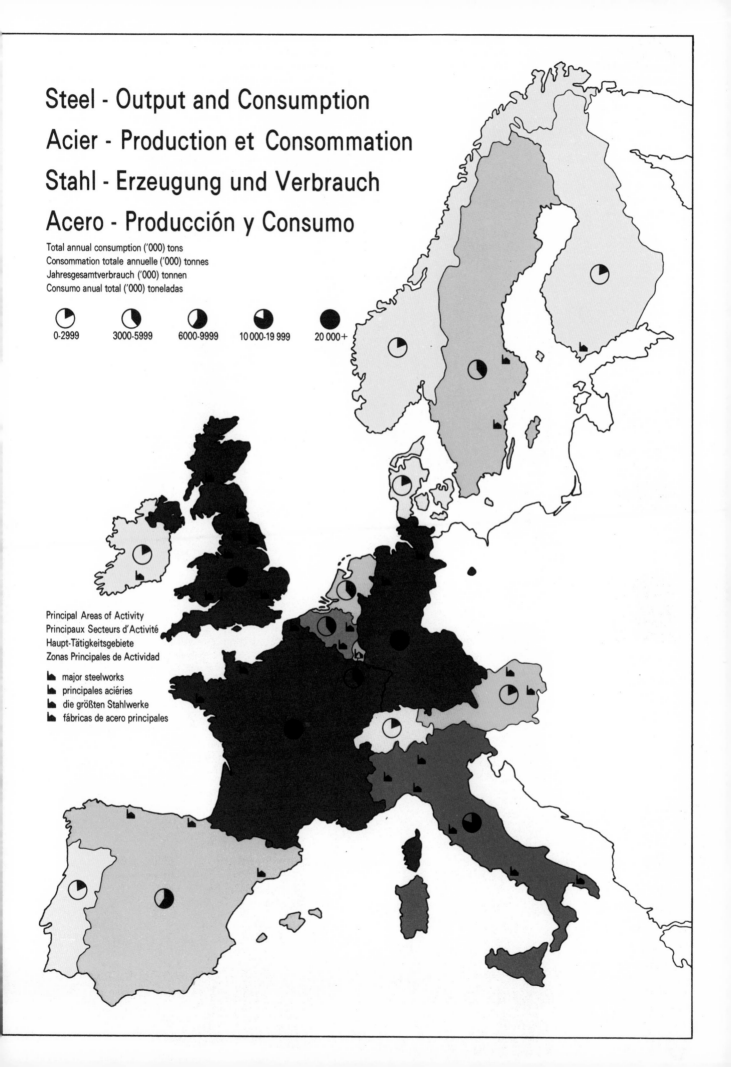

Steel - Output and Consumption
Acier - Production et Consommation
Stahl - Erzeugung und Verbrauch
Acero - Producción y Consumo

Total annual consumption ('000) tons
Consommation totale annuelle ('000) tonnes
Jahresgesamtverbrauch ('000) tonnen
Consumo anual total ('000) toneladas

0-2999   3000-5999   6000-9999   10 000-19 999   20 000+

Principal Areas of Activity
Principaux Secteurs d'Activité
Haupt-Tätigkeitsgebiete
Zonas Principales de Actividad

major steelworks
principales aciéries
die größten Stahlwerke
fábricas de acero principales

Six countries produce over 3m metric tons of non-ferrous metals annually (Norway, Belgium, Netherlands, Italy, West Germany and France) but the relative outputs of the different types of non-ferrous metals vary. For instance 98% of Norway's output is magnesium; while 98% of Netherlands output is tin. Between them, six countries produce nearly 95% of all the non-ferrous metals in Western Europe.

Six pays produisent annuellement plus de 3 millions de tonnes métriques de métaux non-ferreux (la Norvège, la Belgique, les Pays-Bas, l'Italie, l'Allemagne de l'Ouest et la France) mais les productivités relatives des divers types de métaux non-ferreux varient. Par exemple 98% de la productivité de la Norvège est composée de magnésium tandis que 98% de celle des Pays-Bas est l'étain. Entre eux, six pays produisent presque 95% de tous les métaux non-ferreux de l'Europe Occidentale.

Sechs Länder stellen jährlich über 3 Millionen Tonnen NE-Metall her (Norwegen. Belgien, Holland, Italien, Westdeutschland und Frankreich), die Einzel-produktion für NE-Metalle ist jedoch sehr unterschiedlich. 98% der norwegischen Produktion z.B. ist Magnesium, während 98% der holländischen Produktion Zinn ist. Sechs Länder stellen fast alle NE-Metall Westeuropas jährlich her.

Seis paises producen anualmente más de 3 millones de toneladas metricas de metales non-ferricos (Noruega, Bélgica, Holanda, Italia, Alemania Occidental y Francia) pero varian las producciones relativas de los diversos tipos de metales non-ferricos. Por ejemplo el 98% de la produccion Noruega es de magnesio, mientras que el 98% de la Holandesa es de estaño. En Europa Occidental el 95% de todos los metales non ferricos son productos entre esos seis paises.

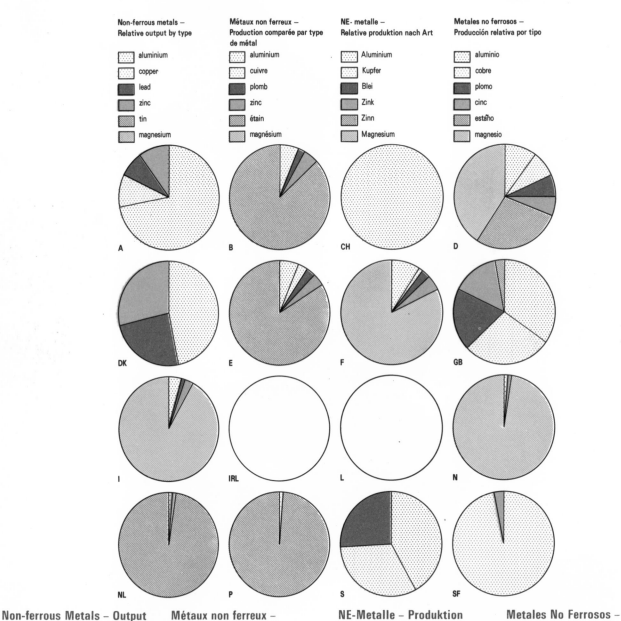

Non-ferrous metals –
Relative output by type

- aluminium
- copper
- lead
- zinc
- tin
- magnesium

Métaux non ferreux –
Production comparée par type de métal

- aluminium
- cuivre
- plomb
- zinc
- étain
- magnésium

NE- metalle –
Relative produktion nach Art

- Aluminium
- Kupfer
- Blei
- Zink
- Zinn
- Magnesium

Metales no ferrosos –
Producción relativa por tipo

- aluminio
- cobre
- plomo
- cinc
- estaño
- magnesio

A   B   CH   D

DK   E   F   GB

I   IRL   L   N

NL   P   S   SF

Non-ferrous Metals – Output

total annual output ('000) metric tons

Métaux non ferreux – Production

production totale annuelle en milliers de tonnes

NE-Metalle – Produktion

Jahres-Gesamtproduktion (in tausend) Tonnen

Metales No Ferrosos – Producción

producción anual total en (miles de) toneladas

('000)				
0-99	100-599	600-2999	3000-6999	7000+

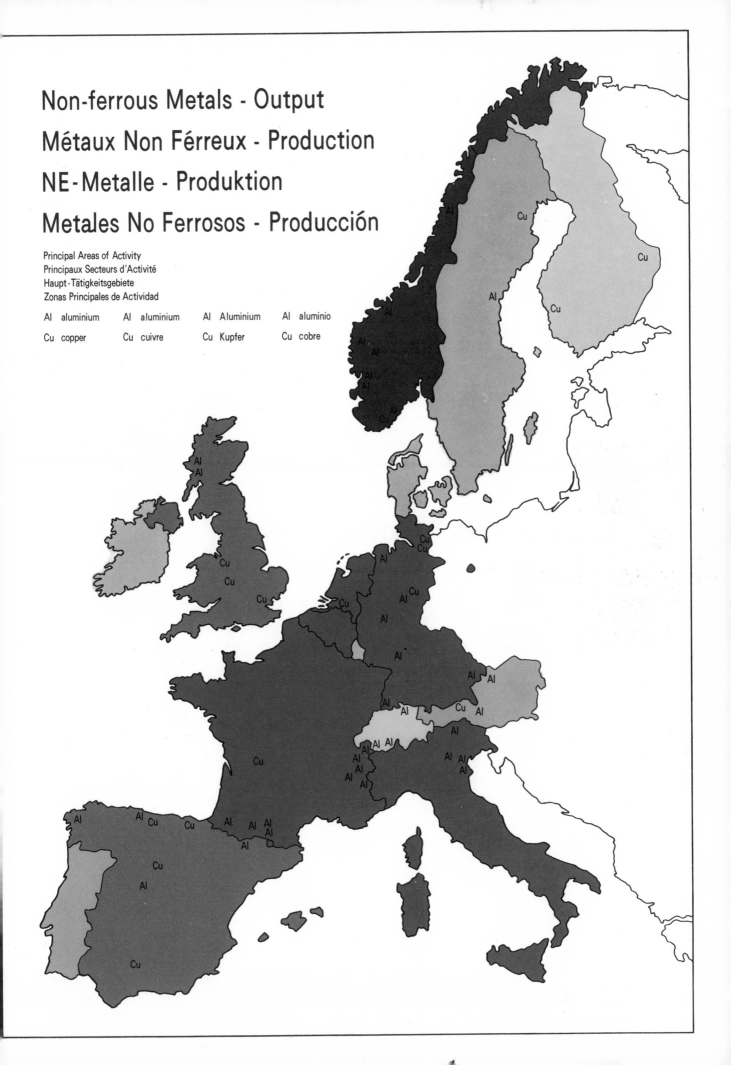

Non-ferrous Metals - Output

Métaux Non Férreux - Production

NE-Metalle - Produktion

Metales No Ferrosos - Producción

Principal Areas of Activity
Principaux Secteurs d'Activité
Haupt-Tätigkeitsgebiete
Zonas Principales de Actividad

| Al | aluminium | Al | aluminium | Al | Aluminium | Al | aluminio |
| Cu | copper | Cu | cuivre | Cu | Kupfer | Cu | cobre |

J

Engineering

La construction mécanique

Technik

Industrias mecánicas

The GEP industry classification of engineering includes mechanical, electrical, electronic, marine engineering, shipbuilding and vehicle manufacture.

Maps and data in this section include:
- Value added per capita.
- Employment distribution.
- Areas of concentrated activity.
- Output of the motor vehicle industry.
- Major engineering companies.

La classification industrielle de la construction mécanique établie par GEP comprend la construction mécanique proprement dite, les industries électronique et électrique, le génie maritime, la construction navale et l'industrie automobile.

Les cartes et les données de cette section comprennent:
- La valeur ajoutée par tête.
- La répartition de la main-d'œuvre.
- Les régions à activité concentrée.
- La production de l'industrie automobile.
- Les principales entreprises de construction mécanique.

In der GEP-Klassifizierung für den Maschinenbau sind Maschinenbau, Elektrotechnik, Elektronik, Schiffsmaschinenbau, Schiffsbau und Fahrzeugbau enthalten.

Aus Karten und Daten dieses Abschnittes können entnommen werden:
- Leistungswert pro Kopf.
- Verteilung der Beschäftigung.
- Gebiete konzentrierter Aktivität.
- Produktion der Kraftfahrzeugindustrie.
- Die größten Maschinenbaufirmen.

En la clasificación GEP de industrias mecánicas se incluye la mecánica, eléctrica, electrónica, naval, construcción naval y fabricación de vehículos.

Los mapas y datos de esta sección incluyen:
- Valor añadido per cápita.
- Distribución de los empleos.
- Áreas de actividad concentrada
- Producción de la industria de vehículos a motor.
- Las principales compañías de construcción mecánica.

Value of output per capita
(US $ per annum)

N.B. Figure for CH is not available

Average for Western Europe $111

Valeur ajoutée par tête
(US $ par an)

N.B. Le chiffre pour CH n'est pas disponible

Moyenne pour l'Europe occidentale $111

Leistungswert pro Kopf
(US $ pro Jahr)

N.B. Für CH liegen keine Angaben vor

Durchschnitt für Westeuropa $111

Valor de la producción por cabeza
(US $ por ano)

N.B. no se cuenta con la cifra para CH

Promedio para Europa Occidental $111

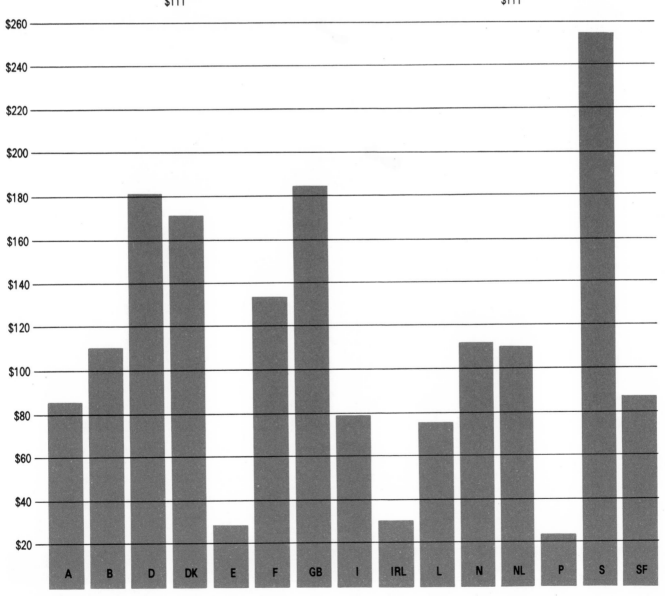

Industry location

Engineering fulfils a vital role in every industrialised country and is the single most important industrial activity in Europe.

West Germany and the UK have the largest engineering sectors in Western Europe. These industries in both countries employ approaching 5m workers and account for over 50% of all manufacturing employment.

In contrast the industries in Spain and Italy, which between them employ over 2.6m workers, are less important in national employment terms. The industries in both countries account for less that 40% of all manufacturing employment.

The more detailed analysis identifies three zones where engineering fulfils a particularly important function. These are:
1 Central UK – including Wales, West and East Midlands.
2 Nordrhein-Westfalen—based on the Ruhr industrial zone.
3 Luxembourg-Saarland.

Other areas of national importance are northern Italy, the Paris region and southern Belgium.

Total Number of Persons Employed in Engineering Industries

calculated to nearest 10,000

Emplacement des industries

L'industrie mécanique remplit un rôle vital dans chaque pays industrialisé et à elle seule représente l'activité industrielle la plus importante de l'Europe Occidentale.

L'Allemagne de l'Ouest et le Royaume-Uni possèdent les plus gros secteurs de construction mécanique de l'Europe Occidentale. Dans chacun de ces deux pays, cette industrie compte près de 5 millions de travailleurs, soit plus de 50% de la main-d'œuvre manufacturière.

Par contre, entre elles, les industries mécaniques de l'Espagne et de l'Italie n'emploient qu'un peu plus de 2,6 millions de travailleurs. Chiffre moins important en terme d'emploi à l'échelle nationale, représentant moins de 40% de la main d'œuvre manufacturière.

Les analyses plus détaillées, identifient trois zones où l'industrie mécanique remplit une fonction particulièrement importante. Ces zones sont:
1 La région centrale du Royaume-Uni-y compris le Pays de Galles, West Midlands and East Midlands.
2 La région Nordrhein-Westfalen-concentrée dans la zone industrielle de la Ruhr.
3 La région Luxembourg-Saarland.

D'autres zones d'importance nationale sont le Nord de l'Italie, la région parisienne et le Sud de la Belgique.

Nombre total de personnes employées dans les industries mécaniques

calcul à 10.000 personnes près

Industriezonen

Für jedes Industrieland is die Technik lebenswichtig. In Europa ist er die bedeutendste Industrie uberhaupt.

In Westeuropa ist die Technik in Westdeutschland und England am stärksten. In beiden Ländern beschäftigt diese Industrie fast 5 Millionen Menschen und bietet über 50% der Stellen in der Fabrikation.

Im Gegensatz dazu ist die Technik in Spanien und Italien mit insgesamt über 2,6 Millionen Arbeitnehmern weniger wichtig im Hinblick auf das Stellenangebot. Die Maschinenbauindustrie bietet in beiden Ländern unter 40% aller Stellen in der Fabrikation.

In der genaueren Analyse werden drei Sektoren herausgestellt, in denen die Technik ein besonders großes Gewicht hat:
1 Mittelengland—einschl Wales, dem West Midlands and East Midlands
2 Nordrhein-Westfalen mit besonderem Gewicht auf dem Ruhrgebiet.
3 Luxembourg und das Saarland.

Weitere wichtige Gebiete sind Norditalien, die Gegend um Paris. und Südbelgien.

Gesamtbeschäftigte in der Technik

auf 10.000 auf- oder abgerundet

Zonas industriales

En todo país industrializado la industria mecánica desempeña un papel vital, e individualmente es la actividad más importante en Europa.

Los sectores de construcción mecánica más amplios en Europa Occidental están situados en Alemania Occidental y en el Reino Unido. En ambos países estas industrias implean cerca de 5 millones de trabajadores, lo cual representa más del 50% de los empleos en industrias fabriles.

Por contraste las industrias en España e Italia, las cuales entre ellas emplean a más de 2,6 millones de trabajadores, son de menor importancia en términos nacionales de empleo. Las industrias en ambos países suman menos del 40% de los empleos en industrias fabriles.

Un análisis más detallado identifica tres zonas donde la industria mecánica desempeña una función particularmente importante. Estas son:
1 Reino Unido Central—Incluidos el País de Gales, West Midlands and East Midlands.
2 Nordrhein-Westfalen—situados en la zona industrial del Ruhr.
3 Luxembourg y el Saarland.

Otras áreas de importancia nacional se encuentran en el Norte de Italia, la región de París, y el Sur de Bélgica.

Número Total de Personas Empleadas en Industrias Mecánicas

cálculo redondeado a la cifra 10.000 más próxima

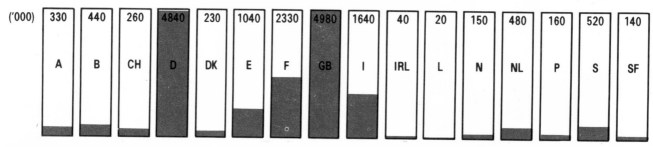

('000)	330	440	260	4840	230	1040	2330	4980	1640	40	20	150	480	160	520	140
	A	B	CH	D	DK	E	F	GB	I	IRL	L	N	NL	P	S	SF

Employment – Engineering

% of manufacturing population in metal manufacture and engineering

Emploi – Industrie mécanique

pourcentage de la population employée à la fabrication dans la métallurgie et l'industrie mécanique

Beschäftigte – Technik

% der in der Produktion Beschäftigten in der Metallherstellung und Technik Für L, NL wurden die Angaben geschätzt

Empleo – Mecánica

% de la población obrera fabril empleada en fabricación de metales y en mecánica

20-34%	35-39%	40-44%	45-49%	50-54%

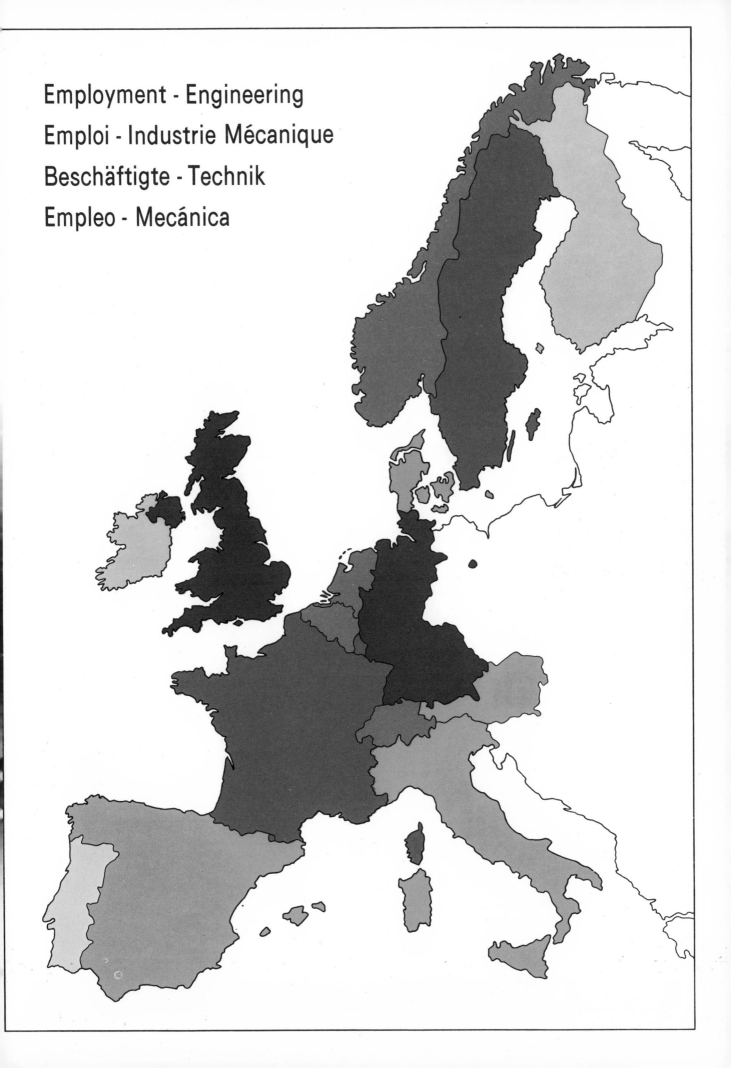

Employment - Engineering

Emploi - Industrie Mécanique

Beschäftigte - Technik

Empleo - Mecánica

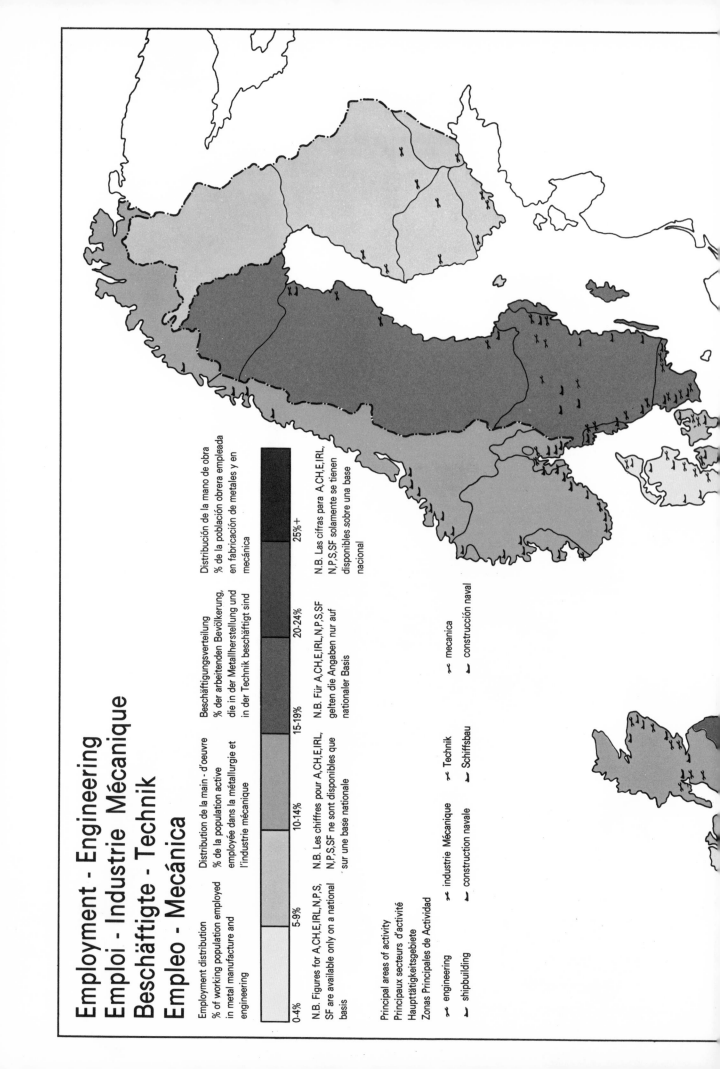

Employment - Engineering
Emploi - Industrie Mécanique
Beschäftigte - Technik
Empleo - Mecánica

Employment distribution

% of working population employed in metal manufacture and engineering

N.B. Figures for A,CH,E,IRL,N,P,S, SF are available only on a national basis

Distribution de la main - d'oeuvre

% de la population active employée dans la métallurgie et l'industrie mécanique

N.B. Les chiffres pour A,CH,E,IRL, N,P,S,SF ne sont disponibles que sur une base nationale

Beschäftigungsverteilung

% der arbeitenden Bevölkerung, die in der Metallherstellung und in der Technik beschäftigt sind

N.B. Für A,CH,E,IRL,N,P,S,SF gelten die Angaben nur auf nationaler Basis

Distribución de la mano de obra

% de la población obrera empleada en fabricación de metales y en mecánica

N.B. Las cifras para A,CH,E,IRL, N,P,S,SF solamente se tienen disponibles sobre una base nacional

| 0-4% | 5-9% | 10-14% | 15-19% | 20-24% | 25%+ |

Principal areas of activity
Principaux secteurs d'activité
Haupttätigkeitsgebiete
Zonas Principales de Actividad

engineering — industrie Mécanique — Technik — mecanica

shipbuilding — construction navale — Schiffsbau — construcción naval

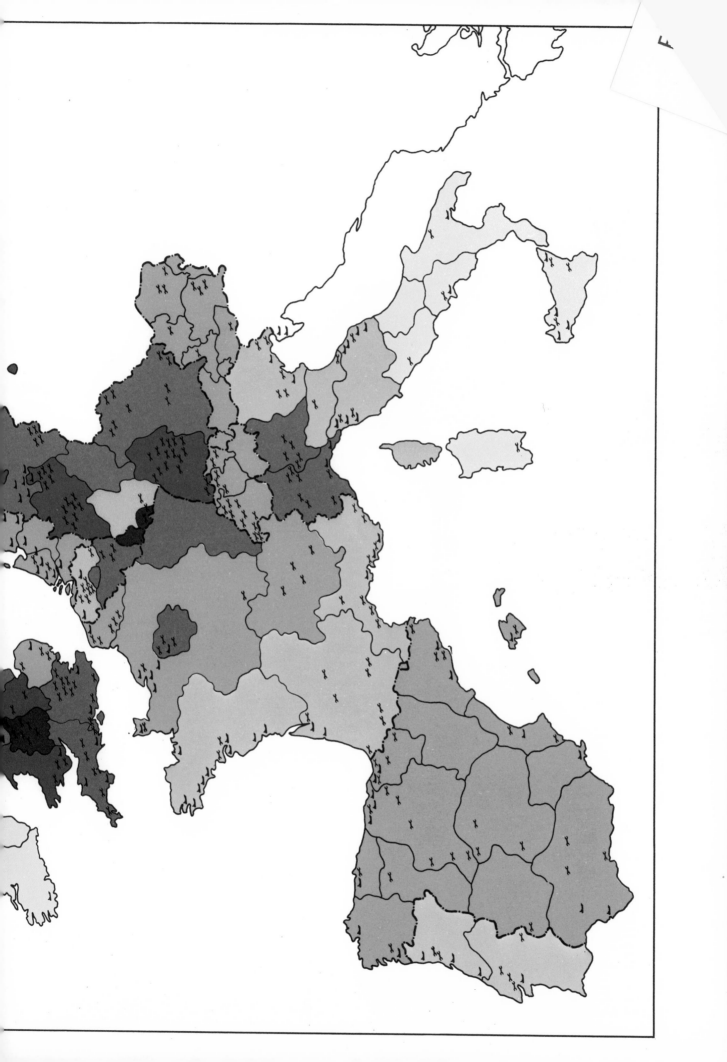

Engineering companies

Sociétés de construction mécanique

Maschinenbau-firmen

Empresas de industrias mecánicas

The following tables list those major European companies operating in the engineering industries. Latest available turnover figures are given; and where possible the proportion of total turnover derived from these activities has been estimated. Where the firm is amongst the 100 major companies of Europe its rank number has been given.

Les tableaux suivants donnent la liste des principales sociétés européennes appartenant au secteur de la construction mécanique. Il sindiquent le dernier montant connu de leur chiffre d'affaires; et, quand cela était possible, la proportion du chiffre d'affaires qui correspond aux activités en question a été évaluée. Dans le cas où la firme se place parmi les 100 premières sociétés d'Europe, son rang a été indiqué.

In der folgenden Tabelle sind die größten europäischen Maschinenbaufirmen aufgeführt. Umsatzzahlen sind angegeben. Wo möglich, wurde der Anteil dieser Produkte am Gesamtumsatz geschätzt. Wenn sich das Unternehmen unter den 100 größten Firmen Europas befindet, ist angegeben, auf welchem Platz es sich befindet.

En la tablas que siguen constan las principales empresas europeas dedicadas a las industrias mecánicas. Se señala las cifras de negocios más recientes que ha habido disponible; y dondequiera haya sido posible, se ha estimado el porcentaje del giro de negocios total derivado de tales actividades. Tratándose de una firma que se cuenta entre las 100 principales empresas de Europa, se indica el puesto que entre ellas ocupa.

General and mechanical engineering / Construction générale et mécanique / Allgemeine Maschinenbau-firmen / Ingenieria mecánica y general			£m	$m	%
Alsthom	F		244·2	586·1	
SA Cockerill-Ougrée-Providence et Espérance-Longdoz	F		326·9	784·6	
Demag AG	D		199·3	478·3	
Deutsche Babcock & Wilcox AG	D		195·8	469·9	50
Flick Group	D	46	699·5	1606·8	
Fried Krupp Huttenwerke AG	D	35	769·3	1846·3	
Gebrüder Sulzer AG	CH		271·1	650·6	
Gränges AB	S		244·9	587·8	43
Guest Keen & Nettlefolds Ltd	GB	59	564·8	1355·5	91
Gutehoffnungshütte Aktienverein	D	30	855·8	2053·9	
Hawker Siddeley Group Ltd	GB	68	472·1	1133·0	30
Klöckner-Humboldt-Deutz AG	D	85	416·8	1000·3	
MAN	D		256·0	614·4	
Mannesman AG	D	29	860·0	2064·0	
Rijn-Schelde-Verlome-Maschinefabrieken	NL		228·6	548·6	
Sears Holdings Ltd	GB		323·6	776·6	22
Tube Investments Ltd	GB	99	366·6	879·8	
Vickers Ltd	GB		181·0	434·4	45
AB Volvo	S	66	490·7	1177·7	
Otto Wolff AG	D	95	378·0	907·3	

Electrical and electronic engineering	Industrie électrique et électronique	Elektro- und Elektronikkonzerne		Ingenieria electrotecnica y electronica		
				£m	$m	%
AEG Telefunken	D	19		1197·8	2874·7	
Allmänna Svenska Electriska-Asea	S			321·6	771·8	
Robert Bosch GmbH	D	45		670·7	1609·7	
British Insulated Callender's Cables Ltd	GB	74		443·0	1063·2	
Brown Boveri & Cie AG	CH	56		580·0	1392·0	80
Brown Boveri & Cie AG	D			263·9	633·4	80
Compagnie Française Thomson-Houston-Hotchkiss-Brandt	F	63		511·6	1227·8	
Compagnie Générale D'Electricité	F	32		811·4	1947·4	
The General Electric Company Ltd	GB	24		974·9	2340·0	87
Gutehoffnungshütte Aktienverein	D	30		855·8	2053·9	
Hawker Siddeley Group Ltd	GB	68		472·1	1133·0	70
IBM Deutschland	D	78		433·9	1041·4	100
Joseph Lucas Industries Ltd	GB			340·0	815·5	92
Montedison SpA	I	26		933·0	2239·2	
Ing C Olivette CSPA	I			310·0	744·0	100
NV Philips' Gloeilampenfabrieken	NL	3		2180·5	5233·3	100
Philips Electronic & Associated Industries Ltd	GB			291·0	698·4	100
Siemens AG	D	8		1633·1	3919·4	63
Thorn Electrical Industries Ltd	GB	86		412·7	990·5	100
Tube Investments Ltd	GB	99		366·6	879·8	17

Motor vehicles

The national distribution of motor vehicle manufacturing follows closely the pattern established in all engineering. Accordingly the UK, France and West Germany, identified in the previous analysis with the highest levels of employment in engineering, have the greatest annual output of motor vehicles. Plants are broadly distributed across these countries with concentrations in the West Midlands and Scotland in the UK and Niedersachsen in West Germany.

Certain countries do, however, fulfil a more important function in motor vehicle manufacturing than the basic engineering structure would suggest, e.g. Italy.

L'industrie automobile

La distribution nationale de l'industrie automobile suit de près celle des industries mécaniques. De ce fait, le Royaume-Uni et l'Allemagne de l'Ouest, identifiés dans l'analyse antérieure comme ayant les plus forts niveaux de main-d'œuvre des industries mécaniques ont des taux de productivités annuelles en véhicules motorisés plus élevés. Les fabriques sont réparties à travers ces pays avec cependant des concentrations dans la région ouest des Midlands et en Ecosse au Royaume-Uni, et à Niedersachsen en Allemagne de l'Ouest.

Toutefois, certains pays jouent un rôle plus important dans la fabrication automobile que ne le laisse penser la structure de leur industrie mécanique. l'Italie en est un example.

Kraftfahrzeuge

Die Verteilung der Kraftfahrzeug-industrie in den einzelnen Ländern gleicht dem Bild des Maschinenbaus. Entsprechend haben auch das Vereinigte Königreich und Westdeutschland, die die größte Beschäftgung im Maschinenbau aufweisen, auch die größte Kraftfahrzeug-produktion. Die Werke sind in diesen Ländern weit gestreut, mit Konzentrationen im west-lichen Mittelengland und Schottland sowie Niedersachsen in Westdeutschland.

Gewisse Länder haben jedoch eine stärkere Kraftfahrzeug-industrie als ihr grundlegendes vermuten ließe. Ein Beispiel dafür ist Italien.

Vehículos a motor

La fabricación nacional de vehículos a motor, sigue de cerca el patrón establecido en el de todas las de la industria mecánica. De acuerdo con ello el Reino Unido, Francia y Alemania Occidental, se identifican con el análisis previo no sólo al tener ambas los niveles más altos de ampleo en ingeniería pero tembién las más altas producciones de vehículos a motor. En estos países las instalaciones están ampliamente distribuidas con concentraciones en el Reino Unido en las Midlands del Oeste y Escocia, y en Alemania en Niedersachsen.

Algunos países, sin embargo, desempeñan un papel más importante en la fabricación de vehículos a motor de lo que sugiere sus estructuras de la industria mecánica básica por ejemplo Italia.

Motor Vehicles – Output

calculated to nearest 1000

Véhicules automobiles – Production

calcul à 1.000 unités près

Motorfahrzeuge – Produktion

auf 1.000 auf- oder abgerundet

Vehículos de Motor – Producción

cálculo redondeado a la cifra 1.000 más próxima

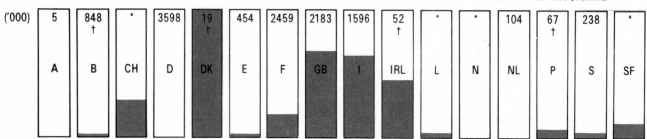

('000)	5	848 †	*	3598	19 †	454	2459	2183	1596	52 †	*	*	104	67 †	238	*
	A	B	CH	D	DK	E	F	GB	I	IRL	L	N	NL	P	S	SF

* less than 1000
† assembly only

* moins de 1000
† assemblée seulement

* unter 1000
† nur Montage

* menos de 1000
† montaje solamente

Motor vehicle companies

Sociétés de l'industrie automobile

Motorfahrzeug-Hersteller

Empresas de vehículos motorizados

The following table lists those major European companies operating in the manufacture of motor vehicles.
Latest available turnover figures are given; and where possible the proportion of total turnover derived from these activities has been estimated.
Where the firm is amongst the 100 major companies of Europe its rank number has been given.

Le tableau suivant donne la liste des principales sociétés européennes engagées dans la manufacture des véhicules automobiles. Il indique le dernier montant connu de leur chiffre d'affaires; et, quand cela était possible, la proportion du chiffre d'affaires qui correspond aux activités en question a été évaluée. Dans le cas où la firme se place parmi les 100 premières sociétés d'Europe, son rang a été indiqué.

In der folgenden Tabelle sind die größten europäischen Hersteller von Motorfahrzeugen aufgeführt.
Umsatzzahlen sind angegeben. Wo möglich, wurde der Anteil dieser Produkte am Gesamtumsatz geschätzt. Wenn sich das Unternehmen unter den 100 größten Firmen Europas befindet, ist angegeben, auf welchem Platz es sich befindet.

En la tabla que sigue constan las principales empresas europeas dedicadas a la fabricación de vehículos motorizados. Se señala las cifras de negocios más recientes que has habido disponible: y dondequiera haya sido posible, se ha estimado el porcentaje del giro de negocios total derivado de tales actividades. Tratándose de una firma que se cuenta entre las 100 principales empresas de Europa, se indica el puesto que entre ellas ocupa.

			£m	$m	%
Alfa Romeo SpA	I		172·4	413·8	
Bayerische Motorenwerke AG	D		228·4	548·2	
British Leyland Motor Corporation Ltd	GB	20	1176·9	2824·6	100
Chrysler UK Ltd	GB		319·5	766·8	100
Citroën SA	F	81	431·0	1034·4	95
Daimler-Benz AG	D	6	1800·0	4320·0	100
Fiat SpA	I	18	1200·5	2881·2	90
Ford Motor Company Ltd	GB	52	589·0	1413·6	90
Ford Werke AG	D	47	662·2	1589·3	
MAN	D		256·0	614·4	
Adam Opel	D	55	583·8	1401·1	
Peugeot SA	F	41	698·3	1675·9	
Regie-Renault	F	28	890·3	2136·7	100
Rheinstahl AG	D	42	682·7	1638·5	
Saab-Scania	S		330·5	793·2	75
SEAT	E		175·4	421·0	
Vauxhall Motors Ltd	GB		287·8	690·7	100
Van Doorne's Automobielfabrieken	NL		115·9	278·2	
Volkswagenwerk AG	D	4	2147·0	5152·8	
AB Volvo	S	66	490·7	1177·7	78

K

Textiles

Les textiles

Textilien

Textiles

The GEP industry classification of textiles, clothing and allied industries includes the manufacture of textiles (natural and synthetic fibres), clothing, footwear, fur and leather products.

Maps and data in this sector include:
- Value added per capita.
- Employment distribution.
- Output of textiles.
- Areas of concentrated activity.

La classification industrielle des textiles, des vêtements et des industries alliées établie par GEP comprend la fabrication des textiles (fibres naturelles et fibres synthétiques), des vêtements, des chaussures, des fourrures et la maroquinerìe.

Les cartes et les données de cette section comprennent:
- La valeur ajoutée par tête.
- La répartition de la main-d'oeuvre.
- La production textile.
- Les régions à activité concentrée.

Die GEP-Klassifizierung für Textilien, Bekleidung und verwandte Industrien enthält Hersteller von Textilien (natürlichen und synthetischen Fasern), Bekleidung, Schuhen, Pelz- und Lederwaren.

Auf Karten und in Angaben dieses Abschnittes sind enthalten:
- Leistungswert pro Kopf.
- Verteilung der Beschäftigung.
- Textilienproduktion.
- Gebiete konzentrierter Aktivitäten.

La clasificación GEP de industrias textiles de vestir y aliadas incluye la fabricación de tejidos (de fibras naturales y sintéticas) prendas de vestir, zapatería, piel y productos del cuero:

Los mapas y datos de este sector incluyen:
- Valor añadido per cápita.
- Distribución de los empleos.
- Produccion textil.
- Áreas de actividad concentrada.

Value of output per capita
(US $ per annum)

N.B. Figure for CH is not available

Average for Western Europe $40

Valeur ajoutée par tête
(US $ par an)

N.B. Le chiffre pour CH n'est pas disponible

Moyenne pour l'Europe occidentale $40

Leistungswert pro Kopf
(US $ pro Jahr)

N.B. Für CH liegen keine Angaben vor

Durchschnitt für Westeuropa $40

Valor de la producción por cabeza
(US $ por ano)

N.B. no se cuenta con la cifra para CH

Promedio para Europa Occidental $40

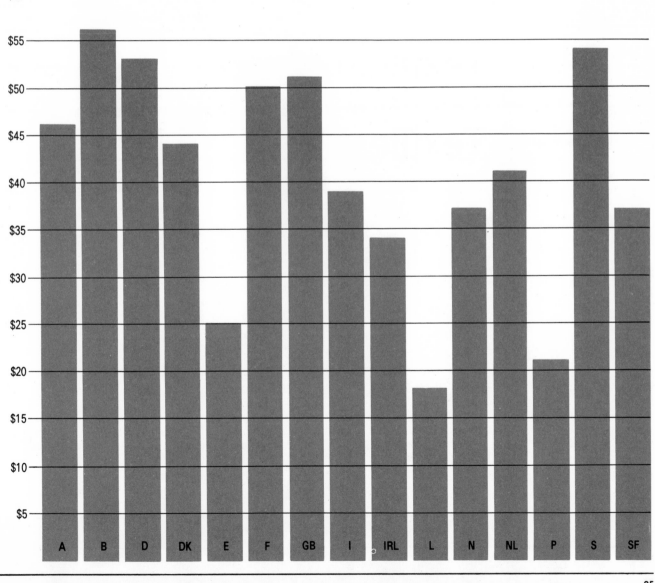

Textile companies

Sociétés textiles

Textilhersteller

Empresas textiles

The following table lists those major European companies operating in the manufacture of textiles. Latest available turnover figures are given; and where possible the proportion of total turnover derived from these activities has been estimated. Where the firm is amongst the 100 major companies of Europe its rank number has been given.

Le tableau suivant donne la liste des principales sociétés européennes engagées dans la manufacture des textiles. Il indique le dernier montant connu de leur chiffre d'affaires; et, quand cela était possible, la proportion du chiffre d'affaires qui correspond aux activités en question a été évaluée. Dans le cas où la firme se place parmi les 100 premières sociétés d'Europe, son rang a été indiqué.

In der folgenden Tabelle sind die größten europäischen Hersteller von Textilien aufgeführt. Umsatzzahlen sind angegeben. Wo möglich, wurde der Anteil dieser Produkte am Gesamtumsatz geschätzt. Wenn sich das Unternehmen unter den 100 größten Firmen Europas befindet, ist angegeben, auf welchem Platz es sich befindet.

En la tabla que sigue constan las principales empresas europeas dedicadas a la fabricación de textiles. Se señala las cifras de negocios más recientes que ha habido disponible; y dondequiera haya sido posible se ha estimado el porcentaje del giro de negocios total derivado de tales actividades. Tratándose de una firma que se cuenta entre las 100 principales empresas de Europa, se indica el puesto que entre ellas ocupa.

			£m	$m	%
Akzo NV	NL	25	969·2	2326·1	
C & A Brenninkmeyer	NL	100	366·2	878·9	
Carrington-Viyella Ltd (ICI)	GB		153·3	367·9	
Coats-Patons Ltd	GB		303·3	727·9	90
Courtaulds Ltd	GB	43	681·5	1635·6	85
English Calico Ltd	GB		162·9	391·0	83
Enka Glanzstoff AG	D	97	371·3	891·1	
Lonrho Ltd	GB		191·9	460·6	9
Imperial Chemical Industries Ltd	GB	9	1524·4	3658·6	13
Snia Viscosa	I		257·3	617·5	80

Employment – Textiles

Emploi – Textiles

Beschäftigte – Textil

Empleo – Textiles

% of manufacturing population employed in textiles, clothing and allied industries

pourcentage de la population employée à la fabrications dans les textiles, l'habillement et les industries connexes.

% der in der Produktion Beschäftigten in Textil-, Bekleidungs- und verwandten Industrien

% de la población obrera fabril empleada en las industrias de textiles, vestimenta y análogos

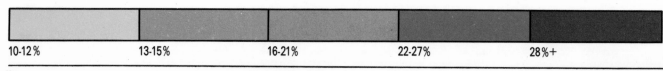

| 10-12% | 13-15% | 16-21% | 22-27% | 28%+ |

Employment - Textiles

Emploi - Textiles

Beschäftigte - Textil

Empleo - Textiles

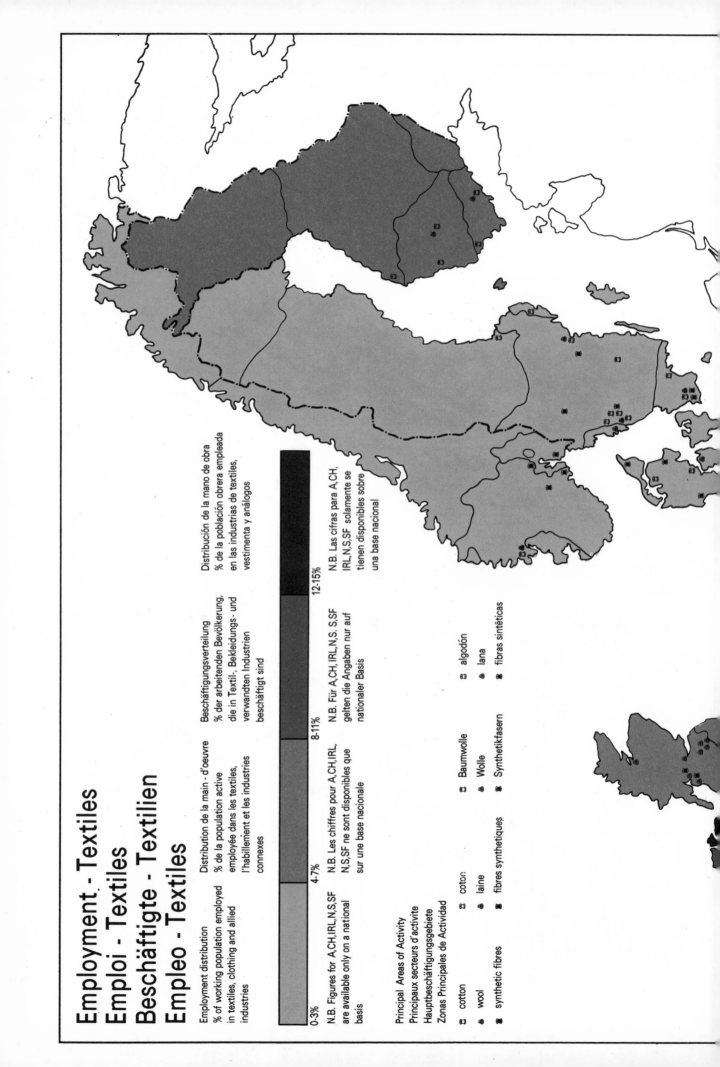

Employment - Textiles
Emploi - Textiles
Beschäftigte - Textilien
Empleo - Textiles

Employment distribution
% of working population employed in textiles, clothing and allied industries

N.B. Figures for A,CH,IRL,N,S,SF are available only on a national basis

Distribution de la main - d'oeuvre
% de la population active employée dans les textiles, l'habillement et les industries connexes

N.B. Les chiffres pour A,CH,IRL, N,S,SF ne sont disponibles que sur une base nacionale

Beschäftigungsverteilung
% der arbeitenden Bevölkerung, die in Textil-, Bekleidungs- und verwandten Industrien beschäftigt sind

N.B. Für A,CH,IRL,N,S, S,SF gelten die Angaben nur auf nationaler Basis

Distribución de la mano de obra
% de la población obrera empleada en las industrias de textiles, vestimenta y análogos

N.B. Las cifras para A,CH, IRL,N,S,SF solamente se tienen disponibles sobre una base nacional

0-3%   4-7%   8-11%   12-15%

Principal Areas of Activity
Principaux secteurs d'activite
Hauptbeschäftigungsgebiete
Zonas Principales de Actividad

cotton	coton:	Baumwolle	algodón
wool	laine	Wolle	lana
synthetic fibres	fibres synthetiques	Synthetikfasern	fibras sintéticas

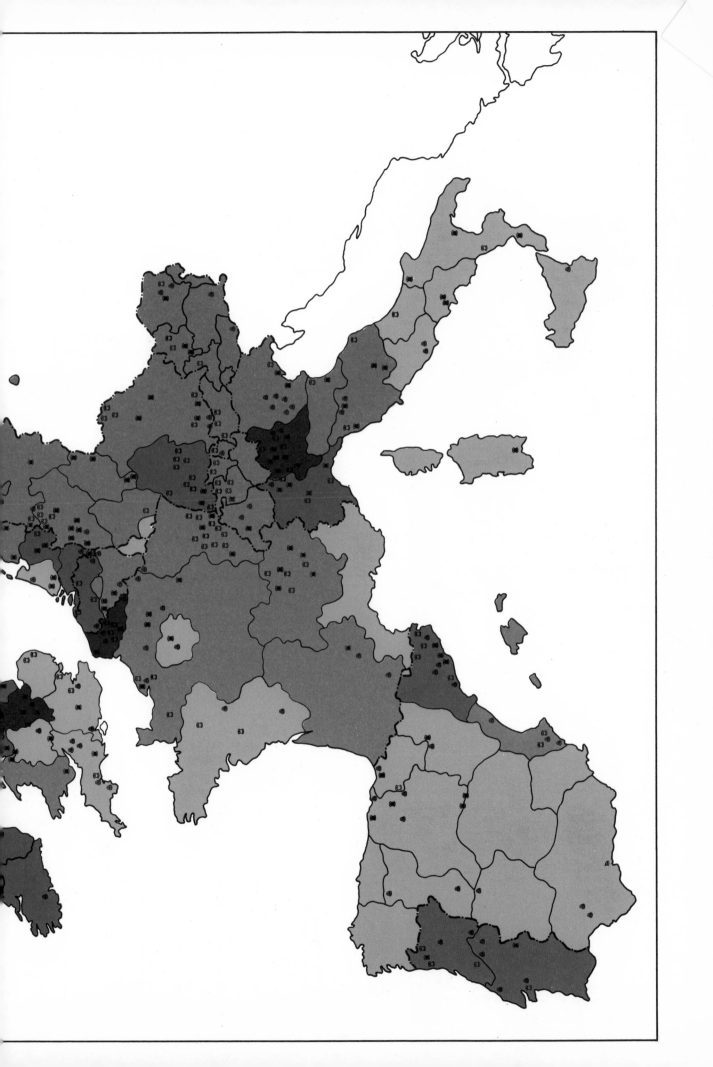

Output of textiles

Germany is the largest producer of textiles in Western Europe with an annual output of approaching 2m. metric tons. It can be seen from the table below that this country, along with the UK and Italy, has over one million employees within the industry classification.

Expressed in terms of share of all manufacturing employment, the industry in Portugal emerges as the only one to employ over 28%. Three countries (Italy, Belgium and Ireland) have between 22% and 27% of the industrial workforce in textiles.

There is a wide variation between the relative output in each country of natural and synthetic fibres. 50% of the output in Austria, Finland and Norway comes from synthetic products whilst in the other countries over 50% still comes from natural fibres especially cotton and wool.

At the regional level the most important areas of textile and clothing production are:
1 Central UK-East Midlands, North West and Yorkshire and Humberside.
2 France-Nord.
3 Italy-Lombardia.
4 Netherlands-Oost and Zuid.

Production de textiles

L'Allemagne est le plus gros producteur de textiles en Europe Occidentale avec une production annuelle de presque 2 millions de tonnes métriques. Comme l'indique le tableau ci-après, ce pays, ainsi que le Royaume-Uni et l'Italie, a plus d'un million d'employés dans cette industrie.

Exprimée sous forme de répartition de toute la main-d'oeuvre manufacturière, l'industrie textile du Portugal est la seule à employer plus de 28 pour cent. Trois pays : l'Italie, la Belgique et l'Irlande ont entre 22 et 27 pour cent de leur main-d'oeuvre industrielle dans les fabriques de textiles.

Il existe une variation marquée entre la production relative des fibres naturelles et des fibres synthétiques dans chaque pays. En Autriche, en Finlande et en Norvège, 50 pour cent de la production sont dérivés de produits synthétiques tandis que dans les autres pays plus de 50 pour cent proviennent de fibres naturelles, surtout le coton et la laine.

Au niveau régional, les emplacements les plus importants pour la production des textiles et des vêtements sont :
1 la région centrale du Royaume-Uni-East Midlands, North West Yorkshire et Humberside.
2 le Nord de la France.
3 la Lombardia en Italie.
4 l'Oost et le Zuid des Pays-Bas.

Textilproduktion

In Westeuropa ist Deutschland mit einer Jahresproduktion von fast 2 Millionen Tonnen der größte Textilhersteller. Aus der untenstehenden Tabelle kann man entnehmen, daß dieses Land zusammen mit dem Vereinigten Königreich und Italien über eine Million Arbeitnehmer in dieser Industrie beschäftigt.

Anteilsmäßig auf alle Arbeitsstellen in der Produktion bezogen ist Portugal das einzige Land, das über 28% in der Textilindustrie beschäftigt. Drei Länder (Italien, Belgien und Irland) beschäftigen zwischen 22 und 27% ihrer Arbeitskräfte in der Textilindustrie.

Die relative Produktion eines jeden Landes von natürlichen und Chemiefasern ist sehr unterschiedlich. 50% der Produktionen von Österreich, Finnland, Norwegen besteht aus Synthetikfasern, in anderen Ländern erfolgt noch über 50% der Produktion aus Naturfasern, besonders Baumwolle und Wolle.

Die größten Gebiete für die Herstellung von Textilien und Bekleidung sind:
1 Mittelengland-östliches Mittelengland, Nordwestengland sowie Yorkshire und am Humber.
2 Nordfrankreich.
3 Die Lombardia in Italien.
4 Ost- und Südholland.

Producción textil

La mayor productora textil de Europa Occidental es Alemania, con una producción anual de casi 2 millones de toneladas métricas. El cuadro de abajo muestra que dicho país conjuntamente con el Reino Unido e Italia, tienen a más de un millon de personas empleadas bajo la clasificación de estas industrias.

Expresado en términos de la participación de los empleos en todas las industrias de fabricación, la industria portuguesa es la que resulta emplear a más del 25%. Tres países (Italia, Bélgica e Irlanda) tienen entre el 22% y el 27% de la mano de obra industrial en productos textiles.

Hay variaciones considerables entre las producciones relativas de fibras naturales y sintéticas en cada país. En Austria, Finlandia y Noruega el 50% de la producción es de productos artificiales, mientras que en otros países más del 50% proviene todavía de fibras naturales, especialmente algodón y lana.

A nivel regional las áreas más importantes en la producción de tejidos y prendas de vestir son:
1 Reino Unido Central, Midlands del Este, Noroeste, Yorkshire y Humberside.
2 El Norte de Francia.
3 Lombardía en Italia.
4 Oost y Zuid en Holanda.

Total Number of Persons Employed in Textile and Clothing Industries

calculated to nearest 10,000

Nombre total de personnes employées dans l'industrie textile et l'habillement

calcul à 10.000 personnes près

Gesamtbeschäftigte in Textil- und Bekleidungsindustrie

auf 10.000 auf- oder abgerundet

Número Total de Personas Empleadas en las Industrias Textiles y de Vestimenta

cálculo redondeado a la cifra 10.000 más próxima

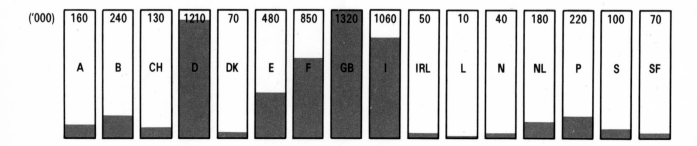

('000)															
	160	240	130	1210	70	480	850	1320	1060	50	10	40	180	220	100	70
	A	B	CH	D	DK	E	F	GB	I	IRL	L	N	NL	P	S	SF

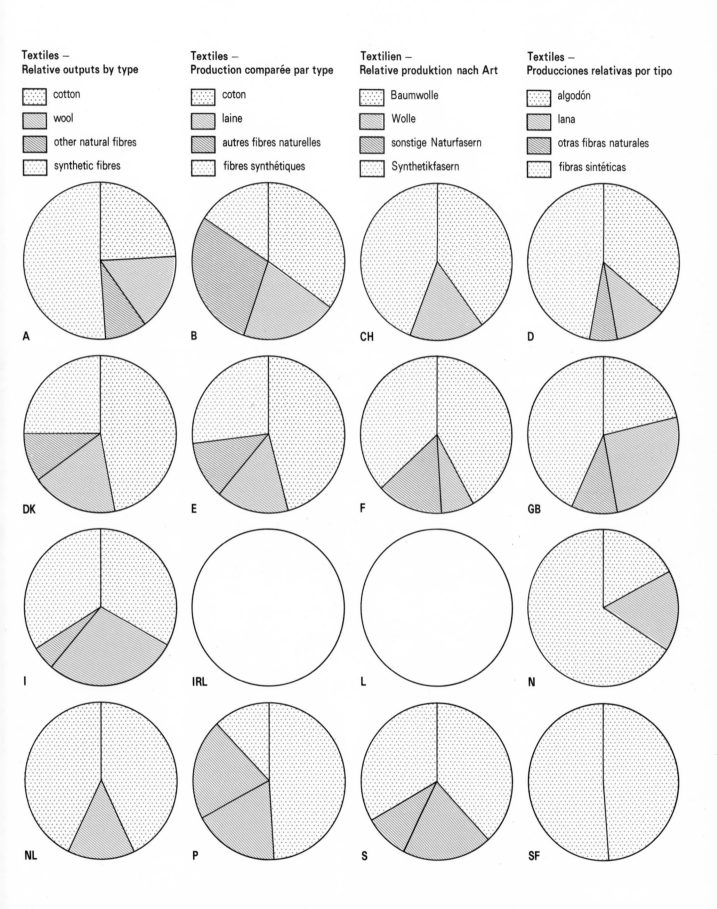

Textiles —
Relative outputs by type

- cotton
- wool
- other natural fibres
- synthetic fibres

Textiles —
Production comparée par type

- coton
- laine
- autres fibres naturelles
- fibres synthétiques

Textilien —
Relative produktion nach Art

- Baumwolle
- Wolle
- sonstige Naturfasern
- Synthetikfasern

Textiles —
Producciones relativas por tipo

- algodón
- lana
- otras fibras naturales
- fibras sintéticas

A

B

CH

D

DK

E

F

GB

I

IRL

L

N

NL

P

S

SF

L

Paper, printing and publishing

Le papier, l'imprimerie et l'édition

Papier, Druck und Verlagswesen

Papel, tipografía y editoriales

The GEP industry classification of paper, printing and publishing includes the manufacture of paper, board and their products, printing, publishing, book-binding and allied activities.

Maps and data in this section include:
● Value added per capita.
● Employment distribution.
● Output of paper and paper products.
● Major paper, printing and publishing companies.

La classification industrielle du papier, de l'imprimerie et de l'édition établie par GEP comprend la fabrication du papier, du carton et de leurs produits associés, l'imprimerie, la publication, la reliure et les activités alliées.

Les cartes et les données de cette section comprennent:
● La valeur ajoutée par tête.
● La répartition de la main-d'oeuvre.
● La production du papier et des produits en papier.
● Les principales entreprises engagées dans la fabrication du papier, dans l'imprimerie et dans l'édition.

In der GEP-Klassifizierung von Papier, Druck und Verlagswesen sind enthalten: Papierherstellung, Pappeherstellung und Neben-produkte, Druckereiwesen, Verlagswesen, Buchbinderei und verwandte Tätigkeiten.

Auf Karten und in Angaben dieses Abschnittes ist folgendes enthalten:
● Leistungswert pro Kopf.
● Verteilung der Beschäftigung.
● Produktion von Papier und Papierprodukten.
● Die größten Hersteller von Papier, Druckereien und Verlage.

En la clasificación GEP de industrias del papel, tipográficas y editoriales se incluye la fabricación de papel, cartón y sus productos, tipografías, editoriales, encuadernaciones y actividades aliadas.

Los mapas y datos de esta sección incluyen:
● Valor añadido per cápita.
● Distribucion de los empleos.
● Producción de papel y productos del papel.
● Los principales periódicos, tipografías y editoriales.

Value of output per capita
(US $ per annum)

N.B. Figure for CH is not available

Average for Western Europe $37

Valeur ajoutée par tête
(US $ par an)

N.B. Le chiffre pour CH n'est pas disponible

Moyenne pour l'Europe occidentale $37

Leistungswert pro Kopf
(US $ pro Jahr)

N.B. Für CH liegen keine Angaben vor

Durchschnitt für Westeuropa $37

Valor de la producción por cabeza
(US $ por ano)

N.B. no se cuenta con la cifra para CH

Promedio para Europa Occidental $37

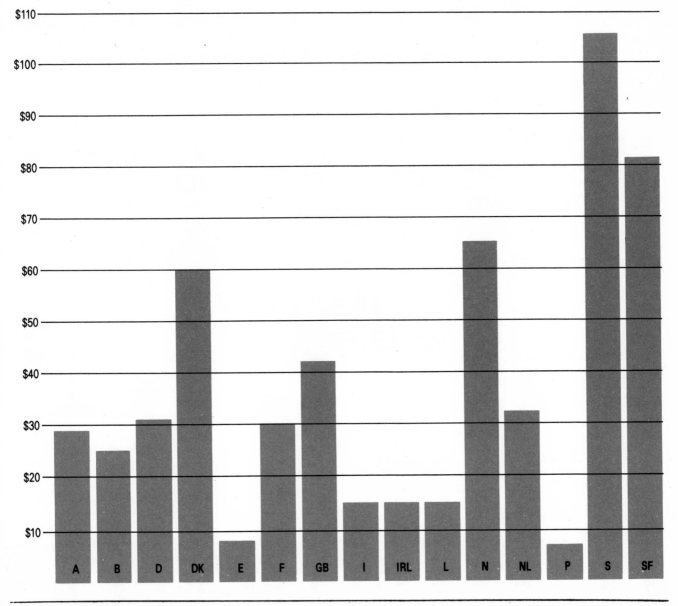

Sweden and Finland form the principal supply area of woodpulp and newsprint. Paper and paperboard output, however, is greatest in the UK and West Germany.

The printing industry is more uniformly distributed throughout Western Europe and is particularly concentrated around the major commercial cities. London, Paris and Roma are the three principal publishing centres in Western Europe.

This industry grouping does not, however, form such a major element within the industrial employment pattern of Western Europe. In only three countries – Finland, Norway and Sweden – does this sector account for over 10% of all manufacturing employment.

La Suède et la Finlande forment le centre principal d'approvisionnement en pâte de bois et en papier-journal. Cependant, la production du papier et du carton est plus élevée au Royaume Uni et en Allemagne de l'Ouest.

L'imprimerie est répartie plus uniformément à travers l'Europe occidentale et elle se concentre surtout autour des principales villes commerciales. London, Paris et Roma sont les trois principaux centres de publication en Europe occidentale.

Toutefois le groupement de cette industrie n'est pas un élément contributif important de la distribution de la main-d'oeuvre industrielle en Europe occidentale. Dans trois pays seulement: la Finlande, la Norvège et la Suède, ce secteur industriel est responsable pour plus de 10 pour cent de toute la main-d'oeuvre manufacturière.

Schweden und Finnland sind die größten Lieferanten für Zellstoff und Zeitungspapier. Das Vereinigte Königreich und Westdeutschland sind jedoch die größten Hersteller von Papier und Pappe.

Das Druckereiwesen ist etwas einheitlicher über Westeuropa verteilt und konzentriert sich um die größeren Handelsstädte. London, Paris und Roma sind die drei großen Verlagszentren Westeuropas.

Diese Industriegruppe hat jedoch in der Beschäftigung von Westeuropa keine so große Bedeutung. Nur in drei Ländern – Finnland, Norwegen und Schweden – beschäftigt diese Branche über 10% der in der Herstellung Beschäftigten.

Las áreas de suministro principales de pulpa leñosa y de papel para imprimir son Suecia y Finlandia. La producción de papel y cartón es sin embargo más grande en el Reino Unido y Alemania Occidental.

La industria tipográfica está distribuida más uniformemente en Europa Occidental y se concentra particularmente alrededor de las principales ciudades comerciales. Los centros principales de Europa Occidental son: London, Paris y Roma.

Este grupo de industrias sin embargo no forma un elemento primario en el patrón de los empleos industriales de Europa Occidental. Sólo en tres países – Finlandia, Noruega y Suecia – este sector suma más del 10% de los empleos industrias fabriles.

Total Number of Persons Employed in Paper, Printing and Publishing

calculated to nearest 10,000

Nombre total de personnes employées dans le papier, l'imprimerie et l'édition

calcul à 10.000 personnes près

Gesamtbeschäftigte in der Papierindustrie, in Druckereiwesen und Verlagen

auf 10.000 auf- oder abgerundet

Número Total de Personas Empleadas en Papel, Impresión y Editoriales

cálculo redondeado a la cifra 10.000 más próxima

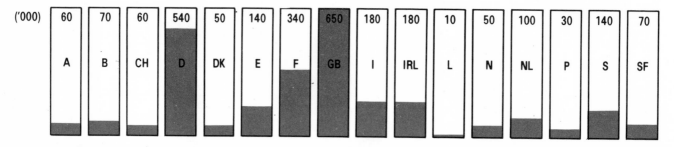

('000)	A	B	CH	D	DK	E	F	GB	I	IRL	L	N	NL	P	S	SF
	60	70	60	540	50	140	340	650	180	180	10	50	100	30	140	70

Employment – Paper, Printing, Publishing

% of manufacturing population employed in paper, printing and publishing

Emploi – Papier, Imprimerie, Edition

pourcentage de la population employée à la fabrication dans le papier, l'imprimerie et l'édition

Beschäftigte – Papier, Druckerei- und Verlagswesen

% der in der Produktion Beschäftigten in der Papierindustrie, Druckerei und Verlagswesen

Empleo – Papel, Impresión Editoriales

% de la población obrera fabril empleada en papel, impresión y editoriales

4-6%	7-9%	10-12%	13-15%	16-18%

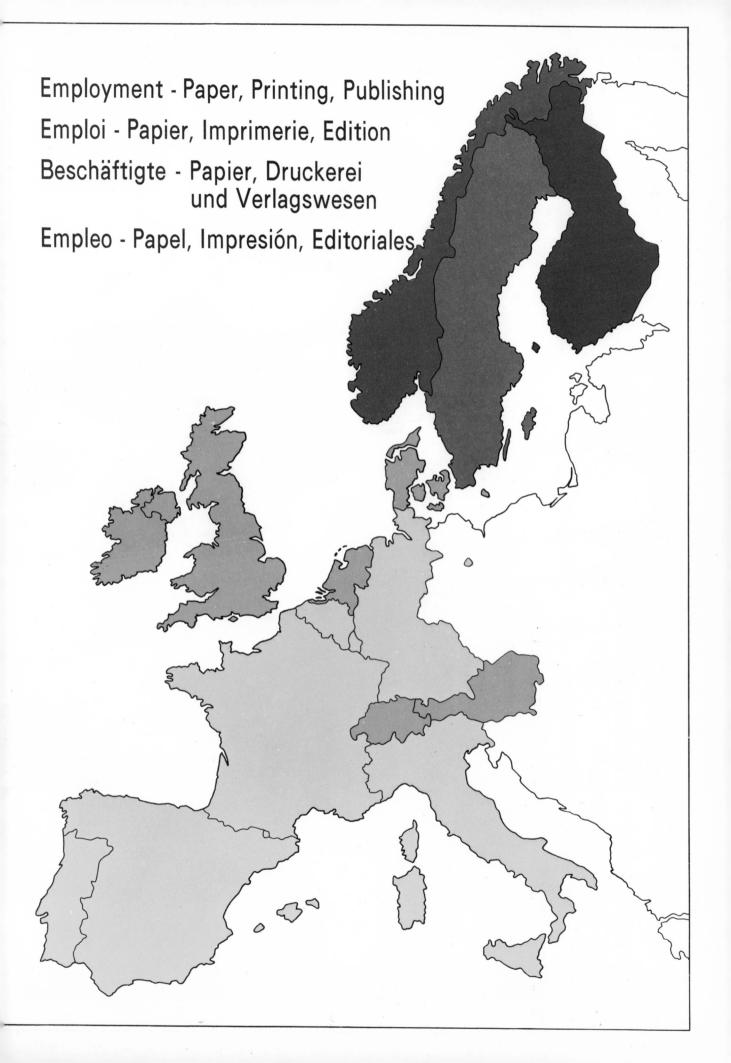

Employment - Paper, Printing, Publishing

Emploi - Papier, Imprimerie, Edition

Beschäftigte - Papier, Druckerei
                 und Verlagswesen

Empleo - Papel, Impresión, Editoriales

Employment - Paper, Printing and Publishing
Emploi - Papier, Imprimerie, Edition
Beschäftigte - Papier, Druckerei- und Verlagswesen
Empleo - Papel, Impresión y Editoriales

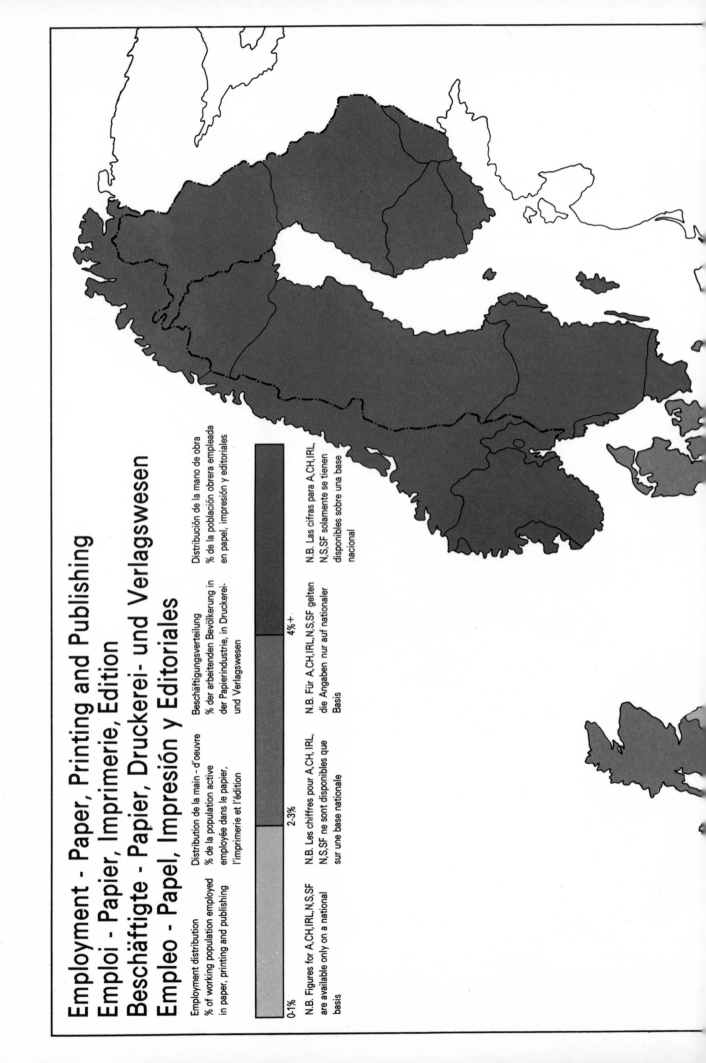

Employment distribution
% of working population employed in paper, printing and publishing

N.B. Figures for A,CH,IRL,N,S,SF are available only on a national basis

Distribution de la main – d'oeuvre
% de la population active employée dans le papier, l'imprimerie et l'édition

N.B. Les chiffres pour A,CH,IRL, N,S,SF ne sont disponibles que sur une base nationale

Beschäftigungsverteilung
% der arbeitenden Bevölkerung in der Papierindustrie, in Druckerei- und Verlagswesen

N.B. Für A,CH,IRL,N,S,SF gelten die Angaben nur auf nationaler Basis

Distribución de la mano de obra
% de la población obrera empleada en papel, impresión y editoriales

N.B. Las cifras para A,CH,IRL, N,S,SF solamente se tienen disponibles sobre una base nacional

0-1%   2-3%   4%+

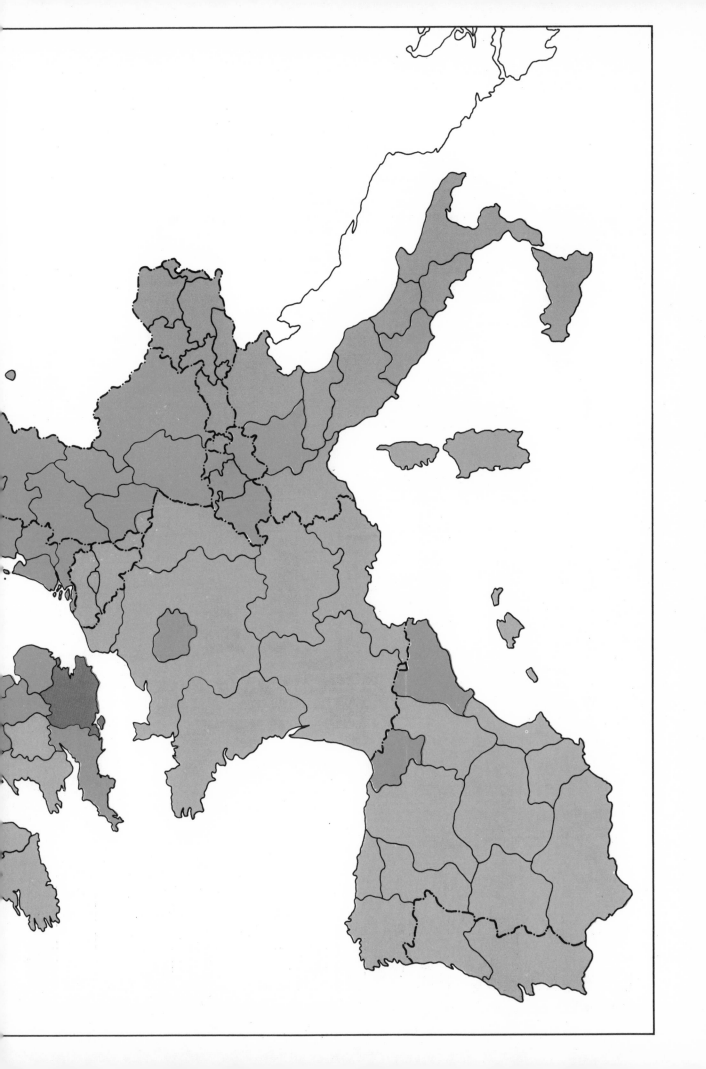

Paper, printing and publishing companies

Sociétés de la papeterie, de l'imprimerie et de l'édition

Druckereien, und Verlage

Empresas impresoras y editoriales

The following table lists those major European companies operating in the paper, printing, publishing and allied industries. Latest available turnover figures are given; and where possible the proportion of total turnover derived from these activities has been estimated. Where the firm is amongst the 100 major companies of Europe its rank number has been given.

Le tableau suivant donne la liste des principales sociétés européennes appartenant aux secteurs de la papeterie, de l'imprimerie, de l'édition et aux industries associées. Il indique le dernier montant connu de leur chiffre d'affaires; et, quand cela était possible, la proportion du chiffre d'affaires qui correspond aux activités en question a été évaluée. Dans le cas où la firme se place parmi les 100 premières sociétés d'Europe, son rang a été indiqué.

In der folgenden Tabelle sind die größten europäischen Firmen in Druck, Papier, Verlagswesen und verwandten Industrien aufgeführt. Umsatzzahlen sind angegeben. Wo möglich, wurde der Anteil dieser Produkte am Gesamtumsatz geschätzt. Wenn sich das Unternehmen unter den 100 größten Firmen Europas befindet, ist angegeben, auf welchem Platz es sich befindet.

En la tabla que sigue constan las principales empresas dedicadas a las industrias del papel, impresoras, editoriales y similares. Se señala las cifras de negocios más recientes que ha habido disponible: y dondequiera haya sido posible, se ha estimado el porcentaje del giro de negocios total derivado de tales actividades. Tratándose de una firma que se cuenta entre las 100 principales empresas de Europa, se indica el puesto que entre ellas ocupa.

			£m	$m	%
Agence Havas	F		148·4	356·2	
Axel Springer Publishing Group	D		118·6	284·6	
The Bowater Paper Corporation Ltd	GB		254·1	609·8	84
Feldmühle AG	D		275·5	661·2	73
Librarie Hachette SA	F		229·1	549·8	
Papierwerke Waldhof Aschaffenburg	S		101·7	244·1	
Reed International Ltd	GB	60	534·4	1282·6	67
Stora Kopparbergs Berglas AB	S		151·7	364·1	33
Svenska Cellulosa AB	S		120·6	298·4	
Uddeholm AB	S		102·5	246·0	29

Paper – Output

total annual output of woodpulp, newsprint, paper and board ('000) metric tons

Papier – Production

production totale annuelle de pâtes de bois, de papier journal, de papier et de carton en milliers de tonnes

Papier – Produktion

Jahres-Gesamtproduktion Halzstoff, Zeitungspapier, Papier und Pappe (in tausend) Tonnen

Papel – Producción

producción anual total de pasta papelera, papel para periódicos, papel y cartón en (miles de) toneladas

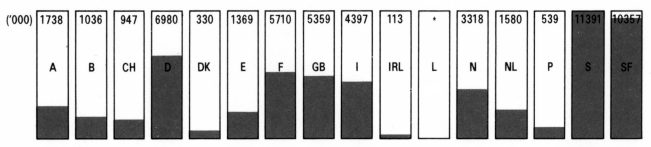

('000)	1738	1036	947	6980	330	1369	5710	5359	4397	113	*	3318	1580	539	11391	10357
	A	B	CH	D	DK	E	F	GB	I	IRL	L	N	NL	P	S	SF

* less than 100 tons   * moins de 100 tonnes   * unter 100 tonnen   * menos de 100 toneladas

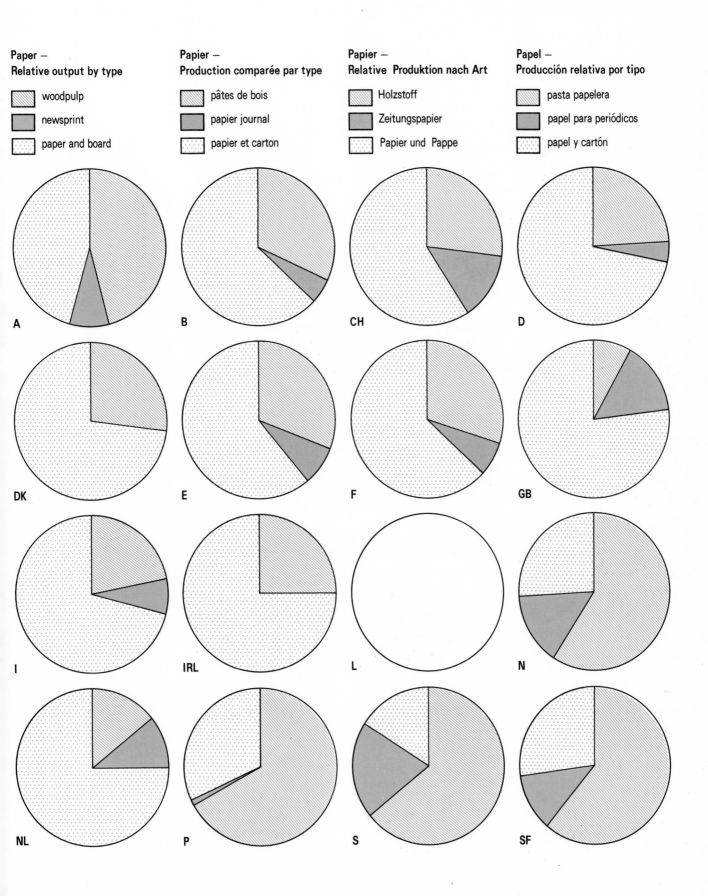

Paper –
Relative output by type

woodpulp
newsprint
paper and board

Papier –
Production comparée par type

pâtes de bois
papier journal
papier et carton

Papier –
Relative Produktion nach Art

Holzstoff
Zeitungspapier
Papier und Pappe

Papel –
Producción relativa por tipo

pasta papelera
papel para periódicos
papel y cartón

A

B

CH

D

DK

E

F

GB

I

IRL

L

N

NL

P

S

SF

3

THE EUROPEAN CONSUMER

LE CONSOMMATEUR EUROPEEN

DER EUROPÄISCHE VERBRAUCHER

EL CONSUMIDOR EUROPEO

Introduction to Part 3

Part 3 is devoted to a study of national and regional variations in consumer standards and market characteristics. It is possible to determine from the following analyses the distribution across Western Europe of differing wealth and consumption patterns.

In standard manner Part 3 is divided into a number of sections which select and analyse various facets of consumer standards. Specifically this part includes information on incomes expenditure, housing, education and publishing.

Introduction de la III ème partie

La troisième partie est consacrée à une étude des variations nationales et régionales des niveaux de consommation et des caractéristiques des marchés. Il est possible d'établir à partir des analyses suivantes la répartition à travers l'Europe Occidentale des modalités de prospérité et de consommation.

Cette troisième partie est d'une façon standardisée, divisée en plusieurs sections et analyse les diverses facettes du genre de vie des consommateurs. D'une façon spécifique, cette partie traite des salaires, des dépenses, du logement, de l'éducation et de la publication.

Einführung zu Teil 3

In Teil 3 werden die nationalen und regionalen Unterschiede im Verbraucherstandard und den Markteigenschaften untersucht. Aus den folgenden Analysen kann man die Verteilung eines unterschiedlichen Wohlstandes und Verbrauchsbildes in West-europa entnehmen.

Wie gehabt ist Teil 3 in mehrere Abschnitte geteilt, die verschiedene Bereiche des Verbraucherstandards auswählen und näher untersuchen. In diesem Teil sind insbesondere Angaben über Einkommen, Ausgaben, Wohnen, Erziehung und Tageszeitungen enthalten.

Introducción a la 3ª Parte

La 3ª Parte se dedica a un estudio de las variaciones en los niveles de los consumidores y características de los mercados tanto nacional como regionalmente. Siguiendo este análisis de distribución a través de Europa Occidental, se puede determinar las diversas riquezas y patronos de consumo.

De forma normal la 3ª Parte se divide en un número de secciones las cuales seleccionan y analizan las varias facetas de los niveles de los consumidores. Esta parte especialmente incluye información sobre los gastos de los ingresos, viviendas, educación y publicaciones.

M

Incomes

Les revenus

Einkommen

Ingresos

Average income per capita is the principal measure of community wealth. This section charts the national and regional variations in this measure across Western Europe together with recent growth trends.

Maps in this section include:
- Distribution of average incomes by region in selected countries.
- Increases in average earnings.

Denmark, West Germany, Luxembourg, Sweden and Switzerland have the highest average annual income per capita. At the regional level, the inhabitants of the Zürich and Basel areas of northern Switzerland and the Bremen and Hamburg areas of northern West Germany enjoy particularly high incomes.

Le revenu par tête est le baromètre de la prospérité d'une communauté. Cette section établit les variations nationales et régionales de cette moyenne des salaires à travers l'Europe Occidentale ainsi que les tendances récentes à l'accroissement.

Les cartes de cette section comprennent:
- La répartition du salaire par région dans certains pays sélectionnés.
- Les augmentations de la moyenne des salaires.

Le Danemark, l'Allemagne de l'Ouest, le Luxembourg, la Suède et la Suisse ont la moyenne de salaire la plus élevée par tête d'habitant. Sur le plan régional, les habitants des environs de Zurich et de Bâle au nord de la Suisse et des régions de Bremen et d'Hambourg au nord de l'Allemagne de l'Ouest jouissent d'un salaire particulièrement élevé.

Der Wohlstand einer Gemeinschaft wird in erster Linie durch das durchschnittliche Pro-Kopf-Einkommen bestimmt. In diesem Abschnitt werden die Unterschiede dieses Einkommens in den Ländern und Gebieten Westeuropas und die heutigen Zuwachstrends behandelt.

Die Karten dieses Abschnittes enthalten:
- Verteilung der Durchschnittseinkommen nach Gebieten in bestimmten Ländern.
- Erhöhung der Durchschnittseinkommen.

Dänemark, Westdeutschland, Luxemburg, Schweden und die Schweiz haben die höchsten Durchschnittseinkommen pro Kopf. In Gebiete aufgeteilt haben die Einwohner Zürichs und Basels in der Nordschweiz und die der Gebiete um Hamburg und Bremen in Westdeutschland besonders hohe Einkommen.

La medida principal de la riqueza de una comunidad es el promedio de los ingresos per cápita. Esta sección pone en relieve las variaciones nacionales y regionales de dichos ingresos a través de Europa Occidental, conjuntamente con las tendencias de crecimiento recientes.

Los mapas en esta seccion incluyen:
- Distribución del promedio de los ingresos por región, en países seleccionados.
- Aumentos en el promedio de ganancias.

Dinamarca, Alemania, Occidental, Luxemburgo, Suecia y Suiza tienen los más altos promedios de ingresos anuales per cápita. A nivel regional los habitantes de Zürich y Basel en el área septentrional de Suiza y los de Bremen y Hamburg en el área norte de Alemania Federal, tienen ingresos particularmente altos.

Growth of Earnings

5 year increase in hourly earnings
N.B. figures for L, P are not available

Evolution des salaires

Augmentation du salaire horaire sur cinq ans
N.B. le chiffre pour L n'est pas disponible

Verdienstzuwachs

5-Jahres-Zuwachs im Stundenverdienst
N.B. Für L liegen keine Angaben vor

Aumento de Salarios

incremento en 5 años de salarios por hora
N.B. no se cuenta con la cifra para L

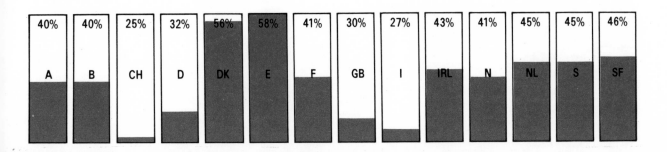

| 40% | 40% | 25% | 32% | 56% | 58% | 41% | 30% | 27% | 43% | 41% | 45% | 45% | 46% |
| A | B | CH | D | DK | E | F | GB | I | IRL | N | NL | S | SF |

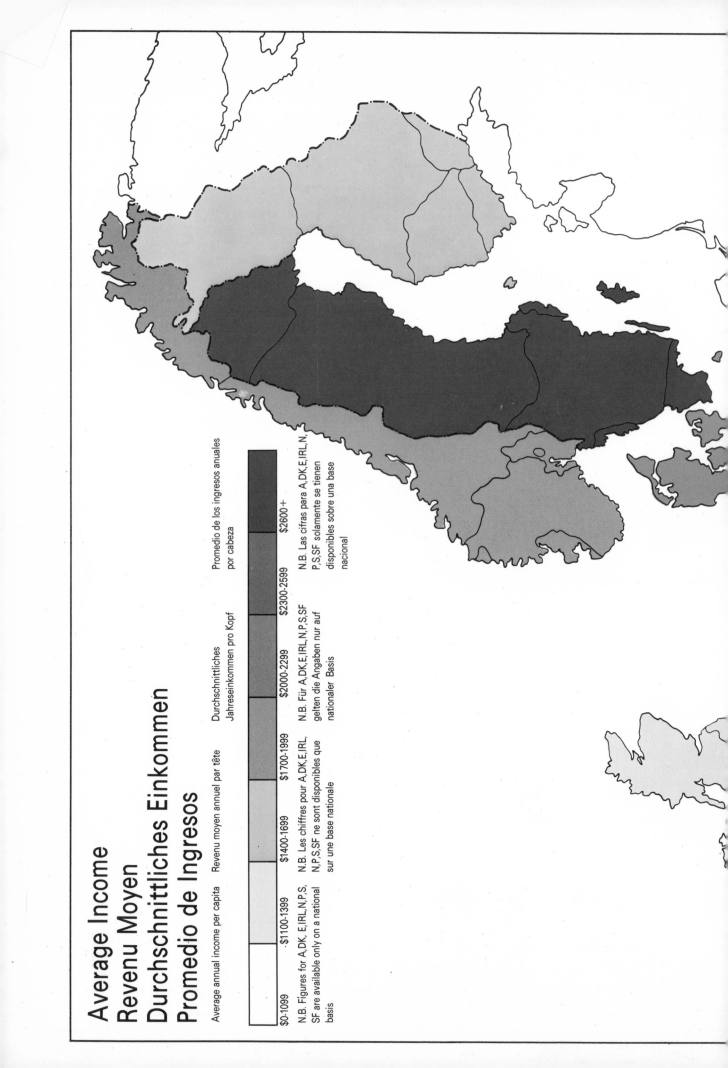

Average Income
Revenu Moyen
Durchschnittliches Einkommen
Promedio de Ingresos

Average annual income per capita   Revenu moyen annuel par tête   Durchschnittliches Jahreseinkommen pro Kopf   Promedio de los ingresos anuales por cabeza

$0-1099	$1100-1399	$1400-1699	$1700-1999	$2000-2299	$2300-2599	$2600+

N.B. Figures for A,DK, E,IRL,N,P,S, SF are available only on a national basis

N.B. Les chiffres pour A,DK,E,IRL, N,P,S,SF ne sont disponibles que sur une base nationale

N.B. Für A,DK,E,IRL,N,P,S,SF gelten die Angaben nur auf nationaler Basis

N.B. Las cifras para A,DK,E,IRL,N, P,S,SF solamente se tienen disponibles sobre una base nacional

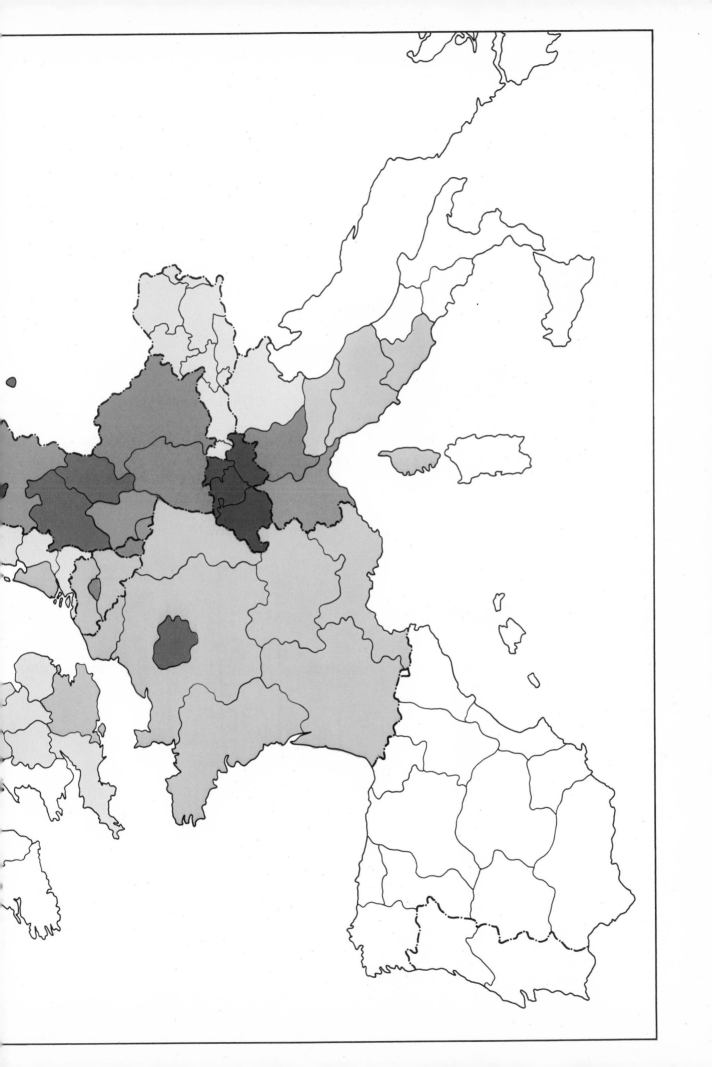

N

Expenditure

Les dépenses

Ausgaben

Gastos

Statistics presented in this section highlight variations in consumer expenditure. It is not the objective to provide detailed information on a wide selection of items, but rather to indicate different levels of consumer wealth.

Maps and data include:
- Television ownership by nation and region.
- Motor car ownership by nation and region.
- Expenditure on furniture.

Les statistiques présentées dans cette section font ressortir les variations du pouvoir d'achat des consommateurs. Le but n'est pas de fournir des renseignements détaillés sur un grand choix d'articles, mais plutôt d'indiquer les différents niveaux de prospérité des consommateurs.

Les cartes et les données comprennent:
- Le nombre de propriétaires de postes de télévision par nation et par région.
- Le nombre de propriétaires de voitures automobiles par nation et par région.
Les dépenses d'ameublement.

Die in diesem Abschnitt enthaltenen Statistiken zeigen, welche Unterschiede in den Verbraucherausgaben bestehen. Sie habeh nicht das Ziel, genaue Informationen über viele Dinge zu geben, sondern sollen zeigen welche Unterschiede im Verbraucherwohlstand bestehen.

In Karten und Angaben sind enthalten:
- Besitz von Fernsehgeräten nach Land und Gebiet aufgeteilt.
- Besitz von Kraftfahrzeugen nach Land und Gebiet aufgeteilt.
- Ausgaben für Möbel.

Las estadísticas presentadas en esta sección secan a relucir las variaciones de gastos en consumos. No tiene el objeto de proveer infomación detallada sobre una amplia selección de artículos, pero más bien indicar los diversos niveles de riqueza en el consumidor.

Los mapas y datos incluyen:
- Propietarios de televisores por país y región.
- Propietarios de coches por país y región.
- Gastos en muebles.

Private Consumption

average annual private consumption per capita

Consommation privée

moyenne annuelle de la consommation privée par tête

Privater Verbrauch

Durchschnittlicher Jahres-verbrauch pro Kopf

Consumo Privado

promedio del consumo privado anual por cabeza

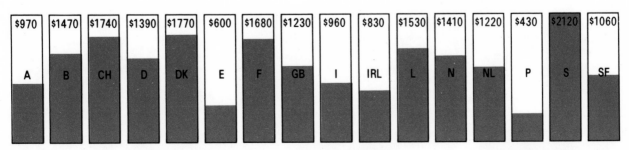

| $970 | $1470 | $1740 | $1390 | $1770 | $600 | $1680 | $1230 | $960 | $830 | $1530 | $1410 | $1220 | $430 | $2120 | $1060 |
| A | B | CH | D | DK | E | F | GB | I | IRL | L | N | NL | P | S | SF |

Average for Western Europe $1234

Moyenne pour l'Europe occidentale $1234

Durchschnitt für Westeuropa $1234

Promedio para Europa Occidental $1234

The consumer goods selected, are considered as 'luxury' items by most of the surveyed countries. The maps display the distribution of expenditure on or ownership of each item taken separately. More important, however, a study of the distribution of the three items taken together provides a general indication of varying levels of prosperity across Western Europe.

On the national scale, Sweden, Denmark, Switzerland and France display the highest rates of personal expenditure. In contrast meagre expenditure on furniture in the United Kingdom is of particular note. This is due to the traditionally low spending in these goods rather than on a general low level of consumer wealth.

Les biens de consommation sélectionnés sont considérés comme des articles ''de luxe'' dans la plupart des pays étudiés. Les cartes montrent la distribution des dépenses ou de la possession pour chaque article pris séparément. Toutefois, une étude de la distribution de ces trois articles pris ensemble a bien plus de valeur pour indiquer d'une façon générale les divers niveaux de prospérité à travers l'Europe Occidentale.

A l'échelle nationale, c'est en Suède, au Danemark, en Suisse et en France que l'on constate les taux les plus élevés pour les dépenses personnelles. Par contre, il convient de noter le faible niveau des dépenses consacrées à l'ameublement dans le Royaume-Uni. Ceci est dû au mode de dépenses traditionnellement restreint de ces marchandises, plutôt qu'à un niveau général de prospérité peu élevé.

Die gewählten Konsumgüter werden von den meisten der untersuchten Länder als 'Luxusgegenstände' angesehen. Die Karten zeigen, wie die Ausgaben für oder der Besitz eines jeden Gegenstandes einzeln verteiltsind. Es ist jedoch noch wichtiger, daß die Verteilung der drei Gegenstände gemeinsam ein allgemeines Bild des unterschiedlichen Wohlstandes in Westeuropa ergeben.

Auf nationaler Stufe zeigen Schweden, Dänemark, die Schweiz und Frankreich das höchste Maß an persönlichen Ausgaben. Im Gegensatz dazu sind die dürftigen Ausgaben für Möbel im Vereinigten Königreich besonders bemerkenswert. Das ist jedoch auf die traditionell niedrigen Ausgaben für diese Güter zurückzuführen und nicht auf den im allgemeinen niedrigeren Verbaucherwholstand.

Los artículos de consumo seleccionados, en la mayoría de los países estudiados se les considera de ''lujo''. Los mapas muestran por cada artículo separadamente, la distribucion de los propietarios o de los gastos en el mismo. Más importante, sin embargo es, el estudio de la distribución de los tres artículos tomados conjuntamente, lo cual da una indicación general de los niveles variantes en la prosperidad de Europa Occidental.

A escala nacional, Suecia, Dinamarca, Suiza y Francia ostentan la proporción más elevada de gestos personales. En contraste, es de observar con particular interés la escasa inversión en mobiliario que se produce en el Reino Unido. Esto se debe al bajo gasto tradicional en esta clase de artículos, más que en un nivel bajo en la riqueza de los consumidores.

Furniture – Expenditure

annual average expenditure per capita
N.B. figures for B, L are combined
N.B. figure for CH is not available

Mobilier – Dépenses

dépenses moyennes annuelles par tête
N.B. les chiffres pour B et L sont combinés
N.B. le chiffre pour CH n'est pas disponible

Möbel – Ausgaben

Durchschnittliche Jahresausgaben pro Kopf
N.B. Die Angaben für B. L sind zusammengefaßt worden
N.B. Für CH liegen keine Angaben vor

Muebles – Gasto

promedio del gasto anual por cabez
N.B. las cifras para B, L, son conjuntas
N.B. no se cuenta con la cifra para CH

$ 7-14 $15-22 $23-30 $30+

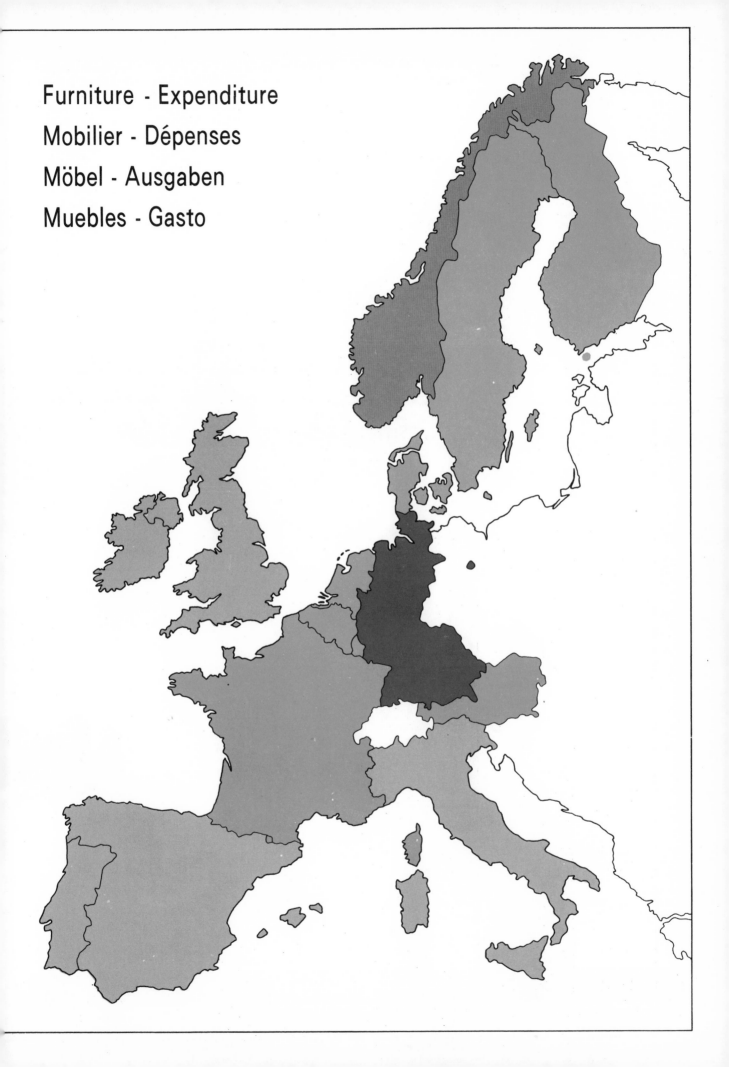

Furniture - Expenditure

Mobilier - Dépenses

Möbel - Ausgaben

Muebles - Gasto

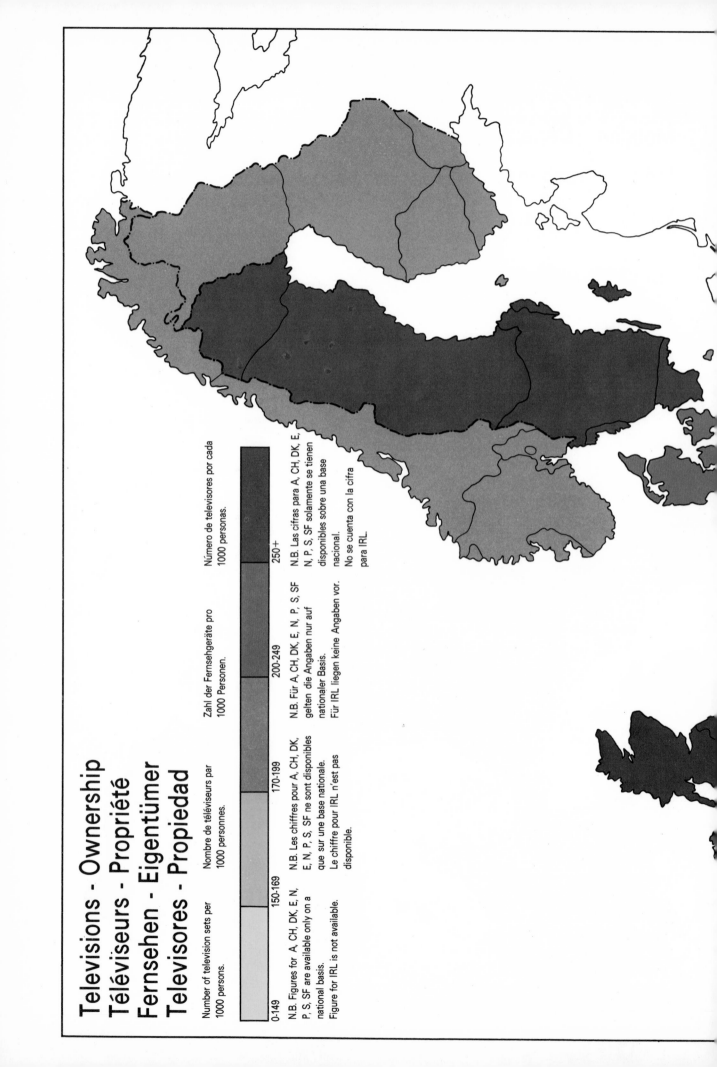

Televisions - Ownership
Téléviseurs - Propriété
Fernsehen - Eigentümer
Televisores - Propiedad

Number of television sets per 1000 persons.

Nombre de téléviseurs par 1000 personnes.

Zahl der Fernsehgeräte pro 1000 Personen.

Número de televisores por cada 1000 personas.

| 0-149 | 150-169 | 170-199 | 200-249 | 250+ |

N.B. Figures for A, CH, DK, E, N, P, S, SF are available only on a national basis.

Figure for IRL is not available.

N.B. Les chiffres pour A, CH, DK, E, N, P, S, SF ne sont disponibles que sur une base nationale.

Le chiffre pour IRL n'est pas disponible.

N.B. Für A, CH, DK, E, N, P, S, SF gelten die Angaben nur auf nationaler Basis.

Für IRL liegen keine Angaben vor.

N.B. Las cifras para A, CH, DK, E, N, P, S, SF solamente se tienen disponibles sobre una base nacional.

No se cuenta con la cifra para IRL.

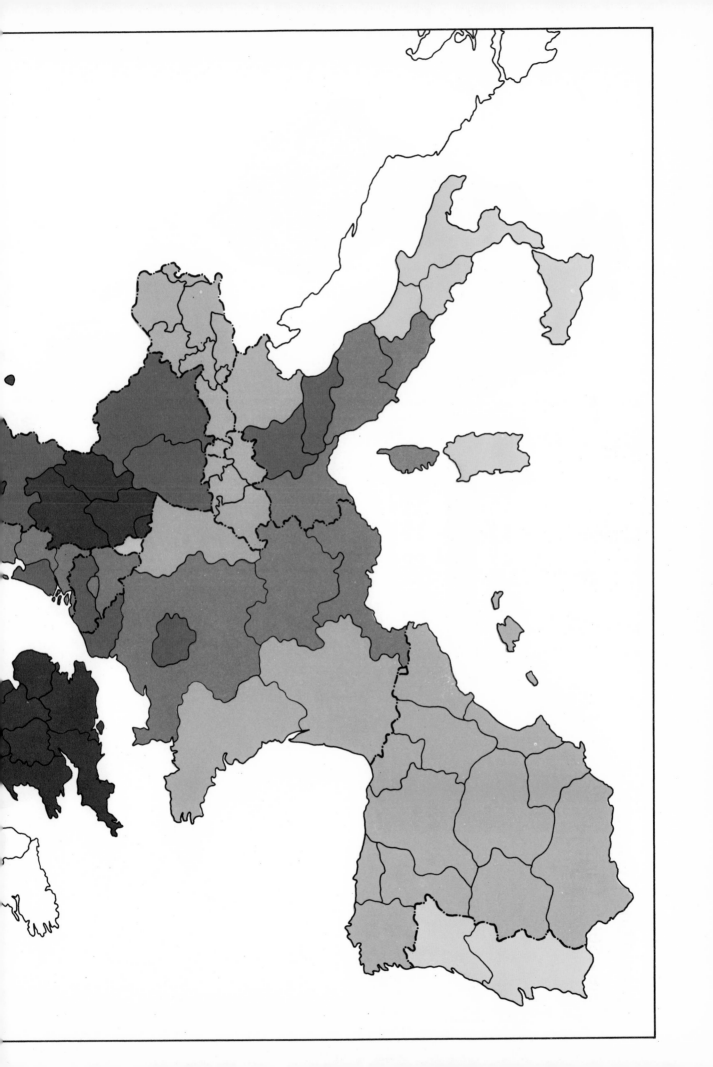

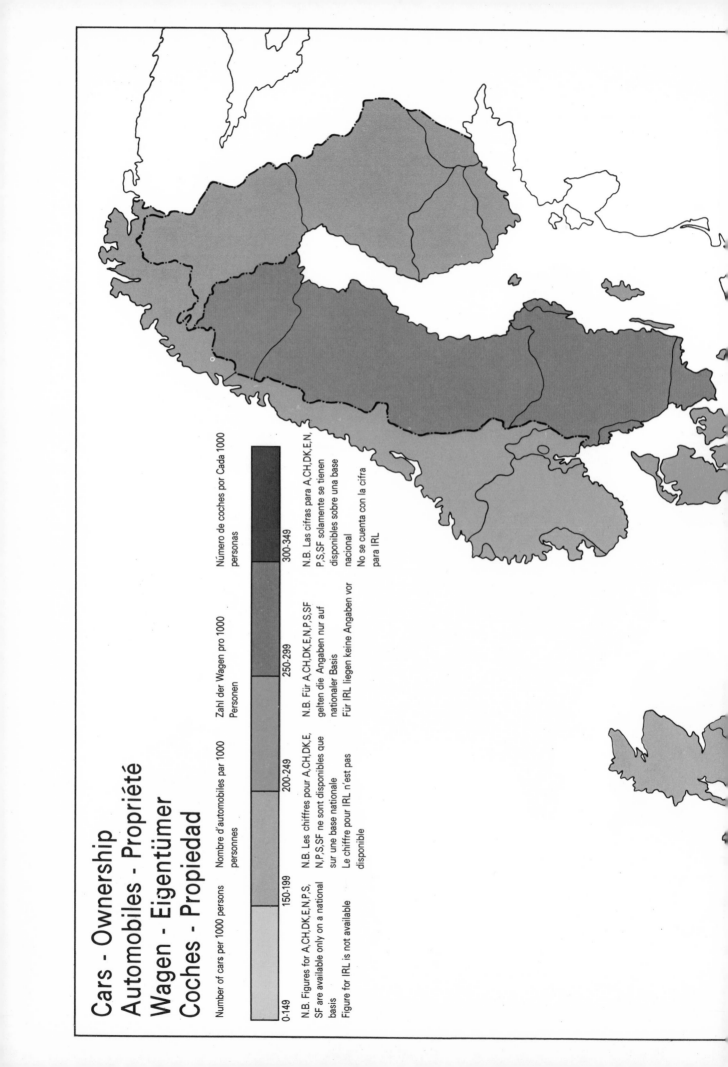

Cars - Ownership
Automobiles - Propriété
Wagen - Eigentümer
Coches - Propiedad

Number of cars per 1000 persons	Nombre d'automobiles par 1000 personnes	Zahl der Wagen pro 1000 Personen	Número de coches por Cada 1000 personas

| 0-149 | 150-199 | 200-249 | 250-299 | 300-349 |

N.B. Figures for A,CH,DK,E,N,P,S, SF are available only on a national basis

Figure for IRL is not available

N.B. Les chiffres pour A,CH,DK,E, N,P,S,SF ne sont disponibles que sur une base nationale

Le chiffre pour IRL n'est pas disponible

N.B. Für A,CH,DK,E,N,P,S,SF gelten die Angaben nur auf nationaler Basis

Für IRL liegen keine Angaben vor

N.B. Las cifras para A,CH,DK,E,N, P,S,SF solamente se tienen disponibles sobre una base nacional

No se cuenta con la cifra para IRL

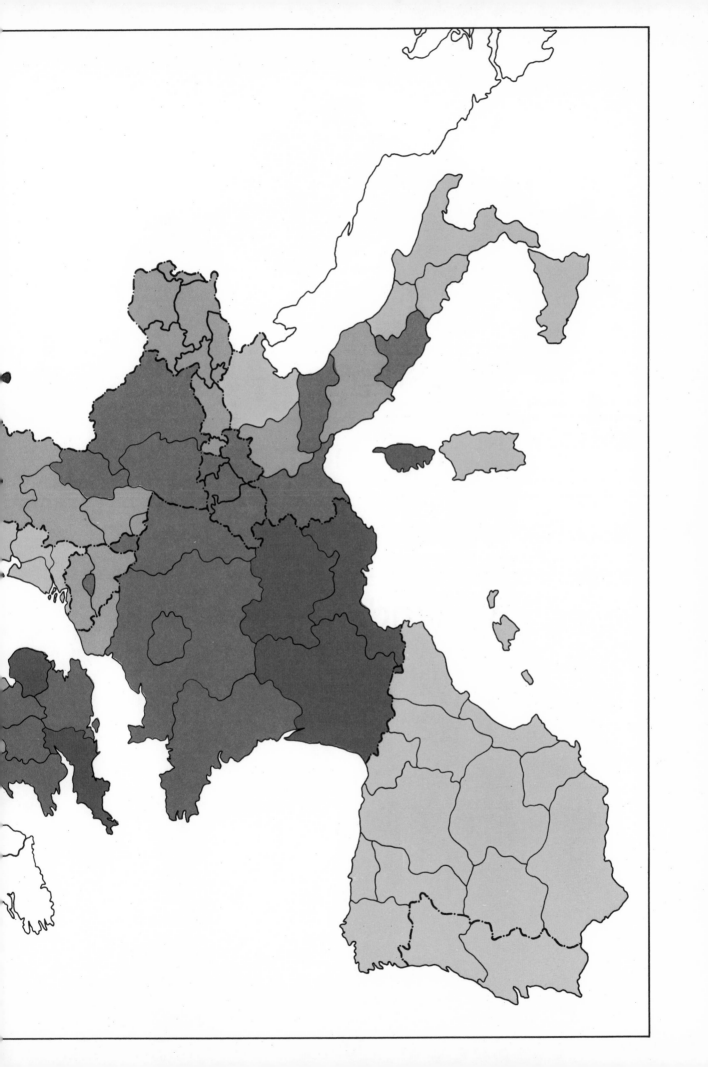

O

Housing

Le logement

Wohnen

Vivienda

The rate of new house construction is a significant indicator to the degree of internal economic development of any country. The section charts the distribution of housebuilding activity in Western Europe.

Maps and data in this section include:
- Contribution of dwellings to investment.
- New dwelling construction.

Le taux de construction de nouvelles maisons est un indice d'importance pour établir le degré de développement économique intérieur d'un pays. Cette section couvre la distribution de l'activité de l'industrie du bâtiment du secteur privé en Europe Occidentale.

Les cartes et les données de cette section comprennent:
- La contribution des logements à l'investissement.
- La construction de nouveaux logements.

Die Erstellung von Neubauten ist ein wichtiges Zeichen für den Grad der innenwirtschaftlichen Entwicklung eines Landes. In diesem Abschnitt sind auf Tabellen Angaben über die Erstellung von Neubauten in Westeuropa enthalten.

Karten und Angaben dieses Abschnittes enthalten:
- Beitrag von Wohnungen zur Investition.
- Erstellung von Neubauten.

La proporción del número de casas en construcción es un indicador significativo del desarrollo económico interno de un país. En esta sección se muestra la distribución de la construcción de viviendas en Europa Occidental.

Los mapas y datos de esta sección incluyen:
- La contribución de las viviendas a la inversión.
- Construcción de nuevas viviendas.

Housing – Investments

gross fixed housing investment as % of gross national product

Habitation – Investissement

Investissement dans l'habitation en pourcentage de la production nationale brute

Wohnen – Anlagen

Anlage in Wohnungen als % vom Bruttosozialprodukt

Vivienda – Inversión

inversion en vivienda como % del producto nacional bruto

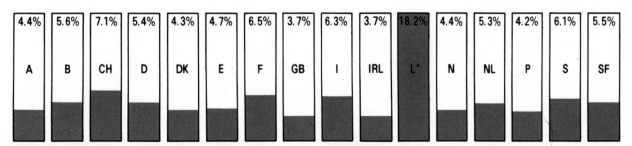

| 4.4% | 5.6% | 7.1% | 5.4% | 4.3% | 4.7% | 6.5% | 3.7% | 6.3% | 3.7% | 18.2% | 4.4% | 5.3% | 4.2% | 6.1% | 5.5% |
| A | B | CH | D | DK | E | F | GB | I | IRL | L* | N | NL | P | S | SF |

* other construction is included

* d'autres formes de construction sont incorporées

* weitere Bauten sind eingeschlossen

* se incluye otra construcción

Dwellings

The extent of each country's housing stock varies in relation to its degree of economic development. The more advanced industrial countries possess in general terms, higher standards of housing.

The analysis of new dwelling completions per 1000 inhabitants pinpoints two Scandinavian countries – Denmark and Sweden – to be enjoying the most active building programmes. It is in France, West Germany, Spain, UK and Italy that the largest total amounts of dwellings have been completed.

Les habitations

Le nombre d'habitations de chaque pays varie par rapport à son degré de développement économique. Les pays fortement industrialisés possèdent en général le nombre le plus élevé de logements.

L'analyse des nouvelles habitations achevées par 1000 habitants indique que deux pays scandinaves – le Danemark et la Suède – font montre de programmes de construction les plus actifs. C'est en France, en Allemagne de l'Ouest, en Espagne, au Royaume-Uni et en Italie que le total le plus élevé d'habitations a été terminé.

Wohnungen

Je nach der wirtschaftlichen Entwicklung ist der Vorrat an Wohnungen in jedem Land unterschiedlich. Die mehr industrialisierten Länder haben im allgemeinen einen hohen Wohnstandard.

Eine Untersuchung der Fertigstellung von Neubauwohnungen pro 1000 Einwohner läßt zwei skandinavische Länder besonders hervortreten – Dänemark und Schweden – wo man die aktivsten Bauprogramme findet. In Frankreich, Westdeutschland, Spanien, dem Vereinigten Königreich und Italien wurden die meisten Neubauwohnungen fertiggestellt.

Viviendas

La cantidad de casas disponibles en cada país, varía en relación al grado de desarrollo económico. Los países industrializados más avanzados, generalmente poseen niveles más altos en viviendas.

El análisis sobre la terminación de viviendas nuevas por 1000 habitantes muestra que dos países Escandinavos – Dinamarca y Suecia – tienen los programas de construcción más activos. Es en Francia, Alemania Occidental, España, Reino Unido e Italia donde se han terminado más viviendas.

Housing – Completions

calculated to nearest 1000
N.B. figure for IRL is not available

Habitation – constructions terminées

calcul à 1.000 unités près
N.B. le chiffre pour IRL n'est pas disponible

Wohnungen – Fertigstellung

auf 1.000 auf- oder abgerundet
N.B. Für IRL liegen keine Angaben vor

Viviendas Construidas

cálculo redondeado a la cifra 1.000 más próxima
N.B. no se cuenta con la cifra para IRL

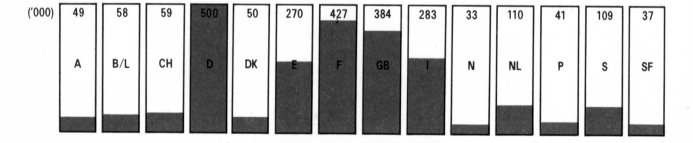

('000)	49	58	59	500	50	270	427	384	283	33	110	41	109	37
	A	B/L	CH	D	DK	E	F	GB	I	N	NL	P	S	SF

Housing – Completions

number of dwellings completed per 1000 persons
N.B. figures for B, L are combined
N.B. figure for IRL is not available

Habitation – constructions terminées

nombre de logements terminés par 1.000 personnes
N.B. les chiffres pour B et L sont combinés
N.B. le chiffre pour IRL n'est pas disponible

Wohnungen – Fertigstellung

Zahl der fertigestellten Wohnungen pro 1.000 Personen
N.B. Für B, L wurden die Angaben zusammengefaßt
N.B. Für IRL liegen keine Angaben vor

Viviendas Construidas

número de viviendas construidas por cada 1.000 personas
N.B. las cifras para B, L, son conjuntas
N.B. no se cuenta con la cifra para IRL

4-6	7-9	10-12	13-15

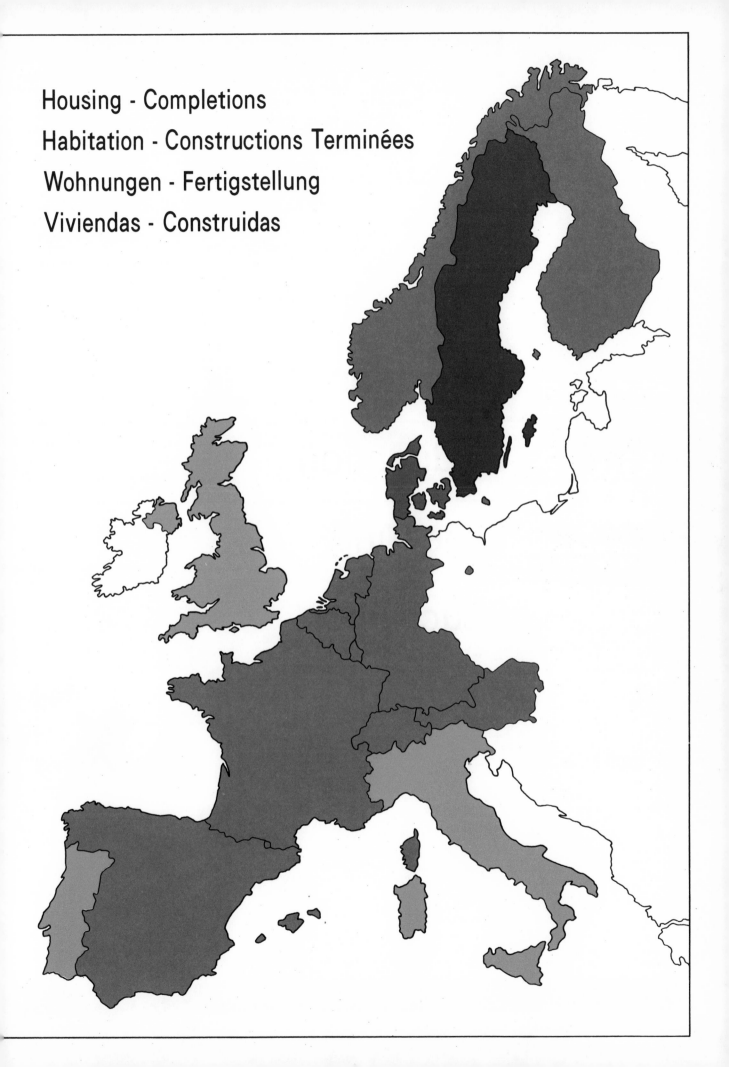

Housing - Completions

Habitation - Constructions Terminées

Wohnungen - Fertigstellung

Viviendas - Construidas

P

Education

L'éducation

Erziehung

Educación

Wide variations exist in the number of pupils and students supported in each country. This section charts the distribution of those receiving full-time education throughout Western Europe.

Maps and data in this section include:
- size of student populations.
- sector analysis of student population.
- location and size of major universities.

In general, it will be seen that the less industrialised countries, i.e. Ireland, Portugal and Spain, have a greater proportion of their students in primary education. Conversely, certain countries of northern Europe, viz., Norway, Netherlands and Sweden, have relatively higher proportions in further education.

Le nombre d'élèves et d'étudiants subventionnés dans chaque pays varie fortement. Cette section établit la répartition de ceux qui reçoivent une éducation à plein temps à travers l'Europe Occidentale.

Les cartes et les données dans cette section comprennent:
- L'effectif des populations estudiantines.
- L'analyse par secteurs de la population estudiantine.
- L'emplacement et l'importance des principales universités.

En général, il est à constater que les pays les moins industrialisés, par exemple l'Irlande, le Portugal et l'Espagne ont un plus grand nombre d'élèves recevant une éducation primaire. Par contre, certains pays de l'Europe du Nord, par exemple le Danemark les Pays-Bas et la Suède, ont des proportions relativement plus fortes d'étudiants poursuivant des études supérieures.

Die in den einzelnen Ländern unterstützten Schüler- und Studentenzahlen variieren stark. Die Tabellen dieses Abschnittes zeigen, wie die im Vollunterricht befindlichen Studenten in Westeuropa verteilt sind.

Karten und Angaben dieses Abschnittes enthalten:
- Umfang der Studenten-bevölkerung.
- Einzelanalyse der Studentenbevölkerung.
- Lage und Größe der größten Universitäten.

Der größere Anteil der Schüler wird in weniger industrialisierten Ländern wie Irland, Portugal und Spanien in der Volksschule angetroffen. Im Gegensatz dazu befinden sich in den nordeuropäischen Ländern wie z.B. Norwegen, Holland und Schweden ein relativ größerer Anteil in höheren Schulen.

Existen grandes variaciones en el número de alumnos y estudiantes que cada país soporta. Esta sección muestra la distribución de aquellos que están recibiendo una educación completa a través de Europa Occidental.

Los mapas y datos de esta sección incluyen:
- Dimensión de la población estudiantil.
- Analísis de sector de la población estudiantil.
- Ubicación y tamaño de las principales universidades.

En general, los países menos industrializados, e.g. Irlanda, Portugal, España, tienen una proporción más elevada de estudiantes en las primarias. Al contrarío, en ciertos países del norte de Europa, viz., Noruega, Holanda y Suecia tienen una proporción más elevada en los estudios superiores.

Total Student Population

calculated to nearest 10,000

Nombre total d'étudiants

calcul à 10.000 étudiants près

Gesamt-Studentenzahl

auf 10.000 auf- oder abgerundet

Población Estudiantil Total

cálculo redondeado a la cifra 10.000 más próxima

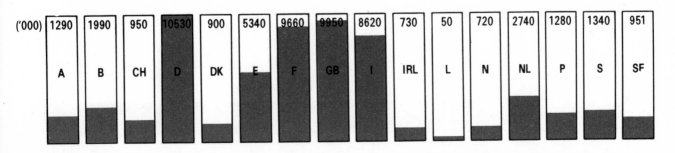

('000)	1290	1990	950	10530	900	5340	9660	9950	8620	730	50	720	2740	1280	1340	951
	A	B	CH	D	DK	E	F	GB	I	IRL	L	N	NL	P	S	SF

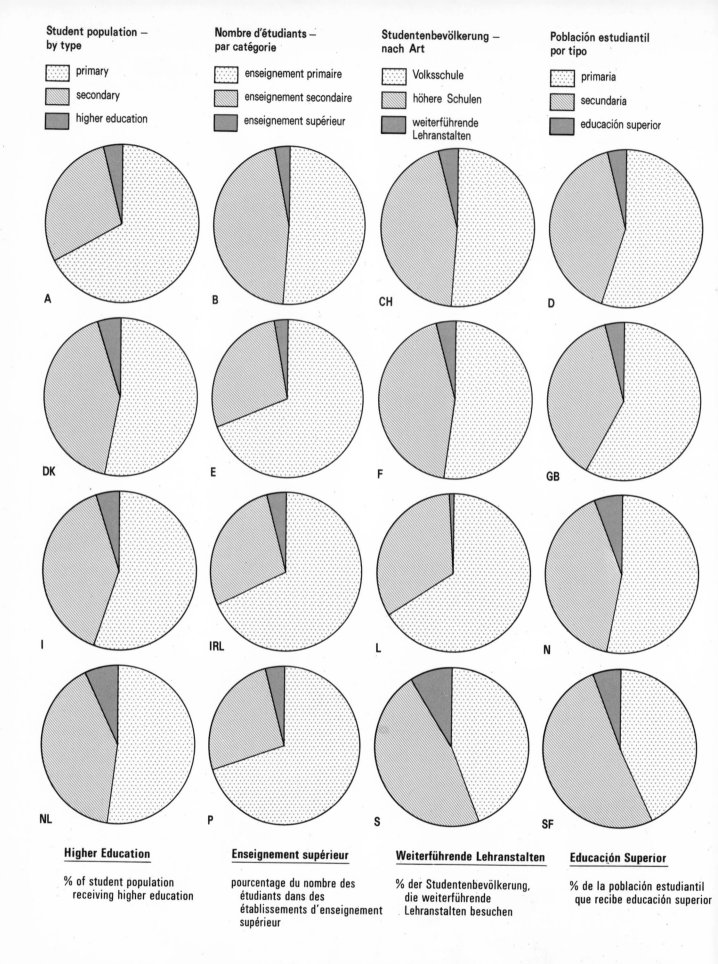

Student population – by type
- primary
- secondary
- higher education

Nombre d'étudiants – par catégorie
- enseignement primaire
- enseignement secondaire
- enseignement supérieur

Studentenbevölkerung – nach Art
- Volksschule
- höhere Schulen
- weiterführende Lehranstalten

Población estudiantil por tipo
- primaria
- secundaria
- educación superior

A B CH D

DK E F GB

I IRL L N

NL P S SF

Higher Education

% of student population receiving higher education

Enseignement supérieur

pourcentage du nombre des étudiants dans des établissements d'enseignement supérieur

Weiterführende Lehranstalten

% der Studentenbevölkerung, die weiterführende Lehranstalten besuchen

Educación Superior

% de la población estudiantil que recibe educación superior

1-4%   4-7%   7-9%

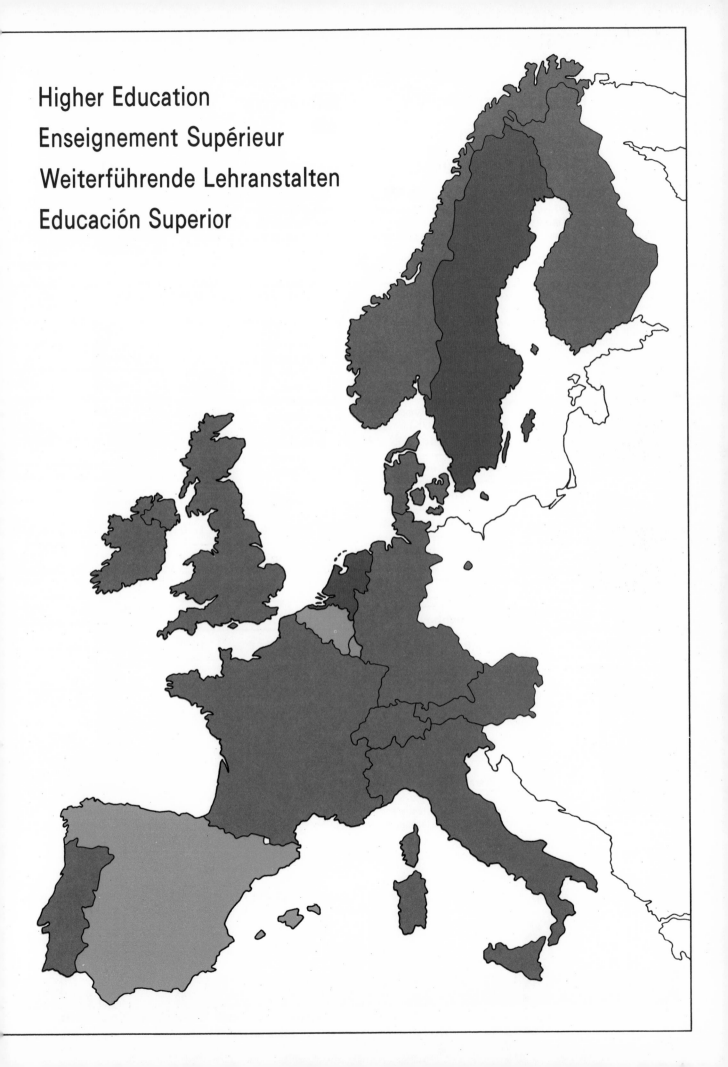

Higher Education

Enseignement Supérieur

Weiterführende Lehranstalten

Educación Superior

The 50 largest universities of Western Europe

Les 50 plus grandes universites d'Europe Occidentale

Die 50 grossten Universitaten Westeuropas

Las 50 universidades mas grandes de Europa Occidental

Set below is a table listing the major universities. They have been ranked in order of the size of their student population.

Le tableau ci-après classe les principales universités. Cette liste a été établie selon l'importance de la population estudiantine.

Die untenstehende Tabelle enthält die größten Universitäten. Ihre Reihenfolge wurde durch ihre Studentenzahl bestimmt.

Abajo se expone un cuadro con la lista de las principales universidades. Estas han sido clasificadas en orden del número de estudiantes.

University / Université / Universität / Universidad	Population / Population / Bevölkerung / Población ('000)
1 Paris	115·0
2 London	70·4
3 Roma	66·0
4 Lyon	49·9
5 Napoli	41·7
6 Toulouse	36·5
7 Bari	35·3
8 Bologna	35·0
9 Padova	34·2
10 Madrid	33·2
11 Stockholm	30·0
12 Marseille	28·6
13 Louvain	27·6
14 Uppsala	25·5
15a Open University (Bucks, UK)	25·0
15b Strasbourg	25·0
17 München	23·3
18 Grenoble	23·1
19 Helsinki	22·9
20a Montpellier	22·0
20b Genova	22·0
22 Lund	21·0
23 København	20·6
24 Lille	20·4
25 Bordeaux	20·3
26 Hamburg	20·2
27 Köln	20·0
28 Milano	19·4
29 Palermo	19·2
30 Wien	19·0
31 Amsterdam	18·4
32 Munster	18·0
33 Torino	17·9
34 Rennes	17·3
35 Firenze	16·5
36 Barcelona	16·0
37 Bonn	15·9
38 Utrecht	15·7
39 Perugia	15·2
40a Nantes	15·0
40b Berlin	15·0
42 Cantania	14·6
43 Lisboa	14·5
44a Parma	14·0
44b Oslo	14·0
46 Clermond-Ferrand	13·9
47 Nancy	13·0
48 Tübingen	12·5
49 Rouens	12·3
50a Granada	12·0
50b Murcia	12·0

Universities

number of universities (including technical universities)

Universités

nombre d'universités (y compris les universités techniques)

Universitäten

Zahl der Universitäten (einschl. techn. Universitäten)

Universidades

número de universidades (incluyendo universidades industriales)

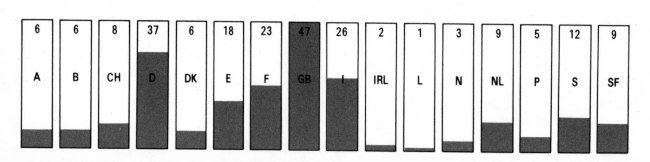

A	B	CH	D	DK	E	F	GB	I	IRL	L	N	NL	P	S	SF
6	6	8	37	6	18	23	47	26	2	1	3	9	5	12	9

Major Universities

Principales Universités

Die Größten Universitäten

Universidades Principales

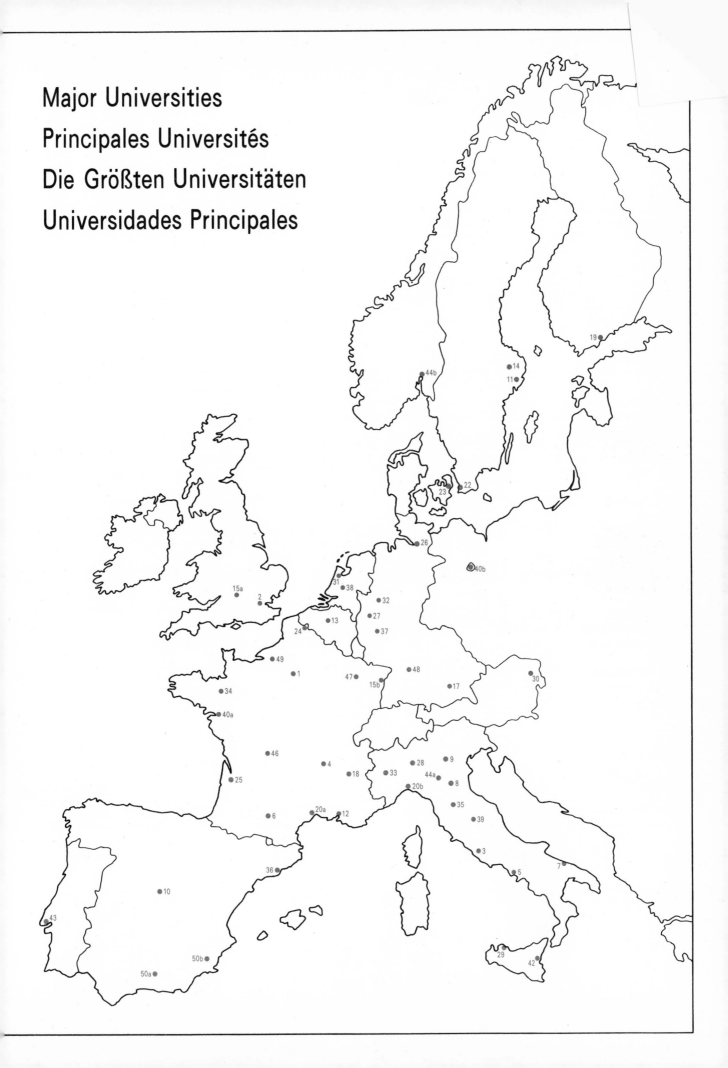

Q

Daily newspapers

Les quotidiens

Tageszeitungen

Diarios

This final section reviews the relative levels of readership of the daily newspapers in each country. The most widely circulated newspapers are identified.

Maps and data in this section include:
- Distribution of newspaper readership.
- Major newspapers by country.

The low levels of newspaper readership in Italy, Portugal and Spain are a reflection of the relatively low literacy rates in these countries. In all countries, however, except Finland, Netherlands, Portugal and Spain, the total number of daily newspapers has declined in recent years.

Cette dernière section analyse les niveaux relatifs du nombre de lecteurs des quotidiens dans chaque pays. Les journaux avec les plus forts tirages sont cités.

Les cartes et les données dans cette section comprennent:
- La répartition des lecteurs de journaux.
- Les principaux quotidiens par pays.

Les niveaux peu élevés du nombre de lecteurs de quotidiens en Italie, au Portugal et en Espagne reflètent les taux relativement peu élevés de lettrés dans ces pays. Cependant, dans tous les pays, sauf en Finlande, aux Pays-Bas, au Portugal et en Espagne, le nombre total de quotidiens a diminué au cours des dernières années.

Dieser letzte Abschnitt enthält die Leserzahlen für die Tageszeitungen eines jeden Landes. Ferner werden die Tageszeitungen mit der größten Auflage aufgeführt.

Karten und Angaben dieses Abschnitts enthalten:
- Verteilung der Zeitungsleser.
- Die größten Zeitungen nach Ländern eingeteilt.

Die niedrigen Leserzahlen für Zeitungen in Italien, Portugal und Spanien sind ein Ergebnis der relativ wenigen Leute, die in diesen Ländern lesen können. In den letzten Jahren hat jedoch die Gesamtauflage aller Tageszeitungen abgenommen, mit Ausnahme von Finnland, Holland, Portugal und Spanien.

Esta sección final pasa revista a los relativos niveles de lectura de diarios en cada país. Se identifican los periódicos de mayor tirada.

Los mapas y datos de esta sección incluye:
- Distribución de los lectores de periódicos.
- Periódicos de mayor tirada por país.

Los niveles bajos en el número de lectores en Italia, Portugal y España denotan las proporciones de analfabetos en los mismos. Sin embargo, en todos los países a exepción de Finlandia, Holanda, Portugal y España el número total de diarios ha bajado en estos últimos años.

Number of daily newspapers per country and total daily circulation (calculated to the nearest 100,000).

Nombre de quotidiens par pays et chiffre total du tirage journalier (calcul à 100,000 exemplaires près).

Anzahl der Tageszeitungen und tägliche Gesamtauflage (berechnet auf die nächsten 100,000 genau).

En la lista a continuación se da el número de diarios, con los nombres y circulación de los principales diarios por país, calculada hasta el número más próximo a 100,000.

Country / Pays / Land / Nacion	No. of daily newspapers / Nombre de quotidiens / Anzahl Tageszeitungen / No. de diarios	Total circulation (daily) / Tirage total (quotidien) / Tägliche Gesamtauflage / Total circulacion (diaria)	Country / Pays / Land / Nacion	No. of daily newspapers / Nombre de quotidiens / Anzahl Tageszeitungen / No. de diarios	Total circulation (daily) / Tirage total (quotidien) / Tägliche Gesamtauflage / Total circulacion (diaria)
A	33	1,800,000	I	70	6,700,000
B	33	2,500,000	IRL	7	7,000,000
CH	121	2,200,000	L	4	1,500,000
D	1098	20,100,000	N	82	1,400,000
DK	59	1,700,000	NL	94	3,900,000
E	116	3,400,000	P	31	6,700,000
F	109	12,150,000	S	115	4,200,000
GB	126	25,600,000	SF	68	1,800,000

Major daily newspapers / Les principaux quotidiens / Die grössten Tageszeitungen / Los principales periodicos diarios

Country / Pays / Land / Nacion	Newspaper / Quotidiens / Tageszeitungen / Diarios	Total daily circulation / Tirage total quotidien / Tägliche Gesamtauflage / Total diaria circulación
A	Neuer Kurier	426,000
	Express	344,000
	Kronen-Zeitung	292,000
B	*French*	
	Le Soir	273,000
	La Libre Belgique	187,000
	Flemish	
	Het Laastete Nieus	300,000
	De Standaard	326,000
CH	Blick	210,000
	Neue Zücher Zeitung	92,000
D	Bild Zeitung	4,700,000
	Westdeutsche Allegemeine	570,000
DK	Berlingske Tidende	180,000
	Politiken	135,000
E	A.B.C.	213,000
	Ya	139,000
F	France-Soir	1,200,000
	Figaro	550,000
	Le Monde	470,000
GB	Daily Mirror	4,700,000
	Daily Express	3,700,000
	Sun	2,100,000
	The Times	345,000
I	Corriere della Sera	600,000
	La Stampa	404,000
IRL	Irish Independent	179,000
	Irish Times	57,000
L	Luxemburger Wort	72,000
N	Aftenposten	220,000
	Dagblodet	107,000
NL	De Telegraaf	450,000
	Het Vrige Volk	285,000
P	Diario De Lisboa	80,000
	Journal De Noticios	75,000
S	Expressen	609,000
	Aftonbladet	500,000
SF	Helsingin Sanomat	272,000
	Turun Sanomat	105,000

Daily Newspapers – Circulation

total daily circulation per 1000 persons

Presse quotidienne – Diffusion

Diffusion totale journalière par 1.000 personnes

Tageszeitungen – Auflage

Tagesgesamtauflage pro 1.000 Personen

Diarios – Circulación

circulación diaria total por cada 1.000 personas

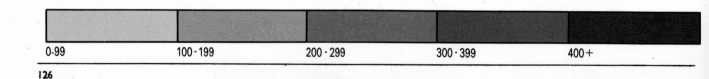

| 0-99 | 100-199 | 200-299 | 300-399 | 400+ |

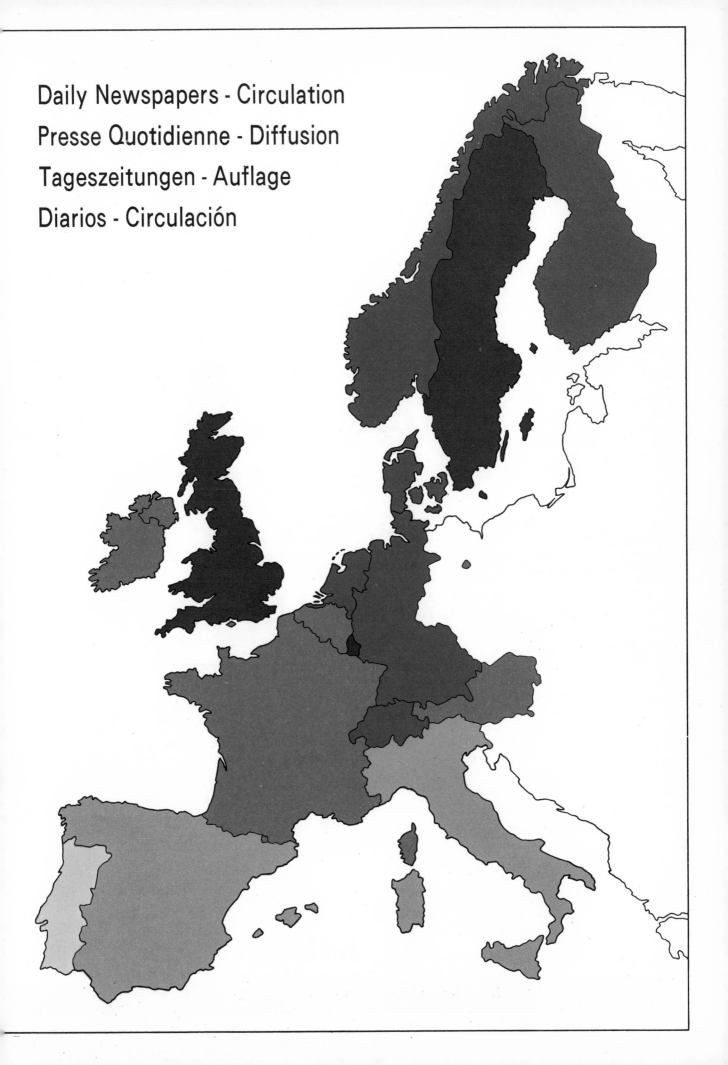

Daily Newspapers - Circulation

Presse Quotidienne - Diffusion

Tageszeitungen - Auflage

Diarios - Circulación

4

SURVEYS OF THE NATIONAL ECONOMIES

ENQUETES SUR LES ECONOMIES NATIONALES

UNTERSUCHUNG DER WIRTSCHAFT DER EINZELNEN LÄNDER

ESTUDIOS DE LAS ECONOMIAS NACIONALES

Austria   Autriche   A   Österreich   Austria

English	Français	A	Deutsch	Español
Population (millions)	Population (en millions)	7·4	Bevölkerung (Mio.)	Población (millones)
Population density (persons per square km)	Densité de la population (en personnes au km²)	88	Bevölkerungsdichte (Personen pro km²)	Densidad de población (habitantes por Km²).
Five year increase in population (%)	Augmentation de la population sur cinq ans (en %)	+1·5	5-Jahreszuwachs der Bevölkerung (%)	Aumento de población en 5 años (%).
Average unemployment rate over five years (%)	Taux moyen du chômage sur 5 ans (en %)	1·8	Durchschnittliche Arbeitslosenzahl der letzten 5 Jahre (%)	Proporción media de desempleo durante 5 años (%).
Gross national product per capita (US $)	Production nationale brute par tête (en dollars américains)	1695	Bruttosozialprodukt pro Kopf (US Dollar)	Producto nacional bruto por cabeza (US $).
Five year increase in gross national product per capita (%)	Augmentation de la production nationale brute par tête sur 5 ans (en %)	+21·0	5-Jahreszuwachs im Bruttosozialprodukt pro Kopf (%)	Aumento en 5 años del producto nacional bruto (%).
Average annual private consumption per capita (US $)	Moyenne annuelle de la consommation privée par tête (en dollars américains)	970	Durchschnittlicher privater Jahresverbrauch pro Kopf (US Dollar)	Promedio del consumo privado anual por cabeza (US $).
Total value of imports (US $ million)	Valeur totale des importations (en millions de dollars américains)	3549	Gesamtwert der Importe (Mio. US Dollar)	Valor total de importaciones (millones de US $).
Five year increase in imports (%)	Augmentation des importations sur 5 ans (en %)	+52·0	5-Jahreszuwachs der Importe (%)	Aumento de importaciones en 5 años (%).
Total value of exports (US $ millions)	Valeur totale des exportations (en millions de dollars américains)	2857	Gesamtwert der Exporte (Mio. US Dollar)	Valor total de exportaciones (millones de US $).
Five year increase in exports (%)	Augmentation des exportations sur 5 ans (en %)	+70·0	5-Jahreszuwachs der Exporte (%)	Aumento de exportaciones en 5 años (%).
Five year increase in hourly earnings (%)	Augmentation du salaire horaire sur 5 ans (en %)	+40·0	5-Jahreszuwachs im Stundenverdienst (%)	Aumento en 5 años de salarios por hora (%).
Five year increase in consumer prices (%)	Augmentation des prix à la consommation sur 5 ans (en %)	+16·0	5-Jahreszuwachs in den Verbraucherpreisen (%)	Aumento en 5 años de precios al consumidor (%).

Major Urban Centres Population ('000)	Principaux Centres Urbains Population ('000)		die größten Städte Einwohnerzahlen ('000)	Centros urbanos principales Población ('000)
		1. Wien	2015	
		2. Graz	252	
		3. Linz	205	
		4. Salzburg	117	
		5. Innsbruck	109	

Belgium   Belgique   B   Belgien   Bélgica

Belgium	Belgique	B	Belgien	Bélgica
Population (millions)	Population (en millions)	9·6	Bevölkerung (Mio.)	Población (millones).
Population density (persons per square km)	Densité de la population (en personnes au km²)	316	Bevölkerungsdichte (Personen pro km²)	Densidad de población (habitantes por Km²).
Five year increase in population (%)	Augmentation de la population sur cinq ans (en %)	+2·0	5-Jahreszuwachs der Bevölkerung (%)	Aumento de población en 5 años (%).
Average unemployment rate over five years (%)	Taux moyen de chômage sur 5 ans (en %)	2·2	Durchschnittliche Arbeitslosenzahl der letzten 5 Jahre (%)	Proporción media de desempleo durante 5 años (%).
Gross national product per capita (US $)	Production nationale brute par tête (en dollars américains)	2360	Bruttosozialprodukt pro Kopf (US Dollar)	Producto nacional bruto por cabeza (US $).
Five year increase in gross national product per capita (%)	Augmentation de la production nationale brute par tête sur 5 ans (en %)	+20·5	5-Jahreszuwachs im Bruttosozialprodukt pro Kopf (%)	Aumento en 5 años del producto nacional bruto (%).
Average annual private consumption per capita (US $)	Moyenne annuelle de la consommation privée par tête (en dollars américains)	1470	Durchschnittlicher privater Jahresverbrauch pro Kopf (US Dollar)	Promedio del consumo privado anual por cabeza (US $).
Total value of imports (US $ million)	Valeur totale des importations (en millions de dollars américains)	*11353	Gesamtwert der Importe (Mio. US Dollar)	Valor total de importaciones (millones de US $).
Five year increase in imports (%)	Augmentation des importations sur 5 ans (en %)	+78·0	5-Jahreszuwachs der Importe (%)	Aumento de importaciones en 5 años (%).
Total value of exports (US $ millions)	Valeur totale des exportations (en millions de dollars américains)	*11595	Gesamtwert der Exporte (Mio. US Dollar)	Valor total de exportaciones (millones de US $).
Five year increase in exports (%)	Augmentation des exportations sur 5 ans (en %)	+82·0	5-Jahreszuwachs der Exporte (%)	Aumento de exportaciones en 5 años (%).
Five year increase in hourly earnings (%)	Augmentation du salaire horaire sur 5 ans (en %)	+36·0	5-Jahreszuwachs im Stundenverdienst (%)	Aumento en 5 años de salarios por hora (%).
Five year increase in consumer prices (%)	Augmentation des prix à la consommation sur 5 ans (en %)	+12·0	5-Jahreszuwachs in den Verbraucherpreisen (%)	Aumento en 5 años de precios al consumidor (%).

*N.B. figures for B, L are combined.

*N.B. les chiffres pour B et L sont combinés.

*N.B. die Angaben für B, L sind zusammengefaßt worden.

*N.B. las cifras para B, L son conjuntas.

Major Urban Centres Population ('000)	**Principaux Centres Urbains** Population ('000)		**die größten Städte** Einwohnerzahlen ('000)	**Centros urbanos principales** Población ('000)
	1. Bruxelles	2070		
	2. Antwerpen	1040		
	3. Liège	575		
	4. Gent	350		
	5. Ostende	58		

Switzerland Suisse CH Schweiz Suiza

English	Français	CH	Deutsch	Español
Population (millions)	Population (en millions)	6·2	Bevölkerung (Mio.)	Población (millones).
Population density (persons per square km)	Densité de la population (en personnes au km²)	149	Bevölkerungsdichte (Personen pro km²)	Densidad de población (habitantes por Km²).
Five year increase in population (%)	Augmentation de la population sur cinq ans (en %)	+3·7	5-Jahreszuwachs der Bevölkerung (%)	Aumento de población en 5 años (%).
Average unemployment rate over five years (%)	Taux moyen du chômage sur 5 ans (en %)		Durchschnittliche Arbeitslosenzahl der letzten 5 Jahre (%)	Proporción media de desempleo durante 5 años. (%).
Gross national product per capita (US $)	Production nationale brute par tête (en dollars américains)	3020	Bruttosozialprodukt pro Kopf (US Dollar)	Producto nacional bruto por cabeza (US $).
Five year increase in gross national product per capita (%)	Augmentation de la production nationale brute par tête sur 5 ans (en %)	+18·0	5-Jahreszuwachs im Bruttosozialprodukt pro Kopf (%)	Aumento en 5 años del producto nacional bruto (%).
Average annual private consumption per capita (US $)	Moyenne annuelle de la consommation privée par tête (en dollars américains)	1740	Durchschnittlicher privater Jahresverbrauch pro Kopf (US Dollar)	Promedio del consumo Privado anual por cabeza (US $).
Total value of imports (US $ million)	Valeur totale des importations en millions de dollars (américains)	6551	Gesamtwert der Importe (Mio. US Dollar)	Valor total de importaciones (millones de US $).
Five year increase in imports (%)	Augmentation des importations sur 5 ans (en %)	+66·0	5-Jahreszuwachs der Importe (%)	Aumento de importaciones en 5 años (%).
Total value of exports (US $ millions)	Valeur totale des exportations (en millions de dollars américains)	5135	Gesamtwert der Exporte (Mio. US Dollar)	Valor total de exportaciones (millones de US $).
Five year increase in exports (%)	Augmentation des exportations sur 5 ans (en %)	+57·0	5-Jahreszuwachs der Exporte (%)	Aumento de exportaciones en 5 años (%).
Five year increase in hourly earnings (%)	Augmentation du salaire horaire sur 5 ans (en %)	+21·0	5-Jahreszuwachs im Stundenverdienst (%)	Aumento en 5 años de salarios por hora (%).
Five year increase in consumer prices (%)	Augmentation des prix à la consommation sur 5 ans (en %)	+13·0	5-Jahreszuwachs in den Verbraucherpreisen (%)	Aumento en 5 años de precios al consumidor (%).

Major Urban Centres Population ('000)	Principaux Centres Urbains Population ('000)		die größten Städte Einwohnerzahlen ('000)	Centros urbanos principales Población ('000)
	1. Zürich		745	
	2. Basel		530	
	3. Genève		335	
	4. Bern		266	
	5. Lausanne		211	

West Germany	Allemagne de l'Ouest	D	Westdeutsch-land	Alemania Occidental
Population (millions)	Population (en millions)	58·7	Bevölkerung (Mio.)	Población (millones).
Population density (persons per square km)	Densité de la population (en personnes au km²)	245	Bevölkerungsdichte (Personen pro km²)	Densidad de población (habitantes por Km²).
Five year increase in population (%)	Augmentation de la population sur cinq ans (en %)	+3·3	5-Jahreszuwachs der Bevölkerung (%)	Aumento de población en 5 años (%).
Average unemployment rate over five years (%)	Taux moyen du chômage sur 5 ans (en %)	0·9	Durchschnittliche Arbeitslosenzahl der letzten 5 Jahre (%)	Proporción media de desempleo durante 5 años (%).
Gross national product per capita (US $)	Production nationale brute par tête (en dollars américains)	2520	Bruttosozialprodukt pro Kopf (US Dollar)	Producto nacional bruto por cabeza (US $).
Five year increase in gross national product per capita (%)	Augmentation de la production nationale grute par tête sur 5 ans (en %)	+23·0	5-Jahreszuwachs im Bruttosozialprodukt pro Kopf (%)	Aumento en 5 años del producto nacional bruto (%).
Average annual private consumption per capita (US $)	Moyenne annuelle de la consommation privée par tête (en dollars américains)	1390	Durchschnittlicher privater Jahresverbrauch pro Kopf (US Dollar)	Promedio del consumo privado anual por cabeza (US $).
Total value of imports (US $ million)	Valeur totale des importations (en millions de dollars américains)	29,814	Gesamtwert der Importe (Mio. US Dollar)	Valor total de importaciones (millones de US $).
Five year increase in imports (%)	Augmentation des importations sur 5 ans (en %)	+65·0	5-Jahreszuwachs der Importe (%)	Aumento de importaciones en 5 años (%).
Total value of exports (US $ millions)	Valeur totale des exportations (en millions de dollars américains)	34,188	Gesamtwert der Exporte (Mio. US Dollar)	Valor total de exportaciones (millones de US $).
Five year increase in exports (%)	Augmentation des exportations sur 5 ans (en %)	+70·0	5-Jahreszuwachs der Exporte (%)	Aumento de exportaciones en 5 años (%).
Five year increase in hourly earnings (%)	Augmentation du salaire horaire sur 5 ans (en %)	+34·0	5-Jahreszuwachs im Stundenverdienst (%)	Aumento en 5 años de salarios por hora (%).
Five year increase in consumer prices (%)	Augmentation des prix à la consommation sur 5 ans (en %)	+10·0	5-Jahreszuwachs in den Verbraucherpreisen (%)	Aumento en 5 años de precios al consumidor (%).

Major Urban Centres Population ('000)	Principaux Centres Urbains Population ('000)		die größten Städte Einwohnerzahlen ('000)	Centros urbanos principales Población ('000)
	1. W. Berlin		5150	
	2. Hamburg		3975	
	3. München		2335	
	4. Köln		1655	
	5. Essen		1625	

Denmark Danemark DK Dänemark Dinamarca

English	French	DK	German	Spanish
Population (millions)	Population (en millions)	4·9	Bevölkerung (Mio.)	Población (millones)
Population density (persons per square km)	Densité de la population (en personnes au km²)	113	Bevölkerungsdichte (Personen pro km²)	Densidad de población (habitantes por Km²).
Five year increase in population (%)	Augmentation de la population sur cinq ans (en %)	+2·7	5-Jahreszuwachs der Bevölkerung (%)	Aumento de población en 5 años (%).
Average unemployment rate over five years (%)	Taux moyen de chômage sur 5 ans (en %)	1·2	Durchschnittliche Arbeitslosenzahl der letzten 5 Jahre (%)	Proporción media de desempleo durante 5 años (%).
Gross national product per capita (US $)	Production nationale brute par tête (en dollars américains)	2860	Bruttosozialprodukt pro Kopf (US Dollar)	Producto nacional bruto por cabeza (US $).
Five year increase in gross national product per capita (%)	Augmentation de la production nationale brute par tête sur 5 ans (en %)	+21·5	5-Jahreszuwachs im Bruttosozialprodukt pro Kopf (%)	Aumento en 5 años del producto nacional bruto (%).
Average annual private consumption per capita (US $)	Moyenne annuelle de la consommation privée par tête (en dollars américains)	1770	Durchschnittlicher privater Jahresverbrauch pro Kopf (US Dollar)	Promedio del consumo privado anual por cabeza (US $).
Total value of imports (US $ million)	Valeur totale des importations (en millions de dollars américains)	4403	Gesamtwert der Importe (Mio. US Dollar)	Valor total de importaciones (millones de US $).
Five year increase in imports (%)	Augmentation des importations sur 5 ans (en %)	+47·0	5-Jahreszuwachs der Importe (%)	Aumento de importaciones en 5 años (%).
Total value of exports (US $ millions)	Valeur totale des exportations (en millions de dollars américains)	3355	Gesamtwert der Exporte (Mio. US Dollar)	Valor total de exportaciones (millones de US $).
Five year increase in exports (%)	Augmentation des exportations sur 5 ans (en %)	+37·0	5-Jahreszuwachs der Exporte (%)	Aumento de exportaciones en 5 años (%).
Five year increase in hourly earnings (%)	Augmentation du salaire horaire sur 5 ans (en %)	+52·0	5-Jahreszuwachs im Stundenverdienst (%)	Aumento en 5 años de salarios por hora (%).
Five year increase in consumer prices (%)	Augmentation des prix à la consommation sur 5 ans (en %)	+29·0	5-Jahreszuwachs in den Verbraucherpreisen (%)	Aumento en 5 años de precios al consumidor (%).

Major Urban Centres Population ('000)	Principaux Centres Urbains Population ('000)		die größten Städte Einwohnerzahlen ('000)	Centros urbanos principales Población ('000)
	1. København	1381		
	2. Århus	190		
	3. Odense	134		
	4. Ålborg	124		
	5. Esbjerg	57		

Spain Espagne E Spanien España

English	French	E	German	Spanish
Population (millions)	Population (en millions)	33·3	Bevölkerung (Mio.)	Población (millones).
Population density (persons per square km)	Densité de la population (en personnes au km²)	65	Bevölkerungsdichte (Personen pro km²)	Densidad de población (habitantes por Km²).
Five year increase in population (%)	Augmentation de la population sur cinq ans (en %)	+4·1	5-Jahreszuwachs der Bevölkerung (%)	Aumento de población en 5 años (%).
Average unemployment rate over five years (%)	Taux moyen du chômage sur 5 ans (en %)	n.a.	Durchschnittliche Arbeitslosenzahl der letzten 5 Jahre (%)	Proporción media de desempleo durante 5 años (%).
Gross national product per capita (US $)	Production nationale brute par tête (en dollars américains)	870	Bruttosozialprodukt pro Kopf (US Dollar)	Producto nacional bruto por cabeza (US $).
Five year increase in gross national product per capita (%)	Augmentation de la production nationale brute par tête sur 5 ans (en %)	+33·0	5-Jahreszuwachs im Bruttosozialprodukt pro Kopf (%)	Aumento en 5 años del producto nacional bruto (%).
Average annual private consumption per capita (US $)	Moyenne annuelle de la consommation privée par tête (en dollars américains)	600	Durchschnittlicher privater Jahresverbrauch pro Kopf (US Dollar)	Promedio del consumo privado anual por cabeza (US $).
Total value of imports (US $ million)	Valeur totale des importations (en millions de dollars américains)	4717	Gesamtwert der Importe (Mio. US Dollar)	Valor total de importaciones (millones de US $).
Five year increase in imports (%)	Augmentation des importations sur 5 ans (en %)	+32·0	5-Jahreszuwachs der Importe (%)	Aumento de importaciones en 5 años (%).
Total value of exports (US $ millions)	Valeur totale des exportations (en millions de dollars américains)	2344	Gesamtwert der Exporte (Mio. US Dollar)	Valor total de exportaciones (millones de US $).
Five year increase in exports (%)	Augmentation des exportations sur 5 ans (en %)	+87·0	5-Jahreszuwachs der Exporte (%)	Aumento de exportaciones en 5 años (%).
Five year increase in hourly earnings (%)	Augmentation du salaire horaire sur 5 ans (en %)	+58·0	5-Jahreszuwachs im Stundenverdienst (%)	Aumento en 5 años de salarios por hora (%).
Five year increase in consumer prices (%)	Augmentation des prix à la consommation sur 5 ans (en %)	+21·0	5-Jahreszuwachs in den Verbraucherpreisen (%)	Aumento en 5 años de precios al consumidor (%).

Major Urban Centres Population ('000)	Principaux Centres Urbains Population ('000)		die größten Städte Einwohnerzahlen ('000)	Centros urbanos principales Población ('000)
	1. Madrid	2900		
	2. Barcelona	2375		
	3. Valencia	765		
	4. Sevilla	549		
	5. Zaragoza	393		

France	France	F	Frankreich	Francia
Population (millions)	Population (en millions)	50·3	Bevölkerung (Mio.)	Población (millones).
Population density (persons per square km)	Densité de la population (en personnes au km²)	91	Bevölkerungsdichte (Personen pro km²)	Densidad de población (habitantes por Km²).
Five year increase in population (%)	Augmentation de la population sur cinq ans (en %)	+3·2	5-Jahreszuwachs der Bevölkerung (%)	Aumento de población en 5 años (%).
Average unemployment rate over five years (%)	Taux moyen du chômage sur 5 ans (en %)	1·7	Durchschnittliche Arbeitslosenzahl der letzten 5 Jahre (%)	Proporción media de desempleo durante 5 años. (%).
Gross national product per capita (US $)	Production nationale brute par tête (en dollars américains)	2770	Bruttosozialprodukt pro Kopf (US Dollar)	Producto nacional bruto por cabeza (US $).
Five year increase in gross national product per capita (%)	Augmentation de la production nationale grute par tête sur 5 ans (en %)	+27·5	5-Jahreszuwachs im Bruttosozialprodukt pro Kopf (%)	Aumento en 5 años del producto nacional bruto (%).
Average annual private consumption per capita (US $)	Moyenne annuelle de la consommation privée par tête (en dollars américains)	1680	Durchschnittlicher privater Jahresverbrauch pro Kopf (US Dollar)	Promedio del consumo Privado anual por cabeza (US $).
Total value of imports (US $ million)	Valeur totale des importations (en millions de dollars américains)	19,114	Gesamtwert der Importe (Mio. US Dollar)	Valor total de importaciones (millones de US $).
Five year increase in imports (%)	Augmentation des importations sur 5 ans (en %)	+61·0	5-Jahreszuwachs der Importe (%)	Aumento de importaciones en 5 años (%).
Total value of exports (US $ millions)	Valeur totale des exportations (en millions de dollars américains)	17,935	Gesamtwert der Exporte (Mio. US Dollar)	Valor total de exportaciones (millones de US $).
Five year increase in exports (%)	Augmentation des exportations sur 5 ans (en %)	+65·0	5-Jahreszuwachs der Exporte (%)	Aumento de exportaciones en 5 años (%).
Five year increase in hourly earnings (%)	Augmentation du salaire horaire sur 5 ans (en %)	+44·0	5-Jahreszuwachs im Stundenverdienst (%)	Aumento en 5 años de salarios por hora (%).
Five year increase in consumer prices (%)	Augmentation des prix à la consommation sur 5 ans (en %)	+22·0	5-Jahreszuwachs in den Verbraucherpreisen (%)	Aumento en 5 años de precios al consumidor (%).

Major Urban Centres Population ('000)	Principaux Centres Urbains Population ('000)		die größten Städte Einwohnerzahlen ('000)	Centros urbanos principales Población ('000)
	1. Paris		8850	
	2. Lyon		920	
	3. Marseille		870	
	4. Toulouse		324	
	5. Nice		293	

United Kingdom	Royaume-Uni	GB	Vereinigtes Königreich	Reino Unido
Population (millions)	Population (en millions)	55·7	Bevölkerung (Mio.)	Población (millones).
Population density (persons per square km)	Densité de la population (en personnes au km²)	228	Bevölkerungsdichte (Personen pro km²)	Densidad de población (habitantes por Km²).
Five year increase in population (%)	Augmentation de la population sur cinq ans (en %)	+1·9	5-Jahreszuwachs der Bevölkerung (%)	Aumento de población en 5 años (%).
Average unemployment rate over five years (%)	Taux moyen du chômage sur 5 ans (en %)	2·3	Durchschnittliche Arbeitslosenzahl der letzten 5 Jahre (%)	Proporción media de desempleo durante 5 años (%).
Gross national product per capita (US $)	Production nationale brute par tête (en dollars américains)	1970	Bruttosozialprodukt pro Kopf (US Dollar)	Producto nacional bruto por cabeza (US $).
Five year increase in gross national product per capita (%)	Augmentation de la production nationale brute par tête sur 5 ans (en %)	+11·0	5-Jahreszuwachs im Bruttosozialprodukt pro Kopf (%)	Aumento en 5 años del producto nacional bruto (%).
Average annual private consumption per capita (US $)	Moyenne annuelle de la consommation privée par tête (en dollars américains)	1230	Durchschnittlicher privater Jahresverbrauch pro Kopf (US Dollar)	Promedio del consumo privado anual por cabeza (US $).
Total value of imports (US $ million)	Valeur totale des importations (en millions de dollars américains)	21,725	Gesamtwert der Importe (Mio. US Dollar)	Valor total de importaciones (millones de US $).
Five year increase in imports (%)	Augmentation des importations sur 5 ans (en %)	+30·0	5-Jahreszuwachs der Importe (%)	Aumento de importaciones en 5 años (%).
Total value of exports (US $ millions)	Valeur totale des exportations (en millions de dollars américains)	19,351	Gesamtwert der Exporte (Mio. US Dollar)	Valor total de exportaciones (millones de US $).
Five year increase in exports (%)	Augmentation des exportations sur 5 ans (en %)	+32·0	5-Jahreszuwachs der Exporte (%)	Aumento de exportaciones en 5 años (%).
Five year increase in hourly earnings (%)	Augmentation du salaire horaire sur 5 ans (en %)	+30·0	5-Jahreszuwachs im Stundenverdienst (%)	Aumento en 5 años de salarios por hora (%).
Five year increase in consumer prices (%)	Augmentation des prix à la consommation sur 5 ans (en %)	+20·0	5-Jahreszuwachs in den Verbraucherpreisen (%)	Aumento en 5 años de precios al consumidor (%).

Major Urban Centres Population ('000)	Principaux Centres Urbains Population ('000)		die größten Städte Einwohnerzahlen ('000)	Centros urbanos principales Población ('000)
	1. London	7379		
	2. Birmingham	1013		
	3. Glasgow	960		
	4. Liverpool	607		
	5. Manchester	541		

Italy   Italie   I   Italien   Italia

Population (millions)	Population (en millions)	53·2	Bevölkerung (Mio.)	Población (millones).
Population density (persons per square km)	Densité de la population (en personnes au km²)	180	Bevölkerungsdichte (Personen pro km²)	Densidad de población (habitantes por Km²).
Five year increase in population (%)	Augmentation de la population sur cinq ans (en %)	+3·1	5-Jahreszuwachs der Bevölkerung (%)	Aumento de población en 5 años (%).
Average unemployment rate over five years (%)	Taux moyen du chômage sur 5 ans (en %)	3·6	Durchschnittliche Arbeitslosenzahl der letzten 5 Jahre (%)	Proporción media de desempleo durante 5 años. (%).
Gross national product per capita (US $)	Production nationale brute par tête (en dollars américains)	1·520	Bruttosozialprodukt pro Kopf (US Dollar)	Producto nacional bruto por cabeza (US $).
Five year increase in gross national product per capita (%)	Augmentation de la production nationale brute par tête sur 5 ans (en %)	+27·5	5-Jahreszuwachs im Bruttosozialprodukt pro Kopf (%)	Aumento en 5 años del producto nacional bruto (%).
Average annual private consumption per capita (US $)	Moyenne annuelle de la consommation privée par tête (en dollars américains)	960	Durchschnittlicher privater Jahresverbrauch pro Kopf (US Dollar)	Promedio del consumo Privado anual por cabeza (US $).
Total value of imports (US $ million)	Valeur totale des importations (en millions de dollars américains)	14,944	Gesamtwert der Importe (Mio. US Dollar)	Valor total de importaciones (millones de US $).
Five year increase in imports (%)	Augmentation des importations sur 5 ans (en %)	+74·0	5-Jahreszuwachs der Importe (%)	Aumento de importaciones en 5 años (%).
Total value of exports (US $ millions)	Valeur totale des exportations (en millions de dollars américains)	13,186	Gesamtwert der Exporte (Mio. US Dollar)	Valor total de exportaciones (millones de US $).
Five year increase in exports (%)	Augmentation des exportations sur 5 ans (en %)	+64·0	5-Jahreszuwachs der Exporte (%)	Aumento de exportaciones en 5 años (%).
Five year increase in hourly earnings (%)	Augmentation du salaire horaire sur 5 ans (en %)	+35·0	5-Jahreszuwachs im Stundenverdienst (%)	Aumento en 5 años de salarios por hora (%).
Five year increase in consumer prices (%)	Augmentation des prix à la consommation sur 5 ans (en %)	+13·0	5-Jahreszuwachs in den Verbraucherpreisen (%)	Aumento en 5 años de precios al consumidor (%).

Major Urban Centres Population ('000)	Principaux Centres Urbains Population ('000)		die größten Städte Einwohnerzahlen ('000)	Centros urbanos principales Población ('000)
	1. Milano		3365	
	2. Roma		2810	
	3. Napoli		1875	
	4. Torino		1480	
	5. Genova		890	

Ireland (Irish Republic)	L'Irlande (République d'Irlande)	IRL	Irland (Republik)	Irlanda (República de Irlanda)
Population (millions)	Population (en millions)	2·9	Bevölkerung (Mio.)	Población (millones).
Population density (persons per square km)	Densité de la population (en personnes au km²)	43	Bevölkerungsdichte (Personen pro km²)	Densidad de población (habitantes por Km²).
Five year increase in population (%)	Augmentation de la population sur cinq ans (en %)	+2·1	5-Jahreszuwachs der Bevölkerung (%)	Aumento de población en 5 años (%).
Average unemployment rate over five years (%)	Taux moyen du chômage sur 5 ans (en %)	5·0	Durchschnittliche Arbeitslosenzahl der letzten 5 Jahre (%)	Proporción media de desempleo durante 5 años (%).
Gross national product per capita (US $)	Production nationale brute par tête (en dollars américains)	1200	Bruttosozialprodukt pro Kopf (US Dollar)	Producto nacional bruto por cabeza (US $).
Five year increase in gross national product per capita (%)	Augmentation de la production nationale brute par tête sur 5 ans (en %)	+20·0	5-Jahreszuwachs im Bruttosozialprodukt pro Kopf (%)	Aumento en 5 años del producto nacional bruto (%).
Average annual private consumption per capita (US $)	Moyenne annuelle de la consommation privée par tête (en dollars américains)	830	Durchschnittlicher privater Jahresverbrauch pro Kopf (US Dollar)	Promedio del consumo privado anual por cabeza (US $).
Total value of imports (US $ million)	Valeur totale des importations (en millions de dollars américains)	1622	Gesamtwert der Importe (Mio. US Dollar)	Valor total de importaciones (millones de US $).
Five year increase in imports (%)	Augmentation des importations sur 5 ans (en %)	+55·0	5-Jahreszuwachs der Importe (%)	Aumento de importaciones en 5 años (%).
Total value of exports (US $ millions)	Valeur totale des exportations (en millions de dollars américains)	1120	Gesamtwert der Exporte (Mio. US Dollar)	Valor total de exportaciones (millones de US $).
Five year increase in exports (%)	Augmentation des exportations sur 5 ans (en %)	+64·0	5-Jahreszuwachs der Exporte (%)	Aumento de exportaciones en 5 años (%).
Five year increase in hourly earnings (%)	Augmentation du salaire horaire sur 5 ans (en %)	+43·0	5-Jahreszuwachs im Stundenverdienst (%)	Aumento en 5 años de salarios por hora (%).
Five year increase in consumer prices (%)	Augmentation des prix à la consommation sur 5 ans (en %)	+26·0	5-Jahreszuwachs in den Verbraucherpreisen (%)	Aumento en 5 años de precios al consumidor (%).

Major Urban Centres Population ('000)	Principaux Centres Urbains Population ('000)		die größten Städte Einwohnerzahlen ('000)	Centros urbanos principales Población ('000)
	1. Dublin		760	
	2. Cork		125	
	3. Limerick		56	
	4. Waterford		30	
	5. Galway		25	

Luxembourg   Luxembourg   L   Luxemburg   Luxemburgo

Population (millions)	Population (en millions)	0·34	Bevölkerung (Mio.)	Población (millones).
Population density (persons per square km)	Densité de la population (en personnes au km²)	131	Bevölkerungsdichte (Personen pro km²)	Densidad de población (habitantes por Km²).
Five year increase in population (%)	Augmentation de la population sur cinq ans (en %)	+3.9	5-Jahreszuwachs der Bevölkerung (%)	Aumento de población en 5 años (%).
Average unemployment rate over five years (%)	Taux moyen de chômage sur 5 ans (en %)	n.a.	Durchschnittliche Arbeitslosenzahl der letzten 5 Jahre (%)	Proporción media de desempleo durante 5 años (%).
Gross national product per capita (US $)	Production nationale brute par tête (en dollars américains)	2266	Bruttosozialprodukt pro Kopf (US Dollar)	Producto nacional bruto por cabeza (US $).
Five year increase in gross national product per capita (%)	Augmentation de la production nationale brute par tête sur 5 ans (en %)	+16·0	5-Jahreszuwachs im Bruttosozialprodukt pro Kopf (%)	Aumento en 5 años del producto nacional bruto (%).
Average annual private consumption per capita (US $)	Moyenne annuelle de la consommation privée par tête (en dollars américains)	1530	Durchschnittlicher privater Jahresverbrauch pro Kopf (US Dollar)	Promedio del consumo privado anual por cabeza (US $).
Total value of imports (US $ million)	Valeur totale des importations (en millions de dollars américains)	*11353	Gesamtwert der Importe (Mio. US Dollar)	Valor total de importaciones (millones de US $).
Five year increase in imports (%)	Augmentation des importations sur 5 ans (en %)	+78·0	5-Jahreszuwachs der Importe (%)	Aumento de importaciones en 5 años (%).
Total value of exports (US $ millions)	Valeur totale des exportations (en millions de dollars américains)	*11595	Gesamtwert der Exporte (Mio. US Dollar)	Valor total de exportaciones (millones de US $).
Five year increase in exports (%)	Augmentation des exportations sur 5 ans (en %)	+82·0	5-Jahreszuwachs der Exporte (%)	Aumento de exportaciones en 5 años (%).
Five year increase in hourly earnings (%)	Augmentation du salaire horaire sur 5 ans (en %)		5-Jahreszuwachs im Stundenverdienst (%)	Aumento en 5 años de salarios por hora (%).
Five year increase in consumer prices (%)	Augmentation des prix à la consommation sur 5 ans (en %)	+14·0	5-Jahreszuwachs in den Verbraucherpreisen (%)	Aumento en 5 años de precios al consumidor (%).
*N.B. figures for B, L are combined.	*N.B. les chiffres pour B et L sont combinés.		*N.B. die Angaben für B, L sind zusammengefaßt worden.	*N.B. las cifras para B, L son conjuntas.

Major Urban Centres Population ('000)	**Principaux Centres Urbains** Population ('000)		**die größten Städte** Einwohnerzahlen ('000)	**Centros urbanos principales** Población ('000)
	1. Esch-sur-Alzette	99		
	2. Luxembourg	97		

Norway   Norvège   N   Norwegen   Noruega

English	French	N	German	Spanish
Population (millions)	Population (en millions)	3·9	Bevölkerung (Mio.)	Población (millones).
Population density (persons per square km)	Densité de la population (en personnes au km²)	12	Bevölkerungsdichte (Personen pro km²)	Densidad de población (habitantes por Km²).
Five year increase in population (%)	Augmentation de la population sur cinq ans (en %)	+3·5	5-Jahreszuwachs der Bevölkerung (%)	Aumento de población en 5 años (%).
Average unemployment rate over five years (%)	Taux moyen du chomage sur 5 ans (en %)	0·9	Durchschnittliche Arbeitslosenzahl der letzten 5 Jahre (%)	Proporción media de desempleo durante 5 años (%).
Gross national product per capita (US $)	Production nationale brute par tête (en dollars américains)	2530	Bruttosozialprodukt pro Kopf (US Dollar)	Producto nacional bruto por cabeza (US $).
Five year increase in gross national product per capita (%)	Augmentation de la production nationale brute par tête sur 5 ans (en %)	+24·0	5-Jahreszuwachs im Bruttosozialprodukt pro Kopf (%)	Aumento en 5 años del producto nacional bruto (%).
Average annual private consumption per capita (US $)	Moyenne annuelle de la consommation privée par tête (en dollars américains)	1410	Durchschnittlicher privater Jahresverbrauch pro Kopf (US Dollar)	Promedio del consumo privado anual por cabeza (US $).
Total value of imports (US million $)	Valeur totale des importations (en millions de dollars américains)	3697	Gesamtwert der Importe (Mio. US Dollar)	Valor total de importaciones (millones de US $).
Five year increase in imports (%)	Augmentation des importations sur 5 ans (en %)	+54·0	5-Jahreszuwachs der Importe (%)	Aumento de importaciones en 5 años (%).
Total value of exports (US $ millions)	Valeur totale des exportations (en millions de dollars américains)	2455	Gesamtwert der Exporte (Mio. US Dollar)	Valor total de exportaciones (millones de US $).
Five year increase in exports (%)	Augmentation des exportations sur 5 ans (en %)	+57·0	5-Jahreszuwachs der Exporte (%)	Aumento de exportaciones en 5 años (%).
Five year increase in hourly earnings (%)	Augmentation du salairé horaire sur 5 ans (en %)	+43·0	5-Jahreszuwachs im Stundenverdienst (%)	Aumento en 5 años de salarios por hora (%).
Five year increase in consumer prices (%)	Augmentation des prix à la consommation sur 5 ans (en %)	+11·0	5-Jahreszuwachs in den Verbraucherpreisen (%)	Aumento en 5 años de precios al consumidor (%).

Major Urban Centres Population ('000)	**Principaux Centres Urbains** Population ('000)		**die größten Städte** Einwohnerzahlen ('000)	**Centros urbanos principales** Población ('000)
	1. Oslo		685	
	2. Bergen		222	
	3. Trondheim		119	
	4. Stavanger		109	
	5. Kristiansand		53	

Netherlands　Pays-Bas　NL　Holland　Holanda

		NL		
Population (millions)	Population (en millions)	13·0	Bevölkerung (Mio.)	Población (millones).
Population density (persons per square km)	Densité de la population (en personnes au km²)	384	Bevölkerungsdichte (Personen pro km²)	Densidad de población (habitantes por Km²).
Five year increase in population (%)	Augmentation de la population sur cinq ans (en %)	+4·5	5-Jahreszuwachs der Bevölkerung (%)	Aumento de población en 5 años (%).
Average unemployment rate over five years (%)	Taux moyen du chômage sur 5 ans (en %)	1·4	Durchschnittliche Arbeitslosenzahl der letzten 5 Jahre (%)	Proporción media de desempleo durante 5 años. (%).
Gross national product per capita (US $)	Production nationale brute par tête (en dollars américains)	2190	Bruttosozialprodukt pro Kopf (US Dollar)	Producto nacional bruto por cabeza (US $).
Five year increase in gross national product per capita (%)	Augmentation de la production nationale brute par tête sur 5 ans (en %)	+25·0	5-Jahreszuwachs im Bruttosozialprodukt pro Kopf (%)	Aumento en 5 años del producto nacional bruto (%).
Average annual private consumption per capita (US $)	Moyenne annuelle de la consommation privée par tête (en dollars américains)	1220	Durchschnittlicher privater Jahresverbrauch pro Kopf (US Dollar)	Promedio del consumo Privado anual por cabeza (US $).
Total value of imports (US $ million)	Valeur totale des importations (en millions de dollars américains)	13,391	Gesamtwert der Importe (Mio. US Dollar)	Valor total de importaciones (millones de US $).
Five year increase in imports (%)	Augmentation des importations sur 5 ans (en %)	+67·0	5-Jahreszuwachs der Importe (%)	Aumento de importaciones en 5 años (%).
Total value of exports (US $ millions)	Valeur totale des exportations (en millions de dollars américains)	11,765	Gesamtwert der Exporte (Mio. US Dollar)	Valor total de exportaciones (millones de US $).
Five year increase in exports (%)	Augmentation des exportations sur 5 ans (en %)	+74·0	5-Jahreszuwachs der Exporte (%)	Aumento de exportaciones en 5 años (%).
Five year increase in hourly earnings (%)	Augmentation du salaire horaire sur 5 ans (en %)	+39·0	5-Jahreszuwachs im Stundenverdienst (%)	Aumento en 5 años de salarios por hora (%).
Five year increase in consumer prices (%)	Augmentation des prix à la consommation sur 5 ans (en %)	+20·0	5-Jahreszuwachs in den Verbraucherpreisen (%)	Aumento en 5 años de precios al consumidor (%).

Major Urban Centres Population ('000)	**Principaux Centres Urbains** Population ('000)		**die größten Städte** Einwohnerzahlen ('000)	**Centros urbanos principales** Población ('000)
	1.	Amsterdam	1805	
	2.	Rotterdam	1095	
	3.	's Gravenhage	840	
	4.	Utrecht	435	
	5.	Eindhoven	280	

Population (millions)	Population (en millions)	9·6	Bevölkerung (Mio.)	Población (millones)
Population density (persons per square km)	Densité de la population (en personnes au km²)	105	Bevölkerungsdichte (Personen pro km²)	Densidad de población (habitantes por Km²).
Five year increase in population (%)	Augmentation de la population sur cinq ans (en %)	+3·9	5-Jahreszuwachs der Bevölkerung (%)	Aumento de población en 5 años (%).
Average unemployment rate over five years (%)	Taux moyen du chômage sur 5 ans (en %)	n.a.	Durchschnittliche Arbeitslosenzahl der letzten 5 Jahre (%)	Proporción media de desempleo durante 5 años (%).
Gross national product per capita (US $)	Production nationale brute par tête (en dollars américains)	600	Bruttosozialprodukt pro Kopf (US Dollar)	Producto nacional bruto por cabeza (US $).
Five year increase in gross national product per capita (%)	Augmentation de la production nationale brute par tête sur 5 ans (en %)	+31·0	5-Jahreszuwachs im Bruttosozialprodukt pro Kopf (%)	Aumento en 5 años del producto nacional bruto (%).
Average annual private consumption per capita (US $)	Moyenne annuelle de la consommation privée par tête (en dollars américains)	430	Durchschnittlicher privater Jahresverbrauch pro Kopf (US Dollar)	Promedio del consumo privado anual por cabeza (US $).
Total value of imports (US $ million)	Valeur totale des importations (en millions de dollars américains)	1556	Gesamtwert der Importe (Mio. US Dollar)	Valor total de importaciones (millones de US $).
Five year increase in imports (%)	Augmentation des importations sur 5 ans (en %)	+52·0	5-Jahreszuwachs der Importe (%)	Aumento de importaciones en 5 años (%).
Total value of exports (US $ millions)	Valeur totale des exporta-tions (en millions de dollars américains)	946	Gesamtwert der Exporte (Mio. US Dollar)	Valor total de exportaciones (millones de US $).
Five year increase in exports (%)	Augmentation des exportations sur 5 ans (en %)	+53·0	5-Jahreszuwachs der Exporte (%)	Aumento de exportaciones en 5 años (%).
Five year increase in hourly earnings (%)	Augmentation du salaire horaire sur 5 ans (en %)	+47·0	5-Jahreszuwachs im Stundenverdienst (%)	Aumento en 5 años de salarios por hora (%).
Five year increase in consumer prices (%)	Augmentation des prix à la consommation sur 5 ans (en %)	+29·0	5-Jahreszuwachs in den Verbraucherpreisen (%)	Aumento en 5 años de precios al consumidor (%).

Major Urban Centres Population ('000)	Principaux Centres Urbains Population ('000)		die größten Städte Einwohnerzahlen ('000)	Centros urbanos principales Población ('000)
	1. Lisboa		1450	
	2. Porto		810	
	3. Coimbra		46	
	4. Setúbal		44	
	5. Braga		41	

Sweden   Suède   S   Schweden   Suecia

Population (millions)	Population (en millions)	8·1	Bevölkerung (Mio.)	Población (millones).
Population density (persons per square km)	Densité de la population (en personnes au km²)	18	Bevölkerungsdichte (Personen pro km²)	Densidad de población (habitantes por Km²).
Five year increase in population (%)	Augmentation de la population sur cinq ans (en %)	+3·1	5-Jahreszuwachs der Bevölkerung (%)	Aumento de población en 5 años (%).
Average unemployment rate over five years (%)	Taux moyen de chômage sur 5 ans (en %)	1·8	Durchschnittliche Arbeitslosenzahl der letzten 5 Jahre (%)	Proporción media de desempleo durante 5 años (%).
Gross national product per capita (US $)	Production nationale brute par tête (en dollars américains)	3570	Bruttosozialprodukt pro Kopf (US Dollar)	Producto nacional bruto por cabeza (US $).
Five year increase in gross national product per capita (%)	Augmentation de la production nationale brute par tête sur 5 ans (en %)	+19·0	5-Jahreszuwachs im Bruttosozialprodukt pro Kopf (%)	Aumento en 5 años del producto nacional bruto (%).
Average annual private consumption per capita (US $)	Moyenne annuelle de la consommation privée par tête (en dollars américains)	2120	Durchschnittlicher privater Jahresverbrauch pro Kopf (US Dollar)	Promedio del consumo privado anual por cabeza (US $).
Total value of imports (US $ million)	Valeur totale des importations (en millions de dollars américains)	7006	Gesamtwert der Importe (Mio. US Dollar)	Valor total de importaciones (millones de US $).
Five year increase in imports (%)	Augmentation des importations sur 5 ans (en %)	+53·0	5-Jahreszuwachs der Importe (%)	Aumento de importaciones en 5 años (%).
Total value of exports (US $ millions)	Valeur totale des exportations (en millions de dollars americains)	6761	Gesamtwert der Exporte (Mio. US Dollar)	Valor total de exportaciones (millones de US $).
Five year increase in exports (%)	Augmentation des exportations sur 5 ans (en %)	+58·0	5-Jahreszuwachs der Exporte (%)	Aumento de exportaciones en 5 años (%).
Five year increase in hourly earnings (%)	Augmentation du salaire horaire sur 5 ans (en %)	+43·0	5-Jahreszuwachs im Stundenverdienst (%)	Aumento en 5 años de salarios por hora (%).
Five year increase in consumer prices (%)	Augmentation des prix à la consommation sur 5 ans (en %)	+17·0	5-Jahreszuwachs in den Verbraucherpreisen (%)	Aumento en 5 años de precios al consumidor (%).

Major Urban Centres Population ('000)	**Principaux Centres Urbains** Population ('000)		**die größten Städte** Einwohnerzahlen ('000)	**Centros urbanos principales** Población ('000)
	1. **Stockholm**	1280		
	2. **Göteborg**	565		
	3. **Malmö**	254		
	4. **Västerås**	109		
	5. **Uppsala**	97		

Finland   Finlande   SF   Finnland   Finlandia

English	Français	SF	Deutsch	Español
Population (millions)	Population (en millions)	4·7	Bevölkerung (Mio.)	Población (millones)
Population density (persons per square km)	Densité de la population (en personnes au km²)	14	Bevölkerungsdichte (Personen pro km²)	Densidad de población (habitantes por Km²).
Five year increase in population (%)	Augmentation de la population sur cinq ans (en %)	+1·3	5-Jahreszuwachs der Bevölkerung (%)	Aumento de población en 5 años (%).
Average unemployment rate over five years (%)	Taux moyen du chômage sur 5 ans (en %)	2·5	Durchschnittliche Arbeitslosenzahl der letzten 5 Jahre (%)	Proporción media de desempleo durante 5 años (%).
Gross national product per capita (US $)	Production nationale brute par tête (en dollars américains)	1940	Bruttosozialprodukt pro Kopf (US Dollar)	Producto nacional bruto por cabeza (US $).
Five year increase in gross national product per capita (%)	Augmentation de la production nationale grute par tête sur 5 ans (en %)	+21·5	5-Jahreszuwachs im Bruttosozialprodukt pro Kopf (%)	Aumento en 5 años del producto nacional bruto (%).
Average annual private consumption per capita (US $)	Moyenne annuelle de la consommation privée par tête (en dollars américains)	1060	Durchschnittlicher privater Jahresverbrauch pro Kopf (US Dollar)	Promedio del consumo privado anual por cabeza (US $).
Total value of imports (US $ million)	Valeur totale des importations (en millions de dollars américains)	2637	Gesamtwert der Importe (Mio. US Dollar)	Valor total de importaciones (millones de US $).
Five year increase in imports (%)	Augmentation des importations sur 5 ans (en %)	+53·0	5-Jahreszuwachs der Importe (%)	Aumento de importaciones en 5 años (%).
Total value of exports (US $ millions)	Valeur totale des exportations (en millions de dollars américains)	2307	Gesamtwert der Exporte (Mio. US Dollar)	Valor total de exportaciones (millones de US $).
Five year increase in exports (%)	Augmentation des exportations sur 5 ans (en %)	+53·0	5-Jahreszuwachs der Exporte (%)	Aumento de exportaciones en 5 años (%).
Five year increase in hourly earnings (%)	Augmentation du salaire horaire sur 5 ans (en %)	+44·0	5-Jahreszuwachs im Stundenverdienst (%)	Aumento en 5 años de salarios por hora (%).
Five year increase in consumer prices (%)	Augmentation des prix à la consommation sur 5 ans (en %)	+19·0	5-Jahreszuwachs in den Verbraucherpreisen (%)	Aumento en 5 años de precios al consumidor (%).

Major Urban Centres Population ('000)	Principaux Centres Urbains Population ('000)		die größten Städte Einwohnerzahlen ('000)	Centros urbanos principales Población ('000)
	1. Helsinki		710	
	2. Turku		190	
	3. Tampere		187	
	4. Lahti		83	
	5. Oulu		81	

the 100 major companies of Europe
les 100 premières sociétés d'Europe
die 100 größten Firmen Europas
las 100 principales empresas de Europa

			£m	$m
51	**Reemstma Group** 2 Hamburg 52, Parkstrasse 51	D	610·9	1466·2
52	**Ford Motor Company Ltd** 88–89 Regent Street, London W1R 6AR	GB	589·0	1413·6
53	**Metallgesellschaft AG** Frankfurt am Main, Reuterweg 14, Postfach 2609	D	586·9	1408·6
54	**Dunlop Holdings Ltd** Dunlop House, 25 Ryder Street, St James's, London SW1Y 6PX	GB	585·0	1404·0
55	**Adam Opel AG** 6090 Russellheim	D	583·8	1401·1
56	**Brown Boveri & Cie AG** Baden	CH	580·0	1392·0
57	**F Hoffman-La Roche** 4002 Basel	CH	580·0	1392·0
58	**Shipping Industrial Holdings Ltd** 15 St Helen's Place, London EC3A 6DQ	GB	578·3	1387·9
59	**Guest Keen & Nettlefolds Ltd** Smethwick, Warley, Worcestershire	GB	564·8	1355·5
60	**Reed International Ltd** Reed House, 82 Piccadilly, London W1A 1EJ	GB	534·4	1282·6
61	**Hoesch AG** Eberhardstrasse 12, Postfach 680, Dortmund	D	519·8	1247·5
62	**Kaufhof AG** Leonhard-Tietz-Strasse 1, Koln	D	516·0	1238·4
63	**Compagnie Francaise Thomson-Houston-Hotchkiss-Brandt** 173 Boulevard Haussman, Paris 8e	F	511·6	1227·8
64	**Societa Finanziaria Telefonica Par Azioni** Piazza Solferino 11, Torino	I	507·9	1219·0
65	**Great Universal Stores Ltd** 100 Wood Street, London EC2P 2AJ	GB	503·1	1207·4
66	**A B Volvo** 58–405 08 Goteborg	S	490·7	1177·7
67	**Allied Breweries Ltd** 156 St John Street, London EC1P 1AR	GB	484·5	1162·8
68	**Hawker Siddeley Group Ltd** 18 St James Square, London SW1Y 4LJ	GB	472·1	1133·0
69	**Salzgitter AG** 3321 Salzgitter-Druttel	D	464·7	1115·3
70	**Marks & Spencer Ltd** Michael House, Baker Street, London W1A 1DN	GB	463·0	1111·2
71	**Gallaher Ltd** 138 York Street, Belfast BT15 1JE	GB	452·9	1087·0
72	**Rio Tinto-Zinc Ltd** 6 St James's Square, London SW1Y 4LD	GB	445·9	1070·2
73	**De Wendel-Sidelor** 57 Rue de Villiers, 92 Neuilly-sur-Seine	F	443·7	1064·9
74	**British Insulated Callender's Cables Ltd** 21 Bloomsbury Street, London WC1B 3QN	GB	443·0	1063·2
75	**The Distillers Company Ltd** 12 Torphichen Street, Edinburgh EH3 8YT	GB	442·6	1062·2